# Taming Alabama

# Taming Alabama

## Lawyers and Reformers, 1804–1929

Paul M. Pruitt Jr.

With an Introduction by G. Ward Hubbs

THE UNIVERSITY OF ALABAMA PRESS
*Tuscaloosa*

Typeface: Caslon

∞

The paper on which this book is printed meets the minimum requirements of American National Standard for Information Sciences—Permanence of Paper for Printed Library Materials, ANSI Z39.48-1984.

Library of Congress Cataloging-in-Publication Data

Pruitt, Paul M.
    Taming Alabama : lawyers and reformers, 1804–1929 / Paul M. Pruitt, Jr. ; with an introduction by G. Ward Hubbs.
        p.    cm.
    Includes bibliographical references and index.
    ISBN 978-0-8173-5601-9 (pbk. : alk. paper) — ISBN 978-0-8173-8328-2 (electronic)
    1. Alabama—History—1819–1950. 2. Social reformers—Alabama—Biography. 3. Alabama—Biography. I. Title.
    F326.P97    2010
    976.1—dc22

                                                                                    2010001035

# Contents

# Preface and Acknowledgments

This book is the product of several years' thought about a group of Alabama reformers, much of it keyed to the question: What did they have in common? Too often, southern reformers have been judged according to the degree of their dissent from the region's racial and political regimes. But it seemed to me that something else, often, was at work. It is clear that several self-assured figures of New South Alabama—Julia S. Tutwiler, Thomas Goode Jones, Henry D. Clayton Jr., and a number of their contemporaries—followed a code of ethics that was conservative, even aristocratic. Yet they also sincerely embraced one or more reformist agendas. One could label these individuals "Bourbon Reformers."[1]

Eventually I realized that across the first century of state history, one can find reformers, many of them lawyers, who were comfortable with the social arrangements of their times. Or they might have been comfortable if Alabama elites had ever put their own best principles into practice. In pursuit of betterment or in response to conscience, these reformers worked to pacify Alabama, to tame, to reconcile. The Populist Joseph C. Manning, different socially and philosophically from his Bourbon contemporaries, was the exception that proves the rule; he exchanged an ideological crusade to overturn the socio-economic order for a less sweeping campaign to secure ballot rights. Like his better-connected counterparts, he persevered in the face of adversity and rejection, sincerely believing in the rule of law.

For more than a year I have enjoyed conversations and email exchanges on the subject of reform with Birmingham-Southern professor Guy Hubbs. For his many valuable insights, for his kindness, for his sarcastic wit, and for his writing the introduction to this volume, I am indebted to him. Likewise, I'm grateful to the perceptive and diligent staff at The University of Alabama Press.

I've been accumulating such debts for thirty years in various settings. To acknowledge my obligations is to pay tribute to a corps of schoolmates, teachers, librarians, and archivists. Some of the people who have befriended me are David Alsobrook, Leah Atkins, Brent Aucoin, Gordon Bond, Ed Bridges, Alfred Brophy, Rickie Brunner, William J. Calvert, C. J. Coley, M. Boyd Coyner, Edward Crapol, Timothy Dixon, Martin Faigel, Allen J. Going, Steve Goodson, Lawrence M. Goodwyn, John Hardin, Patricia Henderson, Robert Bond Higgins, Alan Holland, Glenn House, Milo B. Howard, J. Harvey Jackson, Ludwell H. Johnson, Norwood Kerr, Charles Knighton, Joyce Lamont, Malcolm C. McMillan, Gordon Neavill, Debbie Pendleton, R. B. Roberts, Richard Sherman, H. Eugene Sterkx, Erwin Surrency, Mary Martha Thomas, Michael V. Thomason, James J. Thompson Jr., Ruth Truss, Cam Walker, Robert David Ward, Samuel Webb, Sarah W. Wiggins, Patricia and Calvin Wingo, and Suzanne Wolfe.

I owe debts of gratitude and friendship to many people at The University of Alabama School of Law. Special thanks to Kenneth C. Randall; James Leonard; Tony Freyer; my colleague and frequent collaborator, David I. Durham; and to all my colleagues at the Bounds Law Library, my place of employment since the summer of 1986.

Whatever I have written was made possible by a supportive and stimulating family. Raised by Paul M. Pruitt and Ruth Rogers Pruitt in a small college town in the optimistic 1960s, my brother Shannon and I enjoyed dinner-table conversations given over to literature, history, mathematics, engineering, and the practical small talk of teaching and learning. Likewise, I owe a great deal to the examples set by my uncle William Warren Rogers Sr. (aka Captain Midnight) and my cousin William Warren Rogers Jr. My daughters Juliet Rogers Pruitt and Mary Ruth Pruitt have given me many reasons to dust off the optimism of my upbringing, in addition to good advice and practical help with the manuscript of this and other works. I dedicate this book to my wife, Juliet Bare Pruitt, all in all and over all.

Tuscaloosa, Alabama
June 12, 2009

# Introduction

These biographical essays grow out of a simple yet profound observation by jurist Harry Toulmin: "Some opposition to the will of the majority may be necessary for the purpose of keeping them within the bounds of reason, of justice, and of constituency."[1] It was not only a profound but a prescient observation, for Toulmin was writing in 1804—a year before he set foot in the Tombigbee region of the Mississippi Territory, fifteen years before Alabama would become a state, and over two centuries before his words would be reprinted here. His observation applies as much today as it did then.

Like Toulmin, the settlers who poured into the newly opened southwestern frontier were leaving behind their homes and communities for an unknown future. They left to start anew, to amass wealth, and perhaps to avoid the law. They arrived to find a clean slate, a land of enormous possibilities, but a land without signposts. Alexis de Tocqueville concluded that the American frontier had people but lacked society. Of course, they did have a society of sorts (frontiersmen were known for their friendliness), just not the sort that the Frenchman recognized. What these rapacious and transient Americans lacked was a sense of place and the personal resources to build enduring institutions and traditions. They were ready to pull up stakes and move if a rumor was heard about new lands in the West. To make matters worse, no one knew whether the man with the white collar he just met was a parson praying over his flock or a confidence man preying on unsuspecting victims.

When Judge Toulmin arrived in this anomic wasteland, he recognized that the people needed laws and reputable lawmen if they were to escape anarchy. Toulmin's thousand-page *Digest of the Laws of the State of Alabama* (published in 1823, just four years after statehood) was crucial to creating a functioning society; without the *Digest*, no one could have made sense of the plethora of laws and decisions that were routinely cropping up. One new law might supersede another, or a distant court's judgment might set a precedent applicable to a local case. By organizing and making sense of these developments, Toulmin's *Digest* established the law in Alabama as an (ideally) impartial standard by which disputes could be resolved.

The state emerged from its frontier years under the leadership of Toulmin and others like him. Fewer highwaymen acted in disregard for the legal consequences of their crimes. Successful families started sending their daughters to academies and their sons to universities. Congregations erected churches at nearly every crossroads. And self-interested individualists joined voluntary associations to accomplish together what they could not do alone. People were building rudimentary communities and institutions. But these early social structures were fragile and needed the sort of natural authority that took time to develop. Theirs was a new world, not inherited and ancient, and authority rested in the people. Early Alabamians would not bow to tradition, but they would bow to the people's will.

*Vox populi, vox Dei.* The will of the people was the will of God. That god exerted his power everywhere. The people decided a man's fate through juries. Their elected politicians and judges were expected to set aside their own convictions and implement the people's will. (As subsequent southern history has demonstrated, wily demagogues could retain office by labeling their opponents as "aristocrats" and themselves as "men of the people.") Who dared resist or try to shape the people's will? Who called out in alarm when the people acted unjustly or tyrannically? Who could question something that rested on the most sacred of American values, equality?

Whigs. Until recently, historians have dismissed Whigs as mere opponents of Andrew Jackson and the party he championed. But Whigs represented more than mere opposition to Democrats. Whigs advanced a program that called on individuals to better themselves, and they wanted the government to assist citizens in that endeavor. Schools, penitentiaries, hospitals, churches, and voluntary associations—all were engaged in a great crusade of self-improvement. The result, Whigs believed, would be the moral and economic betterment of all society.

The Whig party folded in the 1850s without ever controlling Alabama's General Assembly or electing a single governor. Still, the Whigs had been crucial in developing the state's educational and moral infrastructure. And that reform impulse continued, in part because Whigs gravitated to certain professions where they exerted great influence: the law, education, journalism, and the church. The overlap is striking. Of the seven reformers whom Pruitt studies here, five were lawyers, three were educators, and at least two were journalists; nearly all were active Christians. Decidedly, all were influenced by the traditions of Whiggish reform. None were farmers.

By focusing on these Alabama reformers, Paul Pruitt has done us a great service. For too long, the role that the Whig tradition performed has been left in the shadows of the blazing events surrounding the Civil War.[2] In his lively portrayals, Pruitt makes the case that these reformers were neither fruitless nor trivial, even if getting people to live reasonably and with concern for the unfortunate is not as glitzy as, say, breaking apart a nation.

These reformers' naïve faith that the law would establish order and temper humankind's capacity to sin looks especially quaint in today's world of jackpot justice and celebrity show trials. One of Toulmin's successors, Benjamin Porter, wrote of the law as "that noble system," that "dispenses reason and justice to the community."[3] Porter set the pattern for the southern Whig reformer as a committed Christian, physician, lawyer, editor, champion of prison reform, and The University of Alabama's first law professor. His life in Alabama spanned the period from settlement into Reconstruction, and he died a Republican.

Once the law created order, reformers believed that educational institutions would liberate the individual from ignorance, freeing him to do better things for himself and his world. Relying on classical works, nineteenth-century teachers drummed into the heads of the state's future leaders the accumulated traditions and wisdom of the past. In looking at the early life of Julia Tutwiler, a life-long educator, Pruitt traces some of the factors that led her to take on reforming the treatment of criminals, especially those in the convict lease program. Tutwiler grew up under the tutelage of her father, himself a renowned educator and friend of Thomas Jefferson. Her views were further broadened by years spent in the north and in Europe. Surely these experiences contributed to making her the state's most famous reformer.

The Whig reform tradition was closely tied to Protestant Christianity. By portraying a transcendent realm demanding service to God and humankind, clergymen sought to lift individuals out of excessive self-regard. The Reverend James F. Smith was in some ways typical. His father began as a non-liturgical Quaker and was later ordained in the schismatic Methodist Protestant Church; James Smith's spiritual quest would bring him to become a priest in the highly liturgical Protestant Episcopal Church. After settling in Talladega, Smith worked to reform and unify a society reeling from the Civil War and trying to cope with the friction resulting from Alabama's rapid industrialization. Like lawyers and educators, the clergy could shape and structure society by promoting learning and civility.

Reformers in Alabama acted within a racially divided society. In their Manichean world of free and unfree, white citizens believed that any breach of the color barrier was a threat to freedom. Rare was the antebellum reformer who even questioned black slavery. Henry Tutwiler—Whig, slaveholder, father of Julia, and friend of abolitionist presidential candidate and sometime Alabamian, James G. Birney—held such faith in self-improvement that he believed that educating the white population would bring about the end of the peculiar institution. He was wrong. During Reconstruction, the Whigs' successors, the Republicans, took on the problem of racial subordination. Violent resistance came from the terrorist wing of the Democratic party, the Ku Klux Klan, which was exemplified by Sumter County's sheriff, Stephen S. Renfroe. First the 1875 and then the notorious 1901 constitution ended what progress the Republicans had made. Yet here and there the reformers persevered.

In courageous, principled opposition stood Joseph C. Manning—Methodist, Republican, and postmaster—who was the only one of the reformers discussed in this volume to challenge openly the white majority's belief in racial superiority. Manning became a political activist, advocating equal opportunity under the law for all men. He suffered for his principles. After being forced out of his job as Alexander City's postmaster, he moved north and used his pen to further the cause of reform by writing for a succession of black newspapers. Manning died in New York City, abandoned not only by his fellow white Alabamians, but by his wife as well.

But by the turn of the century, most reformers were confused. Thomas Goode Jones was raised in a Whiggish family but moved into the dominant Democratic Party and served as governor from 1890 to 1894. He resolved his Whig-Democrat conflict by compartmentalizing his ethical dilemmas. A disciplined lawyer and judge, who venerated the traditions of the bar, Jones used those habits of order and honor to pass regressive laws, including the disfranchising 1901 constitution that he helped to write. Similarly, Judge Henry DeLamar Clayton, a Democrat firmly committed to white supremacy and the 1901 constitution, used his power to steer a jury toward conviction in the notorious Abrams sedition trial; yet Clayton the Progressive vigorously opposed the emergence of the second Ku Klux Klan and continued to believe in the Whiggish notion that the law was a positive force for improving society.

Jones and Clayton were in some ways typical of the conflicted reformist impulse that characterized much of Alabama's second century. Modern reformers would continue to battle the tyranny of the majority and press for improved education, care for the ill, resistance against hate groups, and other causes. But the twentieth century's greatest reform, overcoming racial division, would leave many would-be reformers on the sidelines, consumed with fears of anarchy much like their frontier forebears. Individuals want to do what is right; but, as Toulmin observed, it takes great courage to stand for reason and justice before the will of the god named Majority.

G. Ward Hubbs
Birmingham-Southern College

# I

# Harry Toulmin

## A Frontier Justinian

### Introduction

Harry Toulmin was neither the first nor the only territorial judge to hold court in the future state of Alabama, but his was the most significant record. Toulmin was appointed in 1804 by President Thomas Jefferson to preside over courts in Washington County, Mississippi Territory, a sprawling district of settlements north of Spanish-held Mobile along the Tombigbee, Tensaw, and Alabama rivers. Surrounded by the tribal lands of Creek and Choctaw Indians, this eastern province of Mississippi was isolated and undeveloped; its few officials were hampered by the distances they had to cover. Toulmin continued in his office after the Alabama Territory was carved out, and in all he served from 1804–1819. As late as 1815, he complained that his authority extended over an area that, by his generous estimation, was 340 miles long and 330 miles wide.[1]

Thinking of the early history of Alabama, one easily peoples the political landscape with Jacksonians. This is our default vision, in part, because of the long ascendancy of the Democrats prior to the Civil War. But it is also true that writers of the late antebellum years, many of whom were ironical Whiggish lawyers, have given us such iconic images of frontier raffishness (Simon Suggs and his ilk) that we think one frontier must be like another.[2] Harry Toulmin's career as a territorial judge, however, reminds us that the Jeffersonian southwest was home to several parallel universes, of which the one made by American slaveholders was a likely (but not a certain) winner.[3]

The friction of cultures, races, and economic structures turned Toulmin, who was fundamentally a republican jurist and intellectual, into a borderlands diplomat as much concerned with preventing war as he was in quelling domestic disorders. Society in the Tensaw-Tombigbee districts was too amorphous to be easily tamed—much less brought to that ordered condition in which certain truths seem self-evident. Yet Toulmin's legacy is twofold:

2 / Chapter One

First, he was arguably responsible for the tenuous years of peace prior to the outbreak of the "Redstick" war in 1813; during this time the populous, economically strong United States gathered its strength. Second and most important, he published a significant body of compiled statutes, proto-codes, and notably his Alabama "digest" of 1823. Of these it can be argued that the pen is truly mightier than the sword. Toulmin's legal successors would build upon his work in their own efforts to further the rule of law.

## From the English Enlightenment to the Bluegrass State

Toulmin's early life had prepared him for vicissitudes. Born in 1766 at Taunton, England, he was the son of Joshua Toulmin, a Unitarian minister and a friend of the famous scientist and dissenting clergyman Joseph Priestley. Though he received little formal education, Harry Toulmin drew both information and a love of knowledge from the men of his father's circle—even more, perhaps, from the works he read in a bookstore operated by his mother, Jane Toulmin. Like his father, the young Toulmin became a Unitarian minister, serving two congregations in Lancashire from 1786 to 1793.[4]

The times were dangerous for Englishmen who were either religious or political nonconformists, and Priestley and the Toulmins were both. Indeed they were supporters of the French Revolution, men who applauded the fall of the Bastille, believed in freedom of thought, and hoped that reason could guide humanity toward a state of republican equality. The English government and the Church of England viewed such ideas as a serious threat to the status quo, almost treason; as a result, the authorities did little to prevent violence against Unitarians and republicans. On the second anniversary of Bastille Day (July 14, 1791) a Birmingham mob burned down Priestley's house, destroying his library, laboratory, and personal papers. Priestley began to plan a move to America, as did Harry Toulmin after "a burning effigy of the radical spokesman Thomas Paine disturbed the Joshua Toulmin family doorstep." Toulmin's investigations led him to believe that the newly created state of Kentucky was an ideal destination—in fact Toulmin began to write works promoting immigration there before he ever took ship. In the end, with financial support from his congregation, he sailed to America in the summer of 1793.[5]

Arriving in Virginia, he won the good will of James Madison and Thomas Jefferson (who was a great admirer of Priestley). The Virginians were pleased with Toulmin's political enthusiasms; Jefferson would describe him as a "person of understanding, of science, and of great worth," adding that the young Englishman was "a pure and zealous republican."[6] Armed with encouragement and letters of recommendation Toulmin and his family (he had sailed with his wife, Ann, and four children) traveled to Kentucky. There he made what one scholar calls a "complete redirection," deciding to exchange the life of a clergyman for that of a scholar and teacher.[7] He may have been concerned that a preacher's salary would not bring in enough money. Or perhaps—now that he was away from the presence and expectations of his parents—he may have caught something of the ambitious, worldly spirit of the West.

In February 1794 Toulmin was elected president of Transylvania Seminary in Lexington, Kentucky. There he established a demanding curriculum of languages, science, mathematics, philosophy, and political studies, which he taught to a growing student body. In these years Lexington presented a scene of intellectual and political ferment, with ongoing discussions of republicanism and deism. Thomas Paine's anticlerical *Age of Reason* was available in bookstores and was the object of much discussion, pro and con. It was an atmosphere in which Toulmin might have become a patriarch of Kentucky educators. Yet from his first days at Transylvania he was closely watched by a Presbyterian faction of the school's board of trustees, who viewed him as a heretic and had opposed his election, and by Federalists in the Kentucky legislature. The continuing intervention of these groups in college affairs drove Toulmin to resign in April 1796.[8]

## Law and Politics in the West

As the academic door closed, a political door opened. Shortly after his resignation, Toulmin accepted appointment as Kentucky's secretary of state. He would hold this post for eight years during the administration of Governor James Garrard, a Jeffersonian Republican. One of the secretary's duties was to certify acts of the legislature, and as such Toulmin signed Kentucky's Resolutions of November 1798—by which Kentucky nullified the Federalist-inspired Alien and Sedition Acts.[9] In the intervals of his official work he studied law and sold sets of Blackstone's *Commentaries*.

The knowledge he thus gained stood him in good stead in 1801–1802, when the legislature provided for the appointment of two "revisors" of Kentucky's criminal law. The latter was derived from Virginia law, which in turn was an offshoot of English law—all modified by the statutes and case law of the new state. Toulmin (with attorney James Blair) was appointed to perform the revision and to "collect from the English reporters and from all such other writers on the criminal law as they think proper."[10] The result, a minor classic of arrangement and codification, was the three-volume *A Review of the Criminal Law of the Commonwealth of Kentucky*, published 1804–1806. These books represent Toulmin's first steps as a scholarly lawgiver or (as he would later be called) "frontier Justinian."[11]

Toulmin and Blair laid out the criminal law in a manner similar to but not slavishly dependent on Blackstone. They moved from crimes against individuals (their "persons," their "characters") to those against property, subsequently taking up offenses against public safety, the "public peace," the justice system, religion and morality, and the "public trade" (i.e., usury and related crimes). They provided disquisitions on trial procedure, evidence, and indictments, including diverse examples intended to serve as forms. Unlike Blackstone they stocked their volumes with lengthy verbatim excerpts from English reporters.[12] Yet like Blackstone, Toulmin and Blair wrote in clear, even conversational prose.

The question of style was more than an academic matter to Toulmin, who was a Jeffersonian Republican and no partisan of "technical or cant" terminology. In a sense he and Blair had no choice, for the legislature had instructed them to use "no abbreviations, nor any Latin or French phrases." This was bound to cause some difficulties in dealing with long-established names of actions; but Toulmin met the difficulty by using language designed to provide a "general conception of the nature of the writ alluded to." He and Blair claimed to offer no opinion on the question of simplified language. But while Toulmin claimed "the same latitude as is usually given to our professional men," he admitted "that the obvious meaning of some of the provisions of our constitutions and laws is very different to a plain man, from that which may be placed upon them through the artificial reasoning and subtle refinement of technical men."[13]

Two goals—to state the law plainly and to make it accessible in a new country lacking a well-established legal profession—would provide the justification for most of Toulmin's subsequent writing. In the meantime he dreamed of making money through such works; thus he began to compile a self-help lawbook, which he published in 1806 through Mathew Carey of Philadelphia, one of America's first mass-distribution publishing houses. This pocket-sized book was the ambitiously titled *The Clerk's Magazine and American Conveyancer's Assistant: Being a Collection Adapted to the United States of the Most Approved Precedents.* The book lived up to its title; in just over three hundred pages it delivered 286 forms patterned on those used in England, New York, Massachusetts, Connecticut, New Hampshire, Rhode Island, Pennsylvania, Virginia, Maryland, and (of course) Kentucky. Americans needed guidance, Toulmin wrote, in carrying out simple transactions, for they lived in "a country where property is in a state of incessant fluctuation" and where ordinary citizens carry on more "mercantile intercourse" than anywhere else on earth—with the sad result that "law-suits are multiplied to a most aston-ishing extent."[14]

If Toulmin seemed to have the frontier on his mind it is not surprising. Prior to the publication of *Clerk's Magazine* he had moved to a neighborhood far more isolated than Lexington, Kentucky. In May 1804 he had written to James Madison, asking for appointment to the recently created "Tombig-bee" judgeship in Washington County of the Mississippi Territory.[15] While waiting, he delivered a July 4th address at Frankfort, defending Jefferson's ac-quisition of Louisiana and portraying in darkest terms the ruin that might have followed had the French or English aggressively colonized the new ter-ritory. Fortunately, he said, a "republican" administration had carried the day through well-informed diplomacy, a method preferable to either force or guile—both of which, Toulmin implied, were favored by partisans of Feder-alism. Thus Toulmin laid out the pacific principles he would apply as a fed-eral official serving on an unstable borderland. He was optimistic about the future of republican institutions; yet he understood the turbulence of frontier politics. Certainly he was no supporter of absolute democracy. In the course of his oration he had noted that "Some opposition to the will of the ma-jority may be necessary for the purpose of keeping them within the bounds of reason, of justice, and of constituency."[16]

Toulmin's appointment came through in November. By the summer of 1805 he had brought his family down the Mississippi River by flatboat, then by sailing ship from New Orleans to Mobile. From that Spanish-held port they journeyed upriver to Fort Stoddart, an American military post near the confluence of the Tombigbee and Alabama rivers in Washington County. There they were just above the thirty-first parallel, the northern border of Spanish West Florida. The Toulmins had arrived at a nerve center of con-troversy, an outpost of a vast territory populated sparsely by Native Ameri-cans, white settlers (of Spanish, French, British, and American descent), and African Americans.[17] Toulmin's immediate predecessor described the popu-lation in less than enthusiastic tones as "illiterate, wild and savage, of de-praved morals, unworthy of public confidence or private esteem."[18] At least one faction of white settlers—led by John Caller, a member of an obstreper-ous frontier family—had unsuccessfully proposed their own candidate for the judgeship.[19]

## Law and Diplomacy: Flush Times in the Old Southwest

Toulmin's responsibilities in the Mississippi and Alabama territories were varied; several had little to do with holding court.[20] From 1806 to 1810 he "contracted to operate a mail route from Fort Stoddart to Natchez." At intervals prior to the (impatiently and intemperately awaited) American military occupation of Mobile in 1813, he represented American citizens in their disputes with Spanish officials. The latter controlled the mouth of the district's extensive river system, routinely charging fees as high as 12 percent of the value of crops and goods, and sometimes shutting off trade altogether.[21] As the highest-ranking civilian in his jurisdiction, he also presided over public functions and entertained dignitaries. In 1817 he would welcome French settlers, the beneficiaries of a federal land grant who came with the intention of establishing a "Vine and Olive Colony."[22] Year after year he worked at routine judicial tasks: presiding over criminal cases, addressing grand juries, administering oaths, and taking depositions. Certainly he heard many cases involving disputed titles to land, a type of litigation prevalent in frontier communities. Occasionally he referred his colleagues in the Natchez district to such points of law as "whether a writ of error could stop an execut[io]n" upon property.[23]

Toulmin's commissions from Natchez included one task common to every phase of his mature career: namely, that he compile the young territory's laws. The product of this assignment, his 1807 *Statutes of the Mississippi Territory*, revealed a great deal about both Toulmin's understanding of his work and the varieties of legal business on the borderlands. Clearly, he was determined to blaze a clear path for future judges, for he devoted more than 200 pages to laws and statutes pertaining to judicial proceedings, including such detail-oriented subject headings as "Demurrers, when frivolous" as well as an interesting section on the licensing and conduct of attorneys.[24] The work is otherwise marked by its attention to land laws and criminal laws, especially the latter. Toulmin devoted more than eighty pages to "Crimes and the Public Police" and another forty to crimes punishable by the United States. Of the federal matters singled out for attention, several quasi-military offenses stand out—such as treason, manslaughter in a fort, violating a safe conduct or assaulting a foreign minister, accepting a commission from a foreign power, launching either a military expedition or a ship against a foreign government, confederacy to become pirates, burning a ship at sea, or participating in the international slave trade.[25]

After completing the *Statutes of Mississippi*, Toulmin agreed to write a manual for use by the territory's justices of the peace, elected officials who in the far-flung communities of the Old Southwest were often the local personification of law. Justice manuals based on earlier English works were common in federal-era America. Most of them were notable for a commonsense blending of English and American traditions, so much so that one scholar has called them "the first text-books on Anglo-American law."[26] Toulmin's contribution to the genre was titled *The Magistrate's Assistant: Being an Alphabetical Illustration of Sundry Legal Principles and Usages, Accompanied with a Variety of Necessary Forms.*[27] Like other manuals it contained many references to classical common-law authorities (Edward Coke, Matthew Hale) with few or no concessions to Spanish, French, or Native American practices.[28] And like Toulmin's Mississippi *Statutes*, his *Magistrate's Assistant* was somewhat preoccupied with strategies to put down crimes. Consider the work's list of topics under *A*, consisting of the following topics: Accessories, Affray, Arrest, Assault and Battery, and Assize. Under Arrest there was a separate section, as in the *Statutes*, for federal offenses. Among the latter were provisions for the use of military force "to prevent expeditions from the United States against nations at peace with them."[29]

In spite of—more probably because of—the reality of backwardness, violence, and insurrection, the world as prescribed by the justice manuals was orderly and, in terms of procedures, sophisticated. After all, these books were intended to serve as guides and models for communities suffering through civic adolescence—for places where passions and acquisitiveness were unembarrassed by established churches, schools, or hierarchies of business or planting. A number of Toulmin's neighbors were inclined to resent any authority, whether the Spanish in Mobile or U.S. officials at Fort Stoddart. As such, they embodied the restless energy, self-reliance, and egalitarian social outlook that, to historian Frederick Jackson Turner, were components of frontier democracy.[30] Yet when Toulmin, republican that he was, wrote: "It may be laid down as an invariable rule, that the law favors liberty," he did not equate liberty with freedom from restraint. Indeed, his work presents a regime of choices and gradations for frontier justices, a group that he may have hoped would serve as a republican squirearchy. For their use and the public good use he provided many circumstantial details: citing the occasions when officers could break down doors, listing the types of hearings a coroner could convene, teaching how to interpret the varieties of evidence, providing the (thirty-two) rules of statutory interpretation.[31]

Toulmin's role required that he strike a nice balance between serving citizens of the territory and enforcing the will of his federal superiors. Territorial judges had been given broad federal powers by a congressional act of March 1805,[32] and Toulmin was quite willing to style himself "one of the U.S. Judges for the Mississippi Territory." As such he heard admiralty cases and sought both to prevent and to punish federal crimes, especially those criminal activities likely to have international implications.[33] Toulmin's role in one such case—perhaps the most dramatic, wide-ranging, and ultimately confusing federal prosecution of the era—began in February 1807, when territorial judges at Natchez heard evidence in the matter of the recently surrendered fugitive Aaron Burr. Toulmin was present (as a spectator) as judges and grand jurors struggled to understand Burr's alleged conspiracies against the United States and/or the Spanish Empire. Toulmin, very much the loyal Jeffersonian, viewed Burr as a traitor. Traitor or not, there was every reason to see him as a threat to the peace.

When to Toulmin's distress the Natchez authorities released Burr (who promptly fled eastward), Toulmin issued arrest warrants against the former vice president and his principal allies. Toulmin examined several of the latter and bound them over to grand juries. Burr was eventually captured and briefly confined at Fort Stoddart, Toulmin's home base. There the charismatic adventurer played chess with Toulmin's daughter Frances (the wife of fort commander Edmund Pendleton Gaines) and pursued his schemes before being sent off in March to face trial in Richmond. There is no doubt that many residents of the Tombigbee district would have followed Burr in an expedition against the Spanish in Mobile. Burr had been in contact with territorial legislator James Caller, whose brother John had planned a filibustering raid against Mobile a year earlier. Toulmin had talked John Caller out of that project. Now Toulmin's quick action had deflected another warlike preparation.[34]

However, the root causes of friction between American settlers and Spanish colonials remained unsettled, with the result that Toulmin remained a de facto diplomat. In 1810 he interceded when residents of his district joined the Mobile Society. This group was in sympathy with a little-known revolutionary organization, the Convention of Baton Rouge, whose leaders had recently wrested authority over several "Florida Parishes" (as they are still known in Louisiana) from the Spanish. Though he was determined to keep the peace and avoid international incidents, Toulmin understood his neighbors' frustration with Spanish control over down-river trade. Even as he took every step to discourage lawbreakers, he put out feelers to see if Spanish authorities might relinquish control of Mobile voluntarily.[35]

In the long run Toulmin could not prevent violations of the Spanish boundary, the most annoying of which was a movement against Mobile under the command of Convention agent Reuben Kemper. In November 1810 the latter and his inebriated followers moved into position to attack the Spanish-held town. On December 9 Toulmin was able to arrest several of the filibusters' ringleaders, including Kemper, James Caller, and Joseph Pulaski Kennedy. The following day Governor Vicente Folch (Mobile's Spanish commander) attacked the remaining filibusters' camp, effectively ending the expedition. On December 13 there arrived a copy of President Madison's October 27 proclamation annexing West Florida to the United States. Placed on trial, the ringleaders were acquitted in March 1811 of all charges against them. Such was the state of Tombigbee public opinion that a sizeable faction, including some county and militia officials, considered that Toulmin had been overzealous or even pro-Spanish. He excused himself to President Madison, saying that a judge in a frontier community "must perpetually take a more active part in the early stages of prosecutions than is customary in societies more established, and composed of better materials."[36] Life in the borderlands—six years of judicial diplomacy, meting out "unequal laws unto a savage race"—had somewhat eroded his Jeffersonian enthusiasms.[37]

If Toulmin's prosecutions had angered his filibustrian neighbors, they were even angrier when he was instrumental in preventing a clash between United States troops sent to secure the annexed territory and Spanish forces occupying Mobile. Toulmin and others feared that the Spanish might burn down Mobile if attacked. On reflection, Washington officials agreed; so early in February 1811, federal officials were ordered to leave the port in Spanish hands for the moment.[38] For all such activities Toulmin—though he never lost the support of a core of official and legal friends—became a target for abuse and threats throughout the borderlands. Influenced by his enemies, a Baldwin County grand jury brought a nine-count indictment against him—chiefly accusing him of high-handedness on the bench but also implying that he was carrying on treasonable negotiations with the Spanish.[39]

In November 1811 the territorial legislature forwarded the charges to the U.S. House of Representatives, which referred them to a committee whose members included territorial delegate George Poindexter. Toulmin wrote letters defending his conduct at great length, evidently to the satisfaction of President Madison and the investigating committee, for in May 1812 Poindexter closed the investigation with a report commending Toulmin's "vigilant attention to the duties of his station."[40]

## A Frustrated Founding Father: Toulmin and the Transition to Statehood

Even as Toulmin suffered for damming up the restless acquisitiveness of his neighbors, demographic currents were shifting in his favor. The second decade of the nineteenth century saw river-borne waves of settlement washing over eastern Mississippi. Land sales boomed along the Tombigbee, Alabama, and Tennessee rivers, bringing slave-worked cotton planting to the district that would be known as Alabama's Black Belt and to the Tennessee Valley. These developments led to the growth of several towns, including Huntsville, Selma, Cahawba, Montgomery, and Tuscaloosa. The new communities (like St. Stephens, close to Toulmin's base) began to show such appurtenances of civilization as municipal governments, schools, churches, taverns, and dry-goods stores.[41]

Toulmin surely believed that the advance of "normal American" society would lessen the influence of rascals like Kemper or the Callers.[42] Yet ironically it was the pressure of white settlement that next disrupted the border's fragile peace. A Native American war movement promoted by the charismatic orator Tecumseh found sympathizers among the Creeks of eastern Mississippi; indeed, he had addressed their councils as early as the fall of 1811.[43] When the United States declared war against Great Britain in June 1812 and followed that by seizing Mobile in April 1813, Tecumseh's "Redstick" disciples believed with good reason that both the English and Spanish would support their fight against the Americans.[44]

Toulmin observed the outbreak of war in the summer of 1813 and put pen to paper—assessing the situation for his official contacts, noting the panic that caused white settlers, their slaves, and their Indian allies to cluster in forts ("the people have been fleeing all night," he wrote on July 23), and reporting accurately on the August 30 massacre of soldiers and refugees at Fort Mims.[45] Unlike the filibustering exercises that he had formerly opposed, the Creek War was no comic opera affair; as a result, it was prosecuted with all the force of national authority. Pretenders like James Caller (who had led militia forces to an embarrassing defeat at Burnt Corn Creek) were shoved aside by abler frontiersmen such as the epoch-making Andrew Jackson. Following the latter's crushing March 1814 defeat of Native American forces at Horseshoe Bend, the Creeks ceded huge tracts of land in the south and east of the future state of Alabama.[46] From that point the onrush of settlement resumed.

Antebellum judges were typically stretched very thin, forced to cover long distances via primitive transportation; Toulmin was no exception. After the American takeover of Mobile, he recommended the establishment of a separate federal court there and volunteered to be its judge.[47] He wanted to think of himself (as noted above) as a federal official, and his conduct of office had always been informed by his study of national and international laws. But he was painfully aware that however clear his duties might seem in theory, his authority was ambiguous in practice. This was so because territorial legislatures could pass acts restructuring the staffing and jurisdictions of their courts; the Mississippi assembly did so three times.[48] Another problem, the result of federal stinginess, was that the Mississippi Territory lacked a United

States marshal or attorney until 1813. When necessary, territorial attorneys general represented the United States. Otherwise Toulmin was forced to work with county-level officers, but the latter were reluctant to act in federal matters (which often transcended county boundaries).[49] By the end of 1815, Toulmin's situation was unchanged and uncomfortable. He was performing judicial duties, federal and territorial, in a thriving, litigious, and expanding jurisdiction. Yet in his discouragement he had scaled down his pretensions; he now viewed his court as "merely a territorial court authorized like the state courts to entertain certain suits also belonging to the federal jurisdiction."[50]

As Congress began to entertain petitions for Mississippi statehood, Toulmin was firmly identified with the eastern half of the territory, an area chronically underrepresented in territorial affairs. As early as December 1815, citizens east of the Pearl River had complained to Congress that their counties were more populous than those of the western district but sent "only eight members of the Territorial Legislature, while the Mississippi River Section had sixteen." Though the Tombigbee and Tennessee River settlers had hoped at times to escape from the political clutches of the Natchez group, the rapid growth of the Mobile and Huntsville trading areas convinced them that they would dominate an undivided Mississippi. In October 1816 a convention at John Ford's house on the Pearl River petitioned for the admission of Mississippi as a single state, and sent Toulmin to Washington to represent them. Toulmin appeared before congressional committees, prepared statements, and lobbied as best he could. Still he found that powerful interests had taken the side of the Natchez men. As for the Western Mississippians, they now hoped to escape from their formerly downtrodden neighbors; besides, in the looming sectional conflict over slavery, four U.S. senators were thought to be better than two.[51]

In two acts of March 1817, Congress prepared for Mississippi statehood and established the Territory of Alabama. In the latter, the lawmakers provided three judgeships. The judges, who were to be (as before) presidential appointees, were expected to ride circuit to preside over "superior courts" in the counties and were required to meet twice yearly at St. Stephens (the territorial capital) to hear appeals and to exercise federal jurisdiction within the territory. For the remainder of the pre-statehood period, Toulmin shared these duties with John W. Walker of Madison County, a rising politician who would serve as one of Alabama's first United States senators, and Henry Y. Webb of Perry and Greene counties in the Black Belt, who would serve as a state circuit court judge.[52]

Congress passed an Alabama enabling act in March 1819. Toulmin was elected as a delegate to the constitutional convention that met in July.[53] The membership was distinguished; its forty-four delegates included former congressmen, legislators, and other veteran officials, several of whom would subsequently hold high office in Alabama.[54] Toulmin was not chosen for the Committee of Fifteen that drafted the constitution.[55] Yet it may be significant that its suffrage provisions (white manhood suffrage with no property, militia-service, or taxpaying limitations) were similar to Kentucky's and thereby more liberal than those of other southern states.[56] As a good Jeffersonian, Toulmin was most likely pleased that the convention afforded slaves basic legal protections and trial rights, and empowered the legislature to ban the slave trade, require humane treatments of slaves, and provide for manumissions.[57] Otherwise, he played a modest role, attempting without success "to make more definite the provision guaranteeing religious freedom" and arguing unsuccessfully for the federal (three-fifths) ratio as a basis for apportioning state senate districts. He supported (this time on the winning side) popular election of sheriffs, but failed to turn the convention against the popular election of clerks of court.[58]

Toulmin had acted as a founding father to a state still undergoing its Jacksonian adolescence.[59] Politically he was outdated, superfluous, as the 1819 legislature demonstrated when it failed to elect him to a circuit judgeship. Instead they gave the office (by a vote of 63 to 5) to former territorial legislator Abner Lipscomb.[60] Unemployed, fatigued by duties that had expanded dramatically during the recent land boom years—"attending seven circuit courts twice a year and discharging the duties not only of a Territorial but of a Federal Judge"—Toulmin welcomed an offer from the 1821 legislature to examine, correct, and digest the state's statute law. Even this labor was arduous for a man whose health was failing. He was obliged to attend the 1821 and 1822 sessions of the legislature, to "bring a wagon for the purpose of conveying the digest and original acts of the Legislature," and to hire a clerk.[61] He could base some of the work on his 1807 Mississippi statutes, but he was also forced to deal with a digest published in 1816 by Edward Turner.[62] Toulmin did not admire Turner's work, which he described as "mangling and murdering the laws." Of his own work, *A Digest of the Laws of the State of Alabama,* he declared that it "has brought them to life again."[63]

Toulmin's *Digest* is one of the most impressive works of its kind. Weighing in at nearly a thousand pages of text, it is divided into sixty-seven alphabetical titles that are in turn subdivided into chapters. The latter present major acts pertaining to the topic at hand, arranged in chronological order. Since the *Digest* encompasses statutes of the Mississippi and Alabama territories as well as the acts of the Alabama state legislature, it is unmatched as an historical document of the Old Southwest. Toulmin assured the Alabama legislators, moreover, that he had taken pains to place component parts of multipurpose acts under their proper subject headings.[64] The result, almost as much a code as a digest, is yet another instance of Toulmin, once Jefferson's disciple, shaping the public institutions of the wild frontier. Thus we see that laws enacted against dueling receive their own title, and that instead of a title on slavery per se, Toulmin offers a title on "Negroes and Mulattoes, Bond & Free," with considerable attention devoted to emancipations.[65] On the other hand, Toulmin applied his considerable intelligence to subject groupings that would provide lawyers, politicians, and citizens with information useful in a rapidly growing republic—such as his lengthy title on "Highways, Bridges, and Ferries."[66]

## Conclusion

Toulmin may not have lived to see his final work in print, though he did survive long enough to wrangle a promise of $1500 from the 1822 legislature—no mean political feat for a sick old man, and proof that he still had friends in state government.[67] What he left behind, apart from printed pages, was a legacy pointing toward the supremacy of law. It could be justly said of him that neither distance, hardship, danger, intrigue, politics nor political persecution could shake his faith in the rule of law.[68] Likewise, and marvelously so for a man whose life had been disrupted by mobs and mob mentality from England to Mississippi, he apparently retained his Unitarian, Jeffersonian faith that popular government was the only legitimate foundation for freedom. Did he continue to hope that reason could inform republican decision-making, and so promote freedom under law? Perhaps he did, at least when he speculated over possible events of a distant future. A judge and legal scholar, Toulmin could not suppress the anarchic features of frontier life. But he could help to determine the structures that would stand when chaos had run its course.

# 2

# Benjamin F. Porter

## Whig and Law Reformer

## Introduction

By most accounts, antebellum southern society was permeated by the influence of slavery. Slavery was seen as the opposite of the freedom and honor cherished by white men. The presence of slaves was a continual warning of what could happen to persons who had fallen under the power of men or institutions. Perhaps such fears simply magnified the frontiersman's instinctive resistance to all agencies of power—an instinct that Harry Toulmin had known only too well. African American slavery as practiced in the Old Southwest may have served as a social safety net for poor white folk, and fear of slave insurrections furnished another motive for white solidarity. Given such tensions, it is hardly surprising that white southerners reacted with fury to the rise of a national antislavery movement. Historians have often concluded that the antebellum south was a close-minded society, cut off from reform movements of the day.

This interpretation begs the question of educational and humanitarian reforms that were likewise a product of the Old South. How to explain the schools, insane asylums, schools for the deaf and blind, and penitentiaries launched in a society suspicious of reform and hostile to government initiatives?[1] The following essay traces the life of Benjamin Faneuil Porter, a lawyer, author, and politician who definitely pursued his own interests—together with such a variety of benevolent reforms that he could never hope to bring them all to fruition. In particular, his role in reforming penal institutions in Alabama challenges the notion of a political system caught in the toils of the peculiar institution.

## First Principles

Porter was born in Charleston, South Carolina, in 1808. His father, born in Bermuda, was a craftsman of Irish descent; his mother's family had lived in

South Carolina for generations. The Porters were poor; they could not afford to give Benjamin a complete education. Instead they put him to work, at age fourteen, as a clerk in a counting house. Porter was too restless for such Dickensian drudgery. After a year he found himself a better position under Dr. Thomas Legare, a physician-druggist. Reading in his spare time, Porter prepared for a medical career and commenced a lifelong process of self-education.

Medical study, though, could not satisfy cravings that were central to Porter's personality—a desire to take part in dramatic scenes and, even more important, a need for recognition and acceptance. While a medical student, he made frequent visits to the courts of law. He was excited by the learned conflicts he witnessed, intrigued by the power and influence so openly displayed. Soon Porter was able to persuade attorney William Crafts to take him on as a clerk. Crafts, who "enjoyed an extensive . . . celebrity as a poet and orator," was exactly the sort of man Porter wanted to be.[2]

From his youth Porter was hungry for knowledge. He applied himself to medical books and law books in turn; in addition, probably, he read broadly in literature, philosophy, and history. In 1825 he was admitted to the bar.[3] Forced by the death of his father to support his mother and two sisters, Porter clerked for about two years in a Charleston law office. Next he tried his fortune in the country, moving to Chester Court House, where he formed a partnership and waited in vain for clients. Still, he did not waste his time. During these early professional struggles he fell in love with Eliza Kidd, a durable and intelligent young woman of good family. She agreed to be his bride and, when her parents objected to the match, eloped with him. In June 1828 the couple was married beneath a tree "not far from the paternal residence, and in the presence of the setting sun."[4]

In December 1829 Porter and his wife went west, like many other South Carolinians. After a tense passage through Creek Indian lands in south Alabama, they arrived at Monroe County, where Porter had relatives. They had dreamed of being entertained in a white-pillared mansion, but the reality was that their kinfolk lived in a log house; and so for a time would they. The countryside near Claiborne, then a principal town of the area, was desolate and uncivilized. Violent crime was common. Porter himself was nearly fired upon by a squatter with whom he had a dispute. In such a wide-open setting, Porter appears to have taken no steps to launch a career. Instead, he read such books as he could borrow, wrote poems and essays for a Claiborne newspaper, and spent time with Eliza and an infant son.[5]

Yet a desire for recognition was never far from the surface of Porter's mind. The example set by James Dellet, a South Carolinian who was a leader of the local bar and a fierce anti-Jacksonian, nourished such feelings. Dignified and reserved, Dellet was initially brusque with Porter, at a time when the latter was still wavering between law and medicine. After Porter was admitted to the state bar in November 1830, Dellet listened to him defend an accused murderer, and buttonholing the younger man, advised him to "throw your pillboxes to hell" and offered to take him on as his law partner. Soon they were working together in a practice that covered much of south Alabama.[6]

With Dellet's backing, Porter was soon a county judge and a member of the state House of Representatives. He was proud to be in Tuscaloosa (state capital, 1826–1846) among men of influence. Playing the bored man-of-affairs, he assured Dellet that he was "very sick of legislation";[7] however, in reality there was plenty of excitement.

## Politics, Legislation, Law

Porter had assumed his duties during the fall of 1832 when the great controversy between South Carolina and President Andrew Jackson was a matter of grave concern in the south. Anxious to prove himself a loyal son of the Palmetto State, Porter introduced resolutions that placed him, for the moment, in the states' rights camp. The "Nullifiers" were a mere faction of Alabama's Democratic Party at the time. But by the following year, when Governor John Gayle challenged the Jackson administration in a dispute over Creek Indian tribal lands, the anti-Jackson men were the nucleus of a potentially formidable coalition.[8] In these disputes James Dellet took the Union side—an unpopular stance in Monroe County, where Porter out-shouted his mentor during a debate.[9]

Alabama's party system was in an embryonic state in the 1830s; Porter's political development mirrored the times. He first made his name as a South Carolinian, a states' rights man. On the other hand (proof that sometimes he listened to Dellet?) he soon found that he favored the economic policies put forward by Henry Clay. Before long he was a Whig—defending the Bank of the United States, promoting internal improvements, and resisting efforts to curtail state taxes.[10] Like other critics of Jacksonian politics, he criticized Old Hickory's supporters as his "slaves" and worried that "no man will be retained in office who will not cry out Jackson." Apart from his brief association with Nullification, Porter showed no fear of the power of government. Rather, he saw the state as an agency by which men of good will might improve society. An associate of planters, merchants, and lawyers—why should he worry about rule by an elite?[11]

Still youthful and somewhat emotional, Porter lacked the ponderous consistency so useful in the pursuit of high office.[12] Yet he was safe enough on the bedrock issues of southern rights—including slavery, though he indulged in no flourishes on slavery's morality.[13] On the whole he was a hardworking if mercurial House member who impressed his fellow members. Over the course of his legislative career, Porter would serve on such important committees as Education, Ways and Means, and Judiciary, acting occasionally as chairman of the Committee of the Whole.[14]

Throughout his life Porter practiced and studied law. He had all the inclinations of a scholar, and perhaps for that reason he was chosen to succeed George Stewart as reporter of the Alabama Supreme Court. Porter collaborated with Stewart on five volumes of reports (published 1836–1837) and issued nine volumes by himself (1835–1840). He wrestled with the problem of capturing arguments and decisions faithfully and was critical of his own work; yet "Porter's Reports" are still well regarded.[15] The preface to his sixth volume reveals something of Porter's idealism, grandiloquence, and Whiggery. It was his desire to stand "between the People and the Court—an actor in that noble system, which . . . dispenses reason and justice to the community: thus regulating every conflicting interest of the social system, by the calm, but powerful test of legal principle."[16]

To carry out his duties, Porter in 1835 moved his family to Tuscaloosa, temporarily relinquishing his seat in the legislature. By this time he had attracted the attention of officials at The University of Alabama, who retained him to untangle their financial records. Working over the course of two years, he produced a five-volume work known as the "Porter Report."[17] During these Tuscaloosa years Porter also began to appear regularly as an appellate lawyer. Before the supreme court he handled cases that had originated in issues of a sort common to frontier communities—from criminal charges of burglary or murder to civil disputes over promissory notes, mortgages and insurance, slander, covenants, bills of sale, debt collection, legal residence, and partnership. He was also retained to argue appeals concerning the authority of school commissioners, the relative powers of county and circuit courts, and the right of women to administer estates.[18]

The Porter who practiced before the supreme court in the 1830s and 1840s scarcely resembled the young man who had arrived in Alabama with only "fifty cents in his pocket." Lawyering had made him prosperous, most of the time; though he lost by his own account ten thousand dollars in the Panic of 1837, his income was usually adequate. Politically he had only gained in influence, for Tuscaloosa was a Whiggish county; by 1837 Porter was one of its representatives in the legislature.[19] As for his personal life, it is clear that Porter reveled in the role of a paterfamilias—he and his wife surrounded

themselves with a large family of children and relatives. Though he was profoundly moved by the death of a daughter in 1837, he remained optimistic.[20]

## Philosophy and Crime

In other respects Porter was very much the same man as he had been. He
remained a voracious reader and student, a person possessed both by ideas
and ambition. Thus he sought out works of law, history, philosophy, literature, and science, acquiring a sizeable private library.[21] While he was busy as
a legislator, reporter, practitioner, he was also beginning to produce essays of
his own, filled with historical and literary references, and (especially by the
1840s) adorned with quotations.[22] To some, such erudition may have seemed
mere vanity. Yet his scholarship was the product of a serious curiosity about
the roots of laws and customs.

From his studies and associations with Tuscaloosa intellectuals, Porter absorbed certain political and philosophical ideas.[23] In common with many of
his contemporaries he believed that republican society was the product of a
continuing struggle for freedom and virtue. Yet Porter also trusted to some
extent in progress, assuming the existence of a divine plan for mankind. Like
most Whigs, he was convinced that society could be vastly improved by the
consistent application of reason to humanitarian ends.[24] In short, Porter was
well prepared to receive and understand the currents of reformism that were
sweeping over America in the Jacksonian era. As he fought for clients in
court or battled Democrats on the stump, a corner of his mind was occupied with larger issues. He always loved to act a grand part, believing (for example) that a legislator's first allegiance should be to law and justice—not to
constituents.[25] His personal successes may have convinced him that he could
be a leading force for beneficent change.

During Porter's lifetime, law and justice were subjects of considerable debate in the south. Government was too new, too primitive to exert much
control over citizens, even assuming that the latter, including a fair number
of rowdy pioneers, would have tolerated it. As a result, respectable families
were often horrified by the violence and turbulence around them. Gambling,
swindles, free-for-alls, duels, and highway robberies were common enough to
be part of the folklore and literature of the time.[26] In Tuscaloosa, capital and
university town though it was, men routinely killed each other over debts, in
trifling quarrels, or in fits of insanity.[27]

Residents of Tuscaloosa used various means to promote an atmosphere
of propriety. In peaceful moods, they established primary and secondary
schools, joined temperance societies, sent their children to Sunday schools,

and supported the work of the American Bible Society.[28] Angered or threatened sufficiently, they formed vigilance committees to drive targeted persons or groups out of town. Porter participated in all such activities;[29] but like other lawyers and members of elite groups, he also devoted himself to the reform of the criminal law itself.

In fact, the trend nationwide was to challenge criminal codes that were derived from the common law of England.[30] Punishments under such codes were harsh and were inflicted in public in order to dramatize the triumph of order and the wages of sin.[31] As late as the mid-1830s, Alabama law prescribed death for convicted murderers, rapists, arsonists, burglars, forgers, counterfeiters, and slave stealers, as well as for persons convicted of selling a free person into slavery. Minor crimes were variously punishable by whipping, humiliation in the pillory, and mutilation. Convicted horse thieves, for instance, could be fined, given thirty-nine lashes, branded with the letter "T" on either the face or hand, and imprisoned for up to a year.[32] A law of 1836 revoked the death penalty for white people convicted of felonies that stopped short of murder. Yet executions were still common, and a parade of lesser public brutalities continued unabated.[33]

Common-law punishments had long been targets of reform. William Blackstone's *Commentaries,* so influential among American lawyers, had criticized the law's savagery seventy years before Porter began his legislative career.[34] The Alabama Constitution of 1819, authored by Harry Toulmin and the state's founding fathers, had instructed the legislature to enact as soon as possible a penal code "founded on principles of reformation, and not of vindictive justice."[35] A few years before Porter and others embraced the issue in Alabama, the distinguished Louisiana attorney Edward Livingston had published a model code optimistically entitled *A System of Penal Law for the United States of America.*[36] So it would be fair to say that Porter, by the mid-1830s, was one of many American editors, lawyers, and officials who viewed corporal punishment as a threat to civil order and decorum.[37]

Predicated on the importance of environment, their thinking held that long-term (solitary) confinement, moral education, job training, and disciplined work could reform criminals. New York, Pennsylvania, and other eastern states had already adopted the new system. Its physical emblem was the penitentiary, a facility that to its advocates held out the hope of dealing with lawbreakers in a constructive and relatively private manner.[38] As to this last matter, thoughtful citizens were increasingly anxious to avoid the morbid excitements and degrading tumults of common-law punishments—for as a Tuscaloosa editor put it, additional crimes were often "committed under the very gallows."[39] The adoption of milder punishments might also make

criminal laws more enforceable; since as Porter and others had found by experience, juries often convicted guilty men of lesser offenses rather than in-
flict the death penalty.[40] Thus in the "Flush Times" of the 1830s, the modern
response to crime must have looked better and better to members of the
propertied classes. It is not difficult to imagine that lawyers and politicians
discussed possible approaches to reform as they came together for meetings
of the circuit courts.[41]

Penitentiary bills were debated early in the 1830s without result. By the
1833–1834 session, Governor John Gayle, prominent legislators, and newspapers were behind the proposed reform. Many legislators were undecided
or uncertain, and so it was decided to submit the penitentiary question to
the people. Proponents argued that penal reform would demonstrate Alabama's growing level of civilization, while making punishment more certain
and predictable, and hence more feared. Opponents made fewer statements,
but if they followed the reasoning of their regional counterparts, they feared
giving the state more power and disliked the idea of subjecting white men to
the virtual enslavement of imprisonment.[42] In the event the August 1834 referendum revealed strong support for a penitentiary in such relatively urban
areas as Mobile and Huntsville, where professional elites were more influential. Yet the town votes were more than offset by negative votes from the
countryside.[43]

As Porter emerged from his states' rights phase, his thinking turned increasingly toward Whiggish patterns of reform. As a legislator he voted for
the penitentiary election bill; likewise, in the 1833–1834 session he steered to
passage an act to prevent the imprisonment of females for breach of contract.[44] As he considered the proper responses to more serious crimes, he
was able to draw upon at least one powerful memory—as a youth in South
Carolina, he had been part of a panicky crowd that witnessed the execution of twenty-two men in the aftermath of Denmark Vesey's 1822 slave
conspiracy—and upon his experiences as lawyer and reporter of the supreme
court.[45] There is good evidence that an 1835 Mobile tragedy affected his view
of the death penalty.

Charles Boyington was a printer and sometime poet who had come to
Mobile from New England. Like many young men of that (or any) period,
he was something of a wastrel, and in May 1834, having used up his resources,
he was on his way home when he was arrested for the murder of his friend
Nathaniel Frost. The crime was sensational—Frost's throat had been cut in a
graveyard. Boyington was an outsider and a religious agnostic; Mobile newspapers exploited the case for all it was worth. The state's evidence was circumstantial, but the defense was no match for a prosecution headed by James

Dellet. Boyington appealed his conviction on technical grounds and set about writing a long, persuasive vindication of his innocence. All to no avail—in February 1835 he was taken to the gallows, allowed to make a lengthy and unrepentant speech, and hanged. The hanging was botched, and he died after horrible struggles.[46] Porter, who reported the case for the supreme court, later stated that the scene had caused "a thrill of horror" to run throughout Mobile. His distaste for the execution of an intelligent young man must have changed to disgust when the court, two years later, abandoned the reasoning by which it had denied Boyington's appeal.[47]

Nineteenth-century lawyers liked to believe, with Justice Joseph Story, that law "is a jealous mistress, and requires a long and constant courtship."[48] Porter, as we have seen, was one of those practitioners who brought philosophical and religious speculations to his wooing. The result was that by 1836, as he prepared a speech for the Philomathic Society of the University of Alabama, he was ready to step beyond simple humanitarian reformism into a marriage of natural rights theory and Christianity. His argument before the society was that "life" was a natural right of humanity and, therefore, beyond the reach of governments. Humans, he asserted, had been intended for a life of "benevolence and virtue," but had degraded themselves with violent behavior. Capital punishment was part of that violence.[49] Justifying capital punishment as a long-established practice, he said, was merely "the cant of power." Criminal trials were supposed to preclude private vengeance. Yet as he traced the course of a typical criminal trial for his listeners he was able to show that grudges and prejudices often played a part in the proceedings.[50]

The death penalty, Porter reasoned, was an invasion of God's prerogatives and a violation of the logic of social compacts; in addition, it was a singularly ineffective punishment. It did not deter crime, since robbers often killed witnesses who might (under common law) send them to the gallows. Moreover death (which he said was "frequently one of the kindest privileges of the unfortunate") had fewer terrors than prolonged solitary imprisonment. Above all, death was irrevocable. It stole from sinners' precious time that might be used in repentance, penitence, or even reformation.[51] Despite these appeals to idealism and religion, Porter had little hope of winning a ready acceptance from either the general public or the legislature. Still, he was sanguine. He told the Philomathic students that he looked forward to "the coming age as one of great refinement in the laws," and he invited them to cast off the shackles of the past and make a better world.[52]

These sentiments were all very well, but in the following year (1837) Tuscaloosa suffered a disturbing outbreak of murders. Porter recalled that the residents, infuriated by the killings, demanded that the death penalty be enforced. The result was evidently a series of trials reminiscent of the Boying-ton case. "Vague presumptions took for place of proof," Porter wrote, adding that "[i]t was enough to suspect a man to insure his conviction." One of Porter's clients had been discovered in a drunken stupor with a knife by his side next to the stabbed body of his brother. All expected that he was headed straight for the gallows, but Porter secured his release after a scientific discussion of the brother's wound, showing that "a monomaniac, with whom the deceased had a difficulty, was in a position to give the blow." Not everyone was fortunate enough to be defended by an attorney-physician![53]

Apart from the haphazard nature of the justice system, Porter during these years was much aware of the misery of prisoners. Like other benevolent citizens (see Chapter Three), he made a practice of visiting jails. On one occasion he saw a fifteen-year-old young woman chained to the floor in an entryway because the jail's two cells were full. To Porter it seemed that "her mind was a blank, on which education or parental admonition had impressed no trace of virtue, no principle of knowledge." She was, he judged, "in the infancy of her guilt, but unconscious of morality." The sight of this unfortunate child ("lying upon a miserable pallet," an "object of most terrible human suffering, disgrace, and wretchedness") must have strengthened his resolve that Alabama should have a penitentiary.[54]

Porter's heightened reformist feelings coincided with a busy professional schedule, family crises, and the economic turmoil of the Panic of 1837. When the legislature met that fall, Porter was absorbed by the question of the state's credit. As a Whig, he could simply have pointed his finger at what was arguably the Democrats' disaster. Instead, at the requests of colleagues he spent his time studying the condition of state banks and writing the report of a joint special committee—a labor that consumed his energy.[55] Late in the session the senate passed a penal reform bill and asked the house to agree to another popular referendum on a penitentiary. Apparently the house considered neither seriously.[56]

The 1838–1839 legislature was in a more expansive mood. State finances remained worrisome but for the moment seemed on sounder footing.[57] Porter debated monetary policy endlessly with friends and opponents; but the legislators were also willing to consider a variety of social measures, including bills intended to assist common schools and to regulate the sale of liquor.[58] Moved by the suffering so obvious in hard times, Porter introduced a bill to ban imprisonment for debt and had the pleasure of seeing it become law.[59] Yet his most significant work during the session was his advocacy of legislation that led to the construction of a state penitentiary and to criminal code reform. For the rest of his life, Porter would be proud of that accomplishment.

Porter was a member of the Judiciary Committee, whose membership also included elder statesman Marmaduke Williams (like Harry Toulmin a founding father of the state) and three future congressmen: Henry W. Hilliard, Felix McConnell, and Benjamin G. Shields. The majority of the committee consisted of professional men, and representatives from south Alabama's Black Belt or the Tennessee Valley—the young state's chief plantation districts—occupied twelve of its eighteen seats. At least seven of the committee's members were Whigs.[60] According to a recent study, such propertied, professional, and rather Whiggish men were just the type likely to support the penitentiary system.[61] Apart from humanitarian motives, there were several reasons why they should have done so in 1838–1839. Informed observers, aware of the financial crimes so common before and during the Panic, knew that the state needed a more sophisticated legal machinery. There is also evidence that growing numbers of citizens were anxious to alter a system of punishments that seemed to allow so many lawbreakers to roam at large. Also, neighboring states had recently built penitentiaries.[62]

On December 3, Governor Arthur P. Bagby declared himself in favor of criminal justice reform. Shortly thereafter Porter introduced a bill to revise the penal code.[63] On the floor, Porter was the prime mover of the question, perhaps because of his zeal and ability, or perhaps because the Democratic members were willing to give Whigs a leading role in passing a potentially controversial act. There must have been some consideration of penitentiary construction, since it was clear that code revision along reformist lines required a centralized facility. Yet during the month of December, the maneuvering on these issues was conducted behind closed doors; and Porter's code revision proposals were postponed in favor of more concrete matters.[64]

On January 2, 1839, Porter reported on behalf of the Judiciary Committee a substitute for his own bill, one that provided for the construction of a penitentiary. Under Porter's guiding hand, the substitute survived efforts to postpone it or to tie it to a popular referendum; the sparse nature of the record makes dull reading out of what must have been an interesting debate. At any rate, Porter's bill was read the third time on January 18, 1839, and passed by a margin of 48 to 36. The senate acted speedily and favorably, but in the process it cut a number of sections from the bill. Porter was surely annoyed, but the session was in its waning days and he had learned to take what he could get. On January 22, the house accepted the senate amendments. Four days later Governor Bagby signed the act into law.[65]

Thanks to senate pruning, the penitentiary law was short on particulars. It stated that the purpose of constructing a state prison was to punish and reform criminals, noting that the latter should be put to hard labor in solitary confinement. It required the legislature to elect three commissioners to adapt the state's criminal law to the penitentiary system and three commissioners to oversee construction. With no dissent the house and senate chose supreme court justices Henry W. Collier, Henry B. Goldthwaite, and John J. Ormond to revise the code. Without much difficulty the two houses picked building commissioners and after some maneuvering selected centrally located Wetumpka as the site.[66]

The building commissioners and legislators squabbled endlessly while contractors moved slowly, and the penitentiary was not finished until the fall of 1841. By that time the justices had also done their work, and the legislature had had two sessions to tinker with it.[67] The penal code that emerged was a humane body of laws, indicating that a working majority of legislators were in fundamental agreement with the principles of penal reform. The code did away with the disfigurement of white criminals and refined the use of the death penalty against whites. First-degree murderers, traitors against the state, and inciters of slave rebellion could still be hanged, though even in these instances the code gave jurors a choice between execution and life in prison.[68]

Justices Collier, Goldthwaite, and Ormond—experienced and respected men whose connections ranged from Mobile to the Tennessee Valley—deserve credit for their part in this sweeping reform of law. So does Porter, who authored the 1838–1839 bills and presided over debates on criminal punishments during the 1839–40 legislature. Much credit must also go to Sumter County representative William M. Inge, a Black Belt humanitarian who worked effectively against the death penalty during the 1840–1841 session.[69] In all, the enactment of such a complex project to reform shows that Alabama politicians were capable (at least on occasion) of concerted action despite their doubts about the people's will.

While he was helping the state commence its experiment in reformation, Porter had begun to examine his own career. Reelected to the legislature in 1839, he should have been in fine form. His friend John Phelan was chosen Speaker, and he was appointed to the Judiciary, Education, and Railroads committees. Yet during the session, debates over important issues (the penitentiary, educational affairs, and the banking system) produced no decisive results.[70] Meanwhile, a faction led by Jeremiah Clemens of Madison County undertook a crusade to drive out legislators who had been elected while holding another office. Their targets included Porter, who had been supreme court reporter and agent for the university at the time of his election. He escaped the fate of several members who were forced to relinquish their seats; yet it is hardly surprising that he grew weary of politics.[71]

During the fall of 1839 his thoughts turned often to Mobile, whose residents had recently suffered a yellow fever plague and a series of fires that had destroyed large portions of the town. Early in the session, Porter introduced resolutions designed to secure state financial aid for the destitute and to begin a campaign for improved public health.[72] He was fond of the Whiggish port city and was moved by descriptions of the desolation there, but his motives probably went beyond mere good will. At intervals over the years Porter had dreamed of practicing law in Mobile and of having a summer home in Monroe County near James Dellet and other friends.[73]

At some point during the 1839–1840 session, Porter's daydreams coincided with the reality of a court crisis in south Alabama. Dockets and jails were utterly overcrowded, at least in Mobile. As a result, there was a movement to create a new ("tenth") circuit based in Mobile County. The legislature passed a tenth-circuit act late in January, by which time Porter was already a strong candidate for election to the post. To be sure, circuit judges were elected by the legislature, and the state's constitution prohibited any legislator from holding a "civil office of profit" created during his term.[74] But Porter had been careful not to vote when the tenth-circuit bill came up for passage. Moreover, he resigned his seat on February 3 just prior to his election by a narrow majority over two other candidates. Seven years earlier, judging a case arising out of similar circumstances, the supreme court had declared itself unwilling to second-guess the legislature.[75]

By March 1840 Porter was in Mobile, where he met with a committee of highly respectable citizens, including prominent local politician John Everett. The Mobilians thanked him for his recent services to the city and offered to welcome him with a banquet. Porter, in response, was seized with an awkward fit of legal ethics. He declined, noting that judges must avoid all such "public excitements."[76] Considering that he was an outsider (and that he was arguably ineligible for his position), he might have been more congenial.

Certainly no one could accuse Porter of neglecting his duties. In the spring of 1840 he cleared literally thousands of cases from the books, working with bursts of energy that few judges could rival. Yet he displayed "patience in the investigation of tedious and complicated causes" and preserved an air of urbanity toward attorneys. However, he could also be somewhat impetuous. Just as he was ready to adjourn court for the fever season, he learned by overhearing a conversation that the Mobile jail was full of unfortunate people. Angrily—for he had resolved to leave the jail empty—he summoned the state's attorney. The two men found a "festering" collection of humanity, including sailors jailed to prevent them from deserting and families held as material witnesses. The prisoners included women, one of whom was giving birth, and at least one child sick with fever. Disgusted and touched, Porter decided to take responsibility for letting them all go, though not without sending the sick to a "proper asylum."[77]

Porter did not realize it as he opened the jail doors, but his days of judicial power were numbered. Though his efficiency and humanity were much to his credit, he had caused too much commotion to suit some attorneys, who fretted that he might be removed from office and all his actions nullified.[78] In fact, Attorney General Matthew W. Lindsay—putting on the mantle of righteousness recently worn by Jeremiah Clemens in the legislature—had carried the matter of Porter's eligibility to the supreme court, whose members now proved quite willing to sit in judgment upon legislative elections. At their June session they held that Porter was ineligible to hold the tenth-circuit judgeship. On July 1 Porter sent a letter of resignation to Governor Bagby. In public he kept his dignity, though he was outraged by what he would call the "frail and ridiculous" reasoning of the court.[79]

## Tilting at Windmills: Capital Punishment

After losing his judgeship, Porter pursued an ambivalent course. For months he continued to think of practicing law in Mobile; yet he remained near Tuscaloosa, his political base.[80] Politics, in fact, would take up much of his energy during the next few years—a tumultuous period of partisan strife. In the presidential election of 1840, the Whigs won a majority in three of the state's five congressional districts; Porter's contribution was a burst of letter writing and speechifying.[81] Yet excitement turned to fury as Democrats responded with a "general ticket" act intended to keep Whigs from winning congressional elections. Though it was in force for less than a year, the measure was a success. Thrown off balance, the Whigs remained a minority party.[82] The controversy can only have deepened Porter's disgust for the demagogic side of politics. Still he soldiered on as a loyal Whig, carrying out various party duties and serving three more terms in the legislature.[83]

Yet, with his mixed feelings about public life, Porter took every opportunity to achieve recognition away from politics. He returned to his law practice, appearing often before the Alabama Supreme Court.[84] He served from 1844–1845 as a University of Alabama trustee and in the winter of 1845–1846 was chosen, apparently at his own suggestion, as that institution's first law professor.[85] He had begun to write treatises of Alabama law, and it seems likely that (taking Blackstone as his model) he intended to write a more general work for his students.[86] But the trustees imposed harsh regulations and fees upon the fledgling law school—the academic politics must have been complex and spiteful—and no students enrolled.[87]

Whatever he may have felt about his brushes with pedagogic bureaucracy, Porter did a great deal of writing in the 1840s. In addition to books of law, he produced legal or historical articles, economic commentaries, reformist appeals, and travel pieces, as well as poems and translations. He published in such journals as *DeBow's Review* and *Hunt's Merchants' Magazine,* taking considerable satisfaction in his literary reputation. He was also pleased to have several of his speeches printed. His political opponents thought that he "had some ulterior aim, probably [that of] writing himself into celebrity."[88]

As Porter paid more attention to scholarship, he became a more persistent opponent of capital punishment. He had in addition one very practical reason for doing so—namely, that Alabama's criminal code still mandated the execution of slaves for a variety of offenses.[89] Porter, for his part, believed that shedding human blood was always wrong; he was anxious to see justice done regardless of the defendant's color. During these years he would gain considerable attention from his defense of two black men who were charged with the hanging offense of burglary. The evidence was conclusive, but Porter won a directed acquittal by pointing out inconsistencies in the laws concerning burglary by slaves. Judge and jury were furious with Porter; he remembered that at one point they turned their backs to him.[90]

A personal success aside, Porter was encouraged by the progress of a national anti–capital punishment movement. In many states, as in Alabama, penal reformers had worked to eliminate public executions, thereby limiting the impact of death as spectacle.[91] By the mid-1840s, opponents of the death penalty in New York, Massachusetts, and Pennsylvania had formed a national organization, the Society for the Abolition of the Punishment of Death. Porter probably knew of this group, but since many of its leaders were prominent abolitionists, their support would have done him no good.[92] Still it seems likely that Porter was familiar with the writings of such crusaders as John L. O'Sullivan, whose *Report in Favor of the Abolition of the Punishment of Death by Law* included biblical, theological, logical, sociological, and historical arguments. Presented to New York's legislature in 1841, O'Sullivan's proposals were defeated without debate, a type of rejection with which Porter was all too familiar.[93]

Porter was a member of Alabama's 1842–1843 legislature, which largely concerned itself with probing corruption in the state banks, reducing expenditures, and raising tax revenues.[94] Porter chose to concentrate his efforts on law reform, sponsoring bills to amend courtroom procedure and facilitate the correction of errors. He also took the opportunity to introduce an anti–capital punishment bill, which was referred to the Judiciary Committee. Evidently Porter expected that the house would debate the measure. Yet on January 30, 1843, the Judiciary Committee declared that abolition of the death penalty was "inexpedient"; impatient house members voted 55 to 26 to lay the bill on the table. Supported by six other members, Porter presented a formal "protest."[95]

Barely three pages long, this document was earnest and angry. Porter predicted "that a new era is commencing in criminal justice," which would sweep away "the barbarous and sanguinary enactments of the darker ages"— including the death penalty, which was "the least defensible, because the most cruel" of punishments. Judged by any humane standard of justice, executions were nothing less than an outrage "upon the dearest rights of men." Aware that some persons cited Old Testament scripture in justification of capital punishment, Porter replied that "the Mosaic dispensation was superseded by the milder and more humane schemes of Christ." As a document, the protest is memorable as a resume of reformist arguments and for the paltry number of legislators who were willing to endorse it. Porter was confident that he could have won more support had he been allowed to make a full-blown speech.[96]

Three years later, when Porter was next a member of the house, penal issues were a significant topic of debate. The penitentiary had proved to be a costly reform and had become such a political liability that in 1846 legislators took the fateful step of allowing private contractors to lease it.[97] Porter worried that businessmen-operators would neglect the moral reformation of the hundred or more convicts held by the state. He was one of several legislators who opposed the lease bill and worked to make contracts responsible for the humane treatment of inmates.[98]

During the same session, Porter took the opportunity to introduce another anti–capital punishment bill. He must have been gratified when it was placed on the calendar as a special topic, though the usual crush of affairs postponed its consideration until the latter part of the 1845–1846 session. Porter was under no illusions about the prospects of his bill.[99] Despite changes in criminal justice, hanging was too deeply entrenched in both the legal culture and the popular mind. What Porter wanted was the chance to testify to his convictions and make a few converts.

The "argument" he prepared was at least as emotional as his earlier writings. He mentioned, for example, the savage triumph of society "over a poor chained, criminal, powerless, dead human being."[100] As he had done before,

Porter argued strongly that executions had a corrupting influence on society. By means of well-chosen examples he demonstrated how public furors had often led to ill-considered verdicts, pointing out that the swift course of capital punishment leaves "no time to correct innocent convictions."[101] Noting, on the other hand, that juries frequently refused to convict in capital cases, he said that "men have more humanity than the society which they establish." He had no doubt that imprisonment was both a severe and an effective punishment. He declared idealistically that "the conscience of the prisoner wears away the rough surface of his depraved nature" in a cell.[102]

In the end his bill to abolish the punishment of death was defeated on its third reading by a vote of 63 to 16.[103] Though the measure was hardly likely to have passed the house, Porter's effort was impressive. On the floor and in the lobbies he had served as the nucleus of a group whose members were willing to take a stand on an unpopular issue, at a time when the legislature was turning away from penal reform. Of Porter's supporters (including those who signed his 1843 "protest" as well as those who voted with him in 1846), it should be said that they were independent minded, sure enough of themselves to vote according to conscience. Their number included Democrats and Whigs, both prominent and obscure men, though they were largely from the wealthy counties of the Black Belt or the Tennessee Valley. Likewise, they were well educated by the standards of the time. Of the twenty men who stood with him, nine or more were lawyers and at least two were physicians. Like earlier coalitions of penal reformers, Porter and most of his allies were members of the state's elite. Together they kept alive a core of support for humanitarian justice.[104]

Porter was elected to the 1847–1848 session of the legislature where he chaired the Committee on Internal Improvements and composed a major speech on behalf of a centrally financed public school system.[105] This would be his last term in the house, though he continued to take political stands (he campaigned for Whig presidential candidate Zachary Taylor in 1848).[106] In retrospect it seems clear that life in Tuscaloosa was losing its savor for Porter. By the mid-1840s he was encumbered (not for the first time) with the debts of family members. In the summer of 1845 he lost his kinsman Joseph, a fellow lawyer; the following year his mother died.[107] Some of the personal problems that beset Porter during these years involved his religious life. Always a sincere believer, he had become a Baptist in 1842; by the end of the decade he found it increasingly difficult to keep the commandments of that church. The local Baptist congregation expelled him, in fact, for "dancing on board of a steamboat."[108]

## Tending His Garden

All in all, he felt boxed in, a feeling that was aggravated by the removal of the state capital from Tuscaloosa to Montgomery in 1847. The next year, Porter purchased a summer home at Cave Springs in the mountains of northwest Georgia. During an 1849 trip to Washington, D.C., he was injured and recuperated in the hill country. Late in the summer of that year, in the company of *Charleston Courier* editor Richard Yeadon, he viewed the wonderful Appalachian scenery of north Alabama and was fired with the thought of the mountain country's potential. Yeadon, meanwhile, was urging his restless friend to return to South Carolina. About a year later Yeadon succeeded in luring Porter back, and arranged for him to be editor of the *Charleston Evening News*.[109]

Porter's stay in Charleston lasted about a year. He was a good-humored if outspoken editor, advocating (for instance) reforms in women's education. It may have been that he was too much the nationalistic Whig to prosper as a South Carolina journalist. He practiced law, but apparently his legal business did not flourish.[110] By the early 1850s he was again in northeast Alabama. There he lived for several years, editing local newspapers, practicing law, buying land, supporting educational projects, promoting railroads and industry, and running unsuccessfully for the state senate.[111] In his spare moments he started his memoirs and continued a scholarly project, the translation of a classic commentary on civil law, for which he had diligently studied Latin.[112]

These diverse labors brought only moderate prosperity. The summer of 1860 found Porter, his wife, and six children living near Guntersville in Marshall County. Census records show that they possessed $2,000 worth of real estate and personal property worth $21,090 (including five slaves).[113] That same year the family moved to Greenville, the county seat of Butler County. There Porter carried on a combination of lawyering, doctoring, and writing. Like many old Whigs, he was preoccupied with the crisis of the Union and the possibility of war. He opposed secession; yet when it came, he was a loyal Confederate. He offered his own services to the Confederacy and watched his sons go off to the army. He was chosen mayor of Greenville, and he and his family supported a military hospital.[114]

January 1865 found Porter in a state of mingled shock and grief over the collapse of a cause for which he had expended money, effort, and tragically, the life of a son. After much thought, he poured his feelings into a broadside that reflected the chaotic state of Confederate society. Criticizing politicians who "have been grasping for years, at mere abstractions in politics" until they have "worn out Liberty, in efforts to catch at its visions," he announced his gubernatorial candidacy. He was utterly against the reconstruction of the Union ("I never can fraternize with the murderers of my child") but hoped for peace by means of a treaty by which some European power would protect the Confederacy in return for the gradual emancipation of the slaves. He was still willing to defend slavery though he was aware that "the whole civilized world" condemned it. He warned that the war was destroying the "moral foundations" of black obedience and asked if it was worthwhile "to fight for slave property, till the last man dies, in the last ditch?"[115]

With the coming of peace Porter's hatred of Yankees began to wear off. It had been a natural passion, but Porter was never the man to hold a grudge. During the brief period of "Presidential" Reconstruction, Porter did indeed work with federal officials to relieve the poor and disabled near his home.[116] By 1867 he was pondering his political future in a world seemingly dominated by the Republicans. Nearly sixty years old and in poor health, Porter may have felt that he had little to lose, or he may have sensed one last chance to succeed. By the spring of 1868 he had joined the Republican Party and was rewarded with a circuit judgeship. Scalawags were political and social pariahs in Alabama, as Porter would have found out; but he was never able to stay on the bench for long. In June 1868 he died, leaving projects unfinished and prospects unfulfilled.[117]

The story of Benjamin F. Porter's career goes against many of the stereotypes of deep-south history. Porter was a self-made lawyer, doctor, and businessman; he was just as much a professional reformer. Though he took the righteousness of slavery for granted, he refused to erect an intellectual wall around himself. An early states' rights man, he became a disciple of Whiggery; a Unionist, he worked diligently for the Confederacy. Though he was a spokesman of planting and mercantile interests, he was likewise a zealous guardian of the welfare of common folk.

It seems likely that such persistent reformism, in tandem with his ardent, restless personality, cost Porter the high offices he might have attained. It should not be forgotten, however, that he was popular with the local voters who knew him best and that he worked successfully with like-minded colleagues to make criminal justice more humane. Viewed in context, his life testifies to the existence of a distinct antebellum reformism, the very existence of which was buried beneath the collapse of the slaveholders' world.

# 3
# Julia Tutwiler

## Preparation for a Lifetime of Reform

### Introduction

Julia Strudwick Tutwiler (1841–1916) is one of the best-known reformers in Alabama history. The daughter of Henry Tutwiler, headmaster of the celebrated Greene Springs School, she was raised in an atmosphere of self-conscious preparation for usefulness.[1] Her early abilities marked her as an unusual person; her youthful experiences stimulated in her an appetite for formal education and a delight in distant places. After attending her father's school, she studied at a Philadelphia boarding school, returning to Philadelphia in the post–Civil War era for further study before spending a semester at Vassar College. Tutoring by professors at Washington and Lee University and years of study in Europe completed her training.

Thus prepared, she embarked upon a career of good deeds that would have sufficed for several people. She had taught intermittently at Greene Springs and at other Black Belt schools during her years of education. But in 1881 she began work at what would soon become Alabama Normal College in Livingston. From that post she was a pioneering advocate both of higher education and vocational training for women. She also began to involve herself in many charitable projects, most notably the prison reform work that would, in effect, become her second vocation.

By the 1880s Tutwiler was head of the prison department of the Alabama Women's Christian Temperance Union. In that position she became an influential critic of the state's convict lease system, and a persistent campaigner—for humane treatment of inmates, for prison schools, and for the separation of convicts by age, gender, and type of offense. Untiring, willing to work within written and unwritten rules, she followed her conscience to the squalid mining camps in which the state housed a largely black population of convicts. Careful to pose no overt threat to the established order, she was the first Alabama woman to achieve a degree of political influence.[2] To the extent that she was willing to play at the politics of deference—and to the extent that legislators regarded her, in the 1880s and 1890s, as the spokesperson of her sex—she was for women what Booker T. Washington was for African Americans.[3]

Given her accomplishments, it is not surprising that Tutwiler's works were the stuff of legend, even during her lifetime. Her admirers gave her all the credit for advances in women's education and reforms in the state penal system.[4] A relative remembered her as a lobbyist who conquered by reason and persistence: "When they saw Sister Julia coming, they knew that she would get them to do something."[5] One perceptive writer seemed to see an authentic radical concealed in the trappings of a southern lady: "Her soul," he wrote, "was torn by the social injustice and wrongs suffered by the blacks as well as by the poor of the white race."[6] In general she was viewed as a unique being, the image that her name continues to evoke today.

Tutwiler's background and preparation need to be reexamined. Anne Gary Pannell and Cornelia E. Wyatt published the standard treatment of her life forty years ago. It depicts an idealistic woman who matured in her thirties.[7] Since that time, much more information has come to light on the history of southern women, women's education, the significance of the WCTU, and the role of women in prison reform. It is now possible to assess the attitudes and principles acquired by Julia Tutwiler in her childhood and youth, and to take note of the incidents that pushed her toward her adult careers. Though she was something of an original, she was also the product of identifiable forces and events.

## First Principles: An Academic Childhood

Born in Tuscaloosa, Julia Tutwiler passed her childhood twenty miles to the south at Greene Springs. There she lived in the midst of a throng. She was one of eleven siblings raised among (and educated with) as many as fifty students; by 1860 the family also owned thirty slaves.[8] If not a typical Black Belt childhood, her situation was a wonderful preparation for the life she would choose to live—one in which families (white and black) and students, home and school were thoroughly interconnected. Tutwiler's upbringing also prepared her to understand, personally and psychologically, the young men who would compose the state's elite. Distinguished families sent their sons to Greene Springs; she knew them and in many respects was one of them.

Such familiarity was hardly ordinary, though it was not extraordinary, either. Conventional wisdom, to be sure, declared that women should occupy a "sphere" of domesticity. Within the family circle (so ran the aforesaid wisdom), women would be free from the taint of the world's affairs and so should need little in the way of higher education. Exposure to the competitive world of boys' education might make girls coarse and unwomanly.[9] Many planter-class girls were taught to read and write; then they went to a finishing school or, in the words of Georgia reformer Rebecca L. Felton, were sent "back home for the domestic duties that were imperative."[10] One should not underestimate the ladies' "seminaries" of the antebellum years, however, for many of them provided sound instruction in traditional academic fields as well as lessons in embroidery and china painting. Despite the handicaps imposed by a patriarchal society, female education in the south produced its share of accomplished intellectuals.[11] Julia Tutwiler was one of these.

Henry Tutwiler and his wife Julia Ashe Tutwiler were sufficiently well-off to send their daughters away to be educated. But before allowing other teachers to turn their girls into young ladies, the Tutwilers commenced the process themselves, putting their daughters through the same course of study as paying students. Henry Tutwiler was one of several contemporary southern intellectuals who lamented the poverty of women's educational opportunities. Almost certainly he agreed with the Alabama Whig leader Benjamin F. Porter that women "have intellects entirely equal to the most laborious tasks of the most masculine scholar."[12]

Professor Tutwiler could have had no doubts about Julia's abilities. She was a vibrant child, receptive to ideas and apt to translate them into literary form. Taught to read at an early age by Julia Ashe Tutwiler, the little girl quickly began to spout quotations and to involve family members in impromptu dramatic games. She wrote poetry that seemed advanced for her years, including a piece titled "Lines on Hearing a Violin at Night." She could be precocious and mischievous at once, as when she instructed a younger sister to personify "anger" and steered her toward their mother's flower garden.[13]

The Greene Springs School was an ideal place for such a child. Henry Tutwiler's faculty covered a formidable array of subjects—ancient and modern languages, practical and theoretical mathematics, history, and the various branches of science. When possible, faculty taught by demonstration and experiment. The atmosphere was gentle as well as genteel; amazingly for the era, the Tutwilers did not employ corporal punishment. Like her fellow students, Julia Tutwiler learned how to compose formal essays. But she also participated in her father's relaxed Sunday discussions of religion, where students were encouraged to contribute their own remarks.[14] On the whole, this early training provided Julia Tutwiler with an image of how a community might be run. At the same time her Green Springs training developed her talent for self-expression and brought out in her an unselfconscious faith in God. Though she once rather petulantly dismissed her home education as incomplete and unsystematic, it laid the foundations for her distinguished career in teaching.[15]

Apart from her intellectual progress, Greene Springs furnished Tutwiler with a philosophy of public life. Henry Tutwiler had a deep-rooted belief that love of knowledge, properly cultivated, would lead to industrious habits and love of virtue. He imparted these ideas to his students, together with the Whiggish conviction that privileged young folk had a special duty to prepare themselves for usefulness.[16] Thus throughout her life Julia Tutwiler would assume that the sons of the Black Belt elite could be brought to work for the betterment of society. Why not? She had seen them respond to her father's teachings. Moral campaigning and old school ties were by no means mutually exclusive.

Nor were moral teachings and adolescent romanticism. Like most intelligent schoolchildren, Julia Tutwiler searched in books for role models. It is difficult to tell when Joan of Arc—a warrior saint, bold, naïve, celibate—became a pattern for her life. Yet by her teenage years Tutwiler was able to declaim passages of Friedrich Schiller's *Maid of Orleans*. Once, in a moment of angst, she declared that "she never would marry, and looking at the moon, announced: 'No slumbering babe shall rest upon this breast.'" Then, according to her sister Ida, she "went on about a lonely life . . . given to great deeds."[17]

## Race, Family, and Reform

The youthful Julia Tutwiler may have conceived of life as a stirring contest between good and evil. But it is likely that discussion (and observation) of Alabama politics brought her back to earth, to an interest in practical reforms. Henry Tutwiler was a Whig, and Alabama Whigs, like their counterparts nationally, were willing to support improvements in educational facilities and to back the founding of such "remedial institutions" as a state penitentiary and a state insane asylum.[18] Although the Whig Party never gained control of Alabama government, their influence was important in moving the legislature to experiment with just such human services in the 1840s and 1850s.[19]

One can easily imagine that Julia Tutwiler debated questions of penal and educational policy with her classmates, as well as the wisdom of the temperance and other pre-war reform movements. Henry Tutwiler made sure that they were exposed daily to "whatever subject was at the moment uppermost in the world's mind."[20] One area of controversy, however, may not have been so openly discussed—namely, the moral and political issues attached to the slavery question. Even so, the Tutwiler children were almost certainly exposed to ideas considered radical and dangerous in 1850s Alabama. Some of these ideas were applied within the Tutwiler's family circle, so a good way to approach Julia Tutwiler's evolving views on slavery is to consider them as a part of her training (quite unacademic in nature) in the woman's world of domesticity.

The logistical challenge at Greene Springs was formidable. Family, students, guests, and slaves had to be fed and provided with shelter. Sick people had to be nursed. Someone had to manage these unending affairs, as well as a complex cycle of sewing, mending, and remaking clothes. That someone was Julia Ashe Tutwiler, who also assisted in teaching the children; there is no evidence, one may add, that Henry Tutwiler was as flexible in his domestic expectations as he was in matters of education.[21]

The Tutwiler daughters were observers and participants in household operations. Young Julia developed a typical preoccupation with cloth and its possibilities; also, she was interested in gardening. She was familiar with and resigned to the existence of the "sphere" reserved for white women, an awareness that did not prevent her from hating the drudgery of routine chores. At some point during the 1860s she remarked that she would rather die than do kitchen work for the rest of her life.[22] Previously household slaves, who were scarce by the end of the Civil War, would have performed such physical work. By that time Julia Tutwiler, like many white southerners, had been able to reflect upon her relationship to the black people who served her.

A student of plantation domesticity has observed that white women lived with their female servants in a state of considerable intimacy; that they shared a sense of connectedness, not as sisters nor as equals, but as women carrying out different roles in a society dominated by patriarchal figures.[23] The women of Greene Springs were no exception to this rule, except that their patriarch was not a conventional southerner. As a young man, Henry Tutwiler had been a friend of the abolitionist James G. Burney. He had written to Burney in 1832 that slavery was responsible for "almost all of the moral and political evil in our country." He believed that education of the white population was the key to ending slavery. Yet, as popular hostility to abolitionism mounted (in the general white population and presumably among his students), Tutwiler contented himself with what amounted to a personal slave code.[24] One is tempted to say that Tutwiler followed Voltaire's advice (from *Candide*) to cultivate his garden. But of course in his case, the Tutwiler slaves did the cultivating.

Like the other Tutwiler children, Julia was taught that African Americans were human beings and that, as a Christian, she should measure her treatment of black folk by the Golden Rule.[25] Putting into action his belief that all people are capable of benefiting from an increase of knowledge,

Henry Tutwiler allowed his children to teach the family's slaves to read.[26] Julia Tutwiler received her first teaching experience in such classes—a clear anticipation of her future concerns. She viewed the female slaves as "family." One of her sisters recalled that Julia, during the Civil War, had nursed two black women through long illnesses.[27]

Throughout her life, Julia Tutwiler perceived herself to be part of an organic community in which African Americans had a rightful if (to her) humble place. Her experiences gave her an inner assurance that she "understood" black people—a feeling common among former slaveholders, accompanied by a visceral belief in white superiority. Given her upbringing, Julia Tutwiler was not comfortable with the south's "Peculiar Institution," deeply flawed as she knew it to be. But she was thoroughly accustomed to the role of the young mistress and quite willing to let black hands wash the dishes. Her reaction to emancipation and its aftermath illustrates the ambivalence of her feelings.

Her father had not been a secessionist, but like so many Alabamians of Whiggish leanings the Tutwilers became loyal Confederates. Indeed, various relations fought (and in at least one case died) for the Cause. To Julia Tutwiler, the wartime loss of slave property carried with it the sting of defeat. The jubilant, sometimes rowdy behavior of "ignorant slaves . . . suddenly freed from all restraints" probably confirmed her feeling that most black people were uncivilized. Probably, like other white southerners, she doubted that they could live without help from white people. On the other hand, a number of the former Tutwiler slaves stayed with the family. Here, she thought, were respectable, decent people who deserved a fair chance in life, people whose loyalty seemed to confirm the benevolence of the antebellum regime at Greene Springs.[28]

Henry Tutwiler put his own complicated feelings into an address in which he urged freedmen to make good use of their new-found rights.[29] Julia Tutwiler, for her part, watched as the turbulence of Reconstruction took its toll upon former slaves. In the Black Belt freedmen in large numbers were arrested for petty crimes and sent to work for contractors in convict lease camps. At first she was inclined to think these new arrangements inevitable. The state had no resources with which to build prisons, and most of the convicts were young black men who, to her way of thinking, needed supervision.

She subsequently wrote that "it seemed an injustice to let them suffer when they were willing and able to work for their support." Yet by the early 1880s, reports of wretched conditions and high death rates in the camps had sickened her, convincing her that the system as it existed was a great evil. Having in mind master-slave relations as she had known (or perhaps envisioned) them, she concluded that the convict lease "has been aptly described as having all of the evils of slavery, without one of its ameliorating features."[30]

## Out in the World

Rich as her home experience was, Greene Springs had by no means been the only scene of Julia Tutwiler's education. During her adolescence she had watched male classmates advance to further training and broader use. Why couldn't she do likewise? Sympathetic and willing to let his daughter see more of the world, Henry Tutwiler sent his sixteen-year-old daughter to Madame Maroteau's boarding school in Philadelphia, a city in which he had business interests. Whatever else it was, Madame Maroteau's school was a fair training ground for linguists; her students spoke only French "in the classroom and at table."[31] Such a regimen was doubtless stimulating for Julia Tutwiler, whose academic specialty would be modern languages. But other experiences were just as important—school activities, exposure to other accents and cultures, and the experience of being taught by someone other than her beloved but previously omnipresent father.

If she was like other southern girls who attended boarding schools, Julia Tutwiler was delighted to share a sense of sisterhood with her classmates.[32] Her bubble was burst after two year of study, however, when she was called home not long before the Civil War "for no special reason," as she thought, except that she was considered to be "old enough to leave school." To her family she put on a brave face. Inside she was filled with anger and a rather over-dramatized sense of despair. "I cried my eyes out at the thought of being through life the same ignorant unfinished creature I then felt myself."[33]

Unfinished or not, for the next several years Julia Tutwiler furthered her education on several fronts. Anxious to help in the war effort, she begged to be allowed to serve as a volunteer nurse. Her father refused, but at some point he offered her, her first responsible position, a teaching post at Greene Springs. She must have risen to the challenge, no doubt reflecting on the tactics (acquiescence, patience) necessary to gain concessions from a patriarch. Thus Henry Tutwiler came to see her as a serious person, a potential scholar. Once peace was firmly established, he granted her permission to seek further instruction in the north.[34]

After another stay at Madame Maroteau's, Julia Tutwiler was enrolled in spring 1866 at the recently opened Vassar College in New York. She should have been happy, for she felt within herself "powers which would enable me to learn as much and as well as most men"—powers that she planned to use in service to humanity. Undoubtedly she studied hard (family legend says that she taught French and German, too, at this time); academically, she felt that she was making progress. Moreover she was well liked and respected, for she took a prominent part in the school's first founder's day. Still, she was haunted during her stay by the thought of certain recent, unexplained events that had caused her "great pain and sorrow besides wounded pride and self-respect."[35]

Awkward situations seemed to dog her, for before she left Vassar she had an unpleasant encounter with the oldest of the Harper brothers, a publisher of *Harper's Weekly* and a Vassar trustee. Encountering him, her nerves evidently on edge, she berated him for printing stories that enflamed sectional hatreds. He replied jovially enough that he did not know much about the magazine. But upon meeting her in a corridor the next morning, he spoke to her as if she were a child and asked for a good-bye kiss—not realizing, perhaps, that she was twenty-five years old. In later life she was careful to take a firm but cordial tone with powerful men whose views she opposed.[36]

After returning from the north Julia Tutwiler lived near her family's home for three years as a teacher (eventually head) of the Greensboro Female Academy. For three years after that she taught at the Greene Springs School. If she was restless during these years, it is easy to see why. She was ambitious and skilled, but she lacked credentials and her education had been interrupted repeatedly. Family finances were much reduced since the start of the war. Her work seemed sometimes to be an unending grind; sometimes she worked herself to the point of collapse. Her schoolwork left her so little time for personal study that she despaired of reaching her father's level of culture.[37]

In an effort to address these problems, the Tutwilers decided to try the effect of changes of scenery, coupled with yet more schooling. In 1873, following some useful tutoring in foreign languages by professors in Lexington, Virginia (where one of her brothers was attending Washington and Lee), Julia Tutwiler traveled to Europe with a party of teachers and ministers. First she made a conventional tour of England; then in Brussels, after seeing the Rhineland, she made an unconventional decision. By her own account she had heard a fellow tourist speak of a Lutheran establishment, the Institute of Deaconesses at Kaiserswerth. She had heard of the institute as a school for nurses; now she learned that it also housed a normal (teacher training) department. Hastily she left her party, traveled to Kaiserswerth by railroad, and rented a hack; driving it to the institute's gates, she begged to be accepted as a pupil. She may have had several motives at once—a yearning for peace, a desire to improve her German and her teaching credentials, a wish to prolong her stay abroad. Her sudden apparition must have startled the sisters, but they allowed her to stay.[38]

Julia Tutwiler's year of normal school (1873–1874) shaped the rest of her life. At Kaiserswerth she was exposed to training in "housewifery" and other domestic skills. By this means she acquired an interest in vocational education, which given her frustrations in war-torn Alabama, she must have come to see as an instrument of economic liberation.[39] Meanwhile, she was improving her knowledge of European history and geography, with special attention to German language and literature. The sisters' method of instruction was serious-minded and thorough, infused throughout with a deep but unpretentious piety. Julia Tutwiler learned to admire the "type of woman" the institute produced: "gentle, thoughtful, intelligent women—clear-headed and open-minded, with the power to think accurately and express their thoughts plainly."[40]

Not surprisingly, an atmosphere of sisterhood prevailed at Kaiserswerth, surpassing anything that Julia Tutwiler had experienced. She was conscious of a delightful feeling of purposeful tranquility. In this frame of mind she was receptive to the Kaiserswerth approach to the practical side of life. The deaconesses lived to serve. In the course of living with them Julia Tutwiler found herself among women who worked with orphans, the aged, "Magdalens," prisoners, and hospital patients. Given her upbringing and inclinations, the young Alabamian was bound to admire the sisters' selfless heroism. In this setting, her dreams of a virtuous and successful career began to merge with an attainable reality.[41]

Often, too, it must have seemed that her childhood experiences had prepared her for what she would learn at Kaiserswerth. Henry Tutwiler had preached the benefits of a life devoted to one's fellow man. By his account, he tried to manage his dependents with love and reason. On a daily basis Julia Tutwiler saw the sisters do the same; to their way of thinking, even convicts should be treated as "penitents." Likewise, the sisters offered basic education and vocational training to their charges—just as the Tutwilers, in a more limited sense, had offered similar opportunities to their slaves. Thus in Germany and in the resonance of her memories, Julia Tutwiler found achievable goals for approaching Alabama's racial and educational problems. It was no accident that humane treatment and education of convicts and vocational training for young women were subsequently among her major concerns.[42]

The Julia Tutwiler who emerged from Kaiserswerth was a more settled person, more confident about what women could accomplish within the "sphere" assigned to them—and beyond it. For three years, in all, she lived in Germany—the last two living, for the most part, in or near Berlin. During this time she passed a government teacher's examination. In 1874–1875 she taught at a small boarding school at Steglitz. There, living frugally and working too hard for her own good, she wrote several letters to her sister Netta, pressing her and other family members to come to Germany. The idea (never realized) was that the Tutwilers could bring a sufficient number of American students to make the venture pay for itself.[43]

These letters reveal an imperious, self-justifying side to her character, but they also reflect the tremendous value that Julia Tutwiler placed upon her European experience. She knew that for the rest of her life she would enjoy the glamour of having studied foreign languages in a foreign land. She missed home and family, but she was proud of having made her own way among strangers. Another measure of independence was her success in placing travel letters, sketches, and children's pieces in the American press. She toyed with the idea of writing professionally but recognized that teaching was her calling.[44]

## Finding Her Place(s)

Returning to America in 1876, Julia Tutwiler chose to live near home. The Reconstruction era had passed; public offices and educational institutions in the Black Belt were largely in the hands of white men, a number of whom were Greene Springs graduates or family friends. Also she wanted to be near her elderly parents.[45] Soon she was teaching at the Tuscaloosa Female College, which had recently come under the direction of Alonzo Hill, a graduate of the Greene Springs School and the University of Virginia.[46] The arrangement satisfied her for several years; Hill no doubt regarded her as a prestigious addition to his faculty. In the midst of her Tuscaloosa interlude, however, a bit of the old restlessness erupted. In the summer of 1878 she managed to make another trip abroad.

The second journey was a mere jaunt compared to the first. Tutwiler had received an offer to cover a much-publicized event, the Paris Exposition, for an educational journal; she also tried to place her writings with Alabama newspapermen.[47] In Paris she took the measure of the *ecoles professionnelles*, well-run schools for the vocational and general education of young women. Observing the flow of life in the great city—with its often impersonal, frequently dangerous channels—she decided that much of the misery suffered by women could be traced to their lack of training. She made up her mind that Alabama should take steps to prevent the spread of poverty and criminality among girls.[48]

She was touched, too, to learn of the fine work done in Paris by Ada Leigh, a woman who since 1861 had been working in Paris to provide a homelike, Christian atmosphere for English-speaking girls. Leigh had begun her work by teaching Bible classes. By 1878 she was running shelters for working women, Magdalens, and orphans, and was building a church. Through these "preventive" institutions she was rescuing persons who otherwise might have become prostitutes or died of neglect. Indeed, Miss Leigh was able to solace even hardened sinners, including a woman who had declared: "I hate Christian people because all they give us is good advice." Thinking about Ada Leigh must have heightened Tutwiler's appreciation of the power of personal initiative.[49]

After her return to Tuscaloosa, the world traveler set out to do good works. By 1879 or 1880 she had begun to assist inmates at the local jail. One of her first visits, according to an often-told story, was to aid a "servant girl" who had been arrested. Tutwiler was profoundly affected by what she saw. The Tuscaloosa lockup, like most in the Black Belt, was filled with former plantation field hands awaiting trial on petty charges. To her dismay, Tutwiler soon discovered that no one seemed to care about either their physical or spiritual welfare.[50]

Compared with the housing for unfortunates at Paris or Kaiserswerth, or to any well-run penal institution, this jail was a model of cruel neglect. Prisoners were confined in unheated cells without sewage or "water other than that brought in pails at the pleasure of the jailer." Such conditions were not merely inhumane; they were unjust, inflicted upon men and women who had not yet been convicted and were still presumed innocent. Here was an opportunity for Julia Tutwiler to do her Christian duty; nor did she hesitate to involve the ladies of the town.[51]

Tuscaloosa women, in fact, had long conducted their own charitable activities. One group especially, the Tuscaloosa Female Benevolent Society, had been organized as early as the 1850s. In her jail work Julia Tutwiler enlisted the aid of this group—or a similar body, since her role in the society is not clear.[52] Probably society members conducted Bible classes and saw that the prisoners were more comfortable. At the same time they prepared to make an impact upon the state at large. In the fall of 1880, led by Tutwiler, they began a "labor of love in procuring facts and statistics and placing them before the public."[53]

Their approach was simple, methodical, modern. They sent letters to officials in the state's sixty-six counties, asking specific questions about the welfare of prisoners. The sheriffs were obliging men, for they replied speedily with information showing that only "half a dozen of the county jails were supplied with any means of warmth in winter," while sanitary facilities were primitive or nonexistent. These jails were inspected twice yearly by grand jurors, for whose visits the jailers tended to make "special preparation."[54]

Next the Benevolent Society released its findings to the press—Tutwiler's contacts with newspapermen must have helped here—in an effort to influence public opinion during the legislative session of 1880–1881. Partisan Democrats almost to a man, these journalists were accustomed to dealing roughly with disturbers of the status quo. But they knew Julia Tutwiler (or at least the Tutwiler name) and assumed that the ladies had no political motives.[55] The Eutaw *Mirror*, friendly but tentative, admitted that even criminals "should be made as comfortable as the nature of the case or the ability of the state will permit."[56]

The women of the Benevolent Society had indeed stirred a flurry of interest—with results that must have taken their breath away. The legislature, so often a graveyard of reform proposals, convened on November 9. Three days later, a bill "To Secure the Humane Treatment of Prisoners," introduced by G. R. Farnsworth of Conecuh County, was read in the senate. Referred to the Judiciary Committee, it was reported to the full senate and passed on November 24. Sent to the House, the measure was treated with similar dispatch, passing on December 4. Governor R. W. Cobb promptly signed it into law. Henceforth, sheriffs would be required to heat county jails, provide sanitary facilities, and supply prisoners with "wholesome water for drinking and bathing purposes." Sheriffs, county commissioners, probate judges, and circuit clerks were made accountable for failures in administering the law.[57]

It is hard to say whether Julia Tutwiler had lobbied the legislature personally. If subsequent events are any guide, she used her contacts among Black Belt politicians, relying generally upon her knowledge of the paternalistic psyche. Undoubtedly she was fortunate in this legislature's personnel. A. C. Hargrove, senator from Tuscaloosa and Bibb counties, was a scholarly lawyer with whom she developed a long-term working relationship. In Thomas H. Watts of Montgomery, chairman of the House Judiciary Committee, she found a venerable adviser sympathetic to the expansion of women's rights.[58] The Senate Judiciary Committee, which put the jail bill into final form, was dominated by men from the Black Belt and southwest Alabama, including Daniel S. Troy of Montgomery, son-in-law of T. H. Watts, and Thomas Seay of Hale County, a rising politician and future governor.[59]

Tutwiler and her allies were fortunate in other ways, as well. In the fall of 1880 the convict lease system was almost but not quite a dominant public issue. Abuses inherent in the system were starting to bother the sort of people capable of taking effective action—educated white people like Tutwiler and others of her social class.[60] The poor folk whose kin were being sent to the camps were mostly unable to protest. Governor Cobb, for his part, had several bones to pick with aspects of the system. He worried that the tendency of judges to sentence felons to "hard labor for the county" would disrupt the state's supply of convict labor, thereby reducing revenues. On a more humanitarian note, he was concerned that too many convicts were serving long sentences for nothing more than failure to pay court costs.[61] Cobb was also feuding with the warden of the state penitentiary system, J. G. Bass. By the end of the legislative session the Bass administration was under legislative investigation. From that point on, the convict lease system (its morality, its rules and regulations, its profitability) proved an enduring issue; and Julia Tutwiler was in the thick of it. But from her point of view in the fall of 1880, it was fortunate that jail reform was not lost in the furor of the larger dispute.[62]

Nonetheless, the success of her jail work completed Julia Tutwiler's education in reform and affected her in important ways. First, her faith in the old-time Whig vision of politics was confirmed. More than ever, she believed that public policy could be affected by reasoned debate and that elected officials, particularly gentlemen of the Black Belt, could be brought to make enlightened decisions on behalf of less fortunate persons. She knew that Alabama was a poor state and that some—too many!—Democratic politicians were reluctant to come to the aid of their African American constituents. But for many years to come, she would continue to believe in the efficacy of educational campaigns and persistent lobbying. In this she was anticipating the reformist tactics of the women's organizations that were, over the next two generations, to make quiet but vital contributions to Progressivism and related social movements. When the Women's Christian Temperance Union established itself in Alabama in the mid-1880s, preaching a range of reforms by just such means, Julia Tutwiler was ready to take on leadership roles.[63]

## Forward from Strength

Tutwiler's interest in jail and prison work propelled her into an important arena of the contemporary women's movement. By the 1870s a growing number of northern women were active in prison reform work. Their chief goal was to better the condition of female inmates, who were often subjected to physical and sexual abuse. These reformers responded to Frances E. Willard's "do everything" policy within the WCTU, but they also constituted notable groups within such nascent organizations as the American Prison Association and the National Conference of Charities and Corrections. Their agenda included support for the separation of prisoners by age, gender, and type of offense—essentially the program for which Julia Tutwiler would lobby the Alabama legislature, beginning in the mid-1880s.[64]

A historian of nineteenth-century women prison activists has concluded that many of them were children of well-educated, reformist parents. At their schools, these young women had acquired a sense of female solidarity; yet they were also comfortable with the "separate sphere" concept of woman as guardian of home and morals. They were committed to bringing "unique feminine virtues" into public life, and in order to do so, they—like Julia Tutwiler—utilized hometown networks of women, naturally deriving both satisfaction and confidence from running their own operations.[65] Something of their mingled determination and serenity comes through in a comment Julia Tutwiler made about the value of working through the WCTU. She had been sure, she wrote, that her "suggestions might have more weight" if supported by "so many good women."[66]

Soon after leading the Tuscaloosa Benevolent Society to victory, Julia Tutwiler turned forty. Within a few months she would begin her career at Livingston. Who was she? To be sure, she was still a child of Greene Springs. There she had learned to love knowledge and to have faith in the power of applied reason. There she had absorbed a Whiggish outlook, including a willingness to trust governments and schools with social improvements. Her early education had shown her that Alabama's racial burdens were heavy and almost impossible to discharge equitably. But she had learned to be comfortable with the planter-class men who would lead the state from their secure bastions in the Black Belt. Of course (as argued above) Julia Tutwiler was also a product of formal education and travel. Any one component of her training might have marked her as unusual. As it was, training and personality combined to make her an extraordinary person. It is not hard to see how her contemporaries came to regard her as unique, a saintly eccentric, the state's conscience, one whose "principle aim in life . . . is to alleviate the distress of the poor and needy."[67]

The Julia Tutwiler of 1881 had propelled herself into many situations, emerging as an optimistic, focused person. She had prepared herself well for the roles that she was to play, in which she would simultaneously accept and transcend the traditional image of woman. In addition, she had begun to make contact with like-minded individuals—men and women, politicians, educators, clubwomen, clergy—who were committed to making the social and economic status quo work better. All, perhaps Julia Tutwiler most of all, believed that the existing system should and could be administered with compassion, concern, and a sense of fairness. Together with her allies and counterparts, she would add a touch of plantation gentility to Progressivism. From the standpoint of the 1880s and 1890, it might be more accurate to call her a Bourbon reformer.

# 4
# James F. Smith

## Ordination and Order

## Introduction

It is easy to think of the New South as an epoch of blood and iron, a time of profound material change set upon the ruins of an old order. Julia Tutwiler shows us, however, that some of the social change—change of the type that originates in schools or through the activities of private groups—was rooted in older pathways of thought and action. In many respects, Tutwiler was herself an institution of continuity and change.

James F. Smith, subject of this essay, grew up within institutions, namely denominational churches. Within these worlds were large, mostly coherent sets of principles—ideas designed to move forward through the world, impervious to accidents of politics, economics, or war, overcoming all opposition yet planted on foundations comfortably familiar. For Smith, this world of organized religion made good sense, and he accepted the goals, first of the Methodist Protestant Church and then of the Protestant Episcopal Church. His vision of the good society was similar to Tutwiler's, though he never aspired to set in motion the sweeping changes she contemplated. Smith's was an existence smaller in scale, closer to life as lived in Alabama's small towns.

## Early Life

James Franklin Smith (1821–1899) was the son of Thomas Smith, a settler in Autauga County in south-central Alabama. The elder Smith began as an artisan and farmer, but by 1850 he belonged to that elite group of southerners who owned more than twenty slaves. His several children were raised in the midst of rude plenty and with a sense that they were rising in the world—not yeomen, yet not exactly members of the gentry.[1]

One of Thomas Smith's chief interests was the spread and reform of religion. Raised a Quaker and a convert to Methodism, Smith was by the 1830s a member of the Methodist Protestant Church—itself an offshoot, the product of many years of dispute within the Methodist Episcopal Church. Methodist Protestants opposed the hierarchical power of bishops and elders in the parent body, and the clerical domination of church conferences and meetings.[2] By demanding a greater voice for the laity, Thomas Smith and his cohorts had reenacted the rebellion of eighteenth-century evangelicals against established religion. Viewed in another light, the Methodist Protestant Church was an example of Jacksonian Democracy in religion.[3]

Evangelical churches were the means by which the residents of a sparsely settled society came together in communal worship. Members of diverse ages and social status and of both races were united by the experience of conversion. This was described as the pouring of God's grace into the soul, following the would-be convert's "conviction" of his or her sinful state and his or her understanding of God's freely offered salvation.[4] Thus the religious world into which Thomas Smith introduced his children was one of both shared and private feelings, simultaneously anxious and comfortable, nearly always emotional. For James F. Smith, it seems clear that church life was the central element of his youth, both in a social sense and in terms of the spiritual feelings that would give meaning to his life. Reminiscing many years later, Smith implied that between the ages of sixteen and twenty-two he had embraced a religious vocation. Accepting the challenge of a call to the ministry, he began to preach.[5]

## Initiation to Ministry

In the 1840s the road to ordination in the Methodist Protestant Church was marked by the study of nineteen works, including several by Methodist icon John Wesley.[6] At the same time (and to his lasting pleasure) Smith tackled Latin and Greek, though he previously had little education beyond "the pleasures of the farm."[7] By 1845 Smith was listed among the itinerant preachers of his church; the following year he was fully ordained. During these years, probably, he also began to teach school, a common way for preachers to supplement their inadequate salaries. In all, Smith would spend about ten years teaching the sons of planters and farmers.[8]

Smith had embarked upon a life of creative tension and travel—wrestling with the minds of young folk on weekdays and packing his saddlebags for trips to rural chapels on weekends.[9] Methodist Protestant sermonizing was little different from that of other Methodists. Preachers typically considered it their duty to make clear the burden of sin, explain the "universal atonement" effected by Christ, and emphasize the "free grace" offered by God.[10] A lean, intelligent-looking man with an otherworldly gaze, Smith was described by a Methodist Episcopal historian as a "zealous" preacher. From the pulpit he may have employed the frightening imagery of God's wrath; yet all we know of his later style indicates that he combined earnestness with an appeal to reasonable sentiments.[11]

In general, Smith's career as a clergyman was influenced by his experience as a teacher. He did not think of himself as a man set apart; rather, he was dedicated to spreading both salvation and enlightenment, and it probably would not have occurred to him that the two might be separated. Such a personality was well suited to the period in which Alabama society made the transition from frontier crudity to greater pretensions.[12]

## Turbulence, Change

In 1847 Smith married Martha Hightower, who was only fifteen at the time, but she would demonstrate the emotional and physical strength necessary to bear eleven children and raise five. She took in stride Smith's absences and the many social demands placed upon a clergyman's wife, and allowed her husband to follow his inspiration.[13] By 1850–1851 they had moved across the Alabama River to Lowndes County, where Smith could preach, farm, and teach—all in the thick of a booming plantation society.[14] Social life flourished in town and country, as cotton nabobs mingled with men and women of elevated culture. And though it was true, as Episcopal bishop Nicholas Hamner Cobbs complained, that many persons raised their children "to regard money as the chief good," it was also true that many owners of white-pillared mansions aspired to a high standard of gentility.[15]

Some members of the slaveholding classes were willing to see themselves as members of a paternalistic elite, holding out the benefits of work, discipline, and Christianity to their slaves. Evangelical clergymen—wrestling over the moral ambiguities (to say the least) of slaveholding—encouraged the masters in this attitude and often conducted missionary work on the plantations. Thus at mid-century the Protestant denominations were functionally integrated in established society. Theologically rooted in the spiritual liberation of individuals, they were now attuned to the preservation of peace and order in a slaveholding society.[16]

It is hard to determine whether Smith had any doubts concerning the morality of slavery.[17] The evidence suggests that he was an able worker among slaves, and he took the continuity of the "Peculiar Institution" for granted. By the late 1850s he owned both land and slaves, and was prospering with the good times. By 1860 his real properties alone were worth $28,000—a small fortune, though he could scarcely compete with the leading planters of Lowndes County, some of whom owned multiple plantations and hundreds of human beings.[18] For all his wealth and good work spreading the gospel, the 1850s were trying years for James and Martha Smith. Over these years they would suffer the loss of at least one child.[19] In addition, Smith would undergo a painful disillusionment—not a crisis of faith, but a falling out with the church that had nurtured him.

For Alabama Methodist Protestants, freedom from hierarchy had not brought about internal peace. Indeed they quarreled among themselves to the point of paralysis, holding frequent church trials "upon charges trivial in themselves and notoriously false."[20] Even simple matters of discipline were likely to cause heated divisions, a situation which caused the statewide Annual Conference of 1849 to conclude that its power was "so weakened over its own ministers as to be incapable of proper legislation."[21]

Smith was involved in at least one troubled initiative of the Methodist Protestants. In the 1840s a wealthy layman, Bolling Hall, had received permission to build a Methodist Protestant high school at Robinson's Springs, not too far from Smith's childhood home. As a well-established pastor, Smith served on the school's board of trustees and probably helped to raise funds. But not enough, evidently; and in 1853 disputes broke out over the location and nature of the proposed institution, which in fact was never built.[22]

National church politics were equally unstable, as the abolition controversy, having divided the Methodist Episcopal and Baptist churches in the 1840s, embroiled the Methodist Protestants as well. Northern members objected to regulations that prevented African Americans from holding church offices. In turn, they sought to make "voluntary slave-holding and dealing" a bar to membership itself. The southern response may be gauged by a resolution of Alabama's 1849 Annual Conference. However weak that body's control over its ministers, it instructed the state's national delegates "to oppose, firmly and determinedly, any alteration in our Constitution and *Discipline* on the subject of slavery." Debates over the morality of slavery culminated in 1857–1858, when representatives of northern conferences suspended relations with the remainder of the denomination.[23]

It is likely that Smith was as much disturbed by the national breakup of his church as by its local wrangles. Like other southern evangelicals in a maturing society, he was hoping to make his denomination durable and versatile, a stable religious institution.[24] Schisms among believers—viewed apart from the heat of sectional politics—could only limit the impact of church doctrine and the effectiveness of the church as teacher. Whether he was aware of it or not, Smith had come a great distance from the "come outer" mentality of Methodist Protestants. By the late 1850s, Smith needed a church whose leaders were powerful enough to restrain local squabblers and whose doctrine was broad enough to lessen the impact of sectional crises. As it chanced, it was at the very height of sectional conflict that Smith came under the influence of Nicholas Hamner Cobbs and made the difficult decision to break with his past life.

## New Mission

Cobbs (1796–1861) was born in Virginia and, like Smith, had mixed school teaching and preaching. Cobbs had served parishes in Virginia and Ohio before his election as the first Protestant Episcopal bishop of Alabama in 1844.[25] A man of tremendous energy, Cobbs traveled the state preaching and recruited a corps of clergy who were willing to make rounds like Methodist circuit riders. In the seventeen years of his episcopate he saw the number of parishes increase from a mere handful to more than twenty. Based at St. John's in Montgomery, Cobbs undertook missionary work in several counties, including Lowndes and Autauga.[26]

Smith was a likely candidate for conversion. Under the influence of the culturally ecumenical "Muhlenberg" movement, a number of Episcopal priests were anxious to recruit clergymen from evangelical denominations.[27] Whether or not he was a special target, Smith heard the arguments commonly used by Episcopal missionaries of the day. The latter were accustomed to dealing with evangelical Christians whose spiritual development had moved toward an appreciation of corporate unity in religion—more or less the position that, clearly, appealed to Smith.

Episcopalians claimed that, as members of the Anglican Communion, they were heirs of the purest religious lineage in the Western world. As the authentic descendant of the primitive church (as its spokesmen claimed), the Protestant Episcopal Church was a powerful force for spiritual unity in America. Churchmen might argue fiercely over slavery and other moral issues, but their conception of the church as the sacred body of Christ precluded division. Laboring in a fragmented denomination, Smith may have taken to heart the words of Henry C. Lay, a priest who reminded evangelicals that the Episcopal Church had preserved its unity while other churches had "dug a deep trench all along Mason and Dixon's line."[28]

At some point Smith was initiated into the pleasures of the *Book of Common Prayer*, which was viewed by Cobbs and his priests as an essential guide to religious tradition. A repository of worship and spiritual education, the prayer book was designed to point the way to sincere piety and to shape the characters of those who followed it throughout the church year. Persons so trained were likely to embrace moderation and brotherly love—and would naturally thrive within the polity of the Protestant Episcopal Church, which had established a balance between lay and clerical "orders." To Smith, such a principle may have seemed an ideal compromise between the quarrelsome democracy of the Methodist Protestant Church and the powerful hierarchy of the Methodist Episcopal Church.[29] By the late 1850s, perhaps further influenced by the stratified society of the Black Belt, Smith had fully accepted hierarchy as an appropriate organizing principle.

To be sure, Smith must have been aware that many Alabamians disliked the Episcopal Church. To these persons, the Episcopal Church was a preserve of the rich, of hypocrites who were satisfied with a formal devotion, of those unspontaneous and lacking in "heart religion." It was true that Episcopalians often refused to join in the revival movements that, at intervals, swept up whole communities. A number of priests were actively opposed to revivals—like Henry C. Lay, who implied that sinners were pressured by public scrutiny into dubious conversions.[30] Under these circumstances, Cobbs probably viewed Smith as a man who would be skilled at building bridges for converts.

Whatever thoughts were swirling through his mind, Smith affiliated with the Protestant Episcopal Church in late 1857 or early 1858. He was not alone in making such a decision; several Lowndes County Methodist Protestants became Episcopalians in that year.[31] After producing the necessary testimonials, Smith was admitted as a candidate for Holy Orders in May 1858 and ordained a deacon in July. Cobbs noted that Smith's labors demonstrated "the most flattering prospects of usefulness and success," and in July 1859 the bishop presided at Smith's ordination to the priesthood.[32]

Thereafter, Smith would pursue his career for nearly four decades as a devoted Episcopalian; though shortly after his ordination, he would reveal something of the psychic price he had paid in leaving his former communion. In September 1860, Smith gave the sermon at the ordination of James S. Jarratt, like himself a former Methodist Protestant. A correspondent of the *Church Intelligencer* noted that "the speaker's allusions to the trials and experiences through which both had passed, were exceedingly impressive, and the occasion was one of deep interest." Smith chose Acts 20:31 as his text: "Therefore watch, and remember, that by the space of three years I ceased not to warn every one day and night with tears."[33]

Like other Alabamians, Smith was caught up in the drama of secession. Cobbs was one of the state's most distinguished opponents of disunion, but like other Union men, he was outmaneuvered in the days following Abraham Lincoln's election. In fact, Cobbs died on January 11, 1861, the day Alabama seceded from the Union.[34] His successor, Richard Hooker Wilmer, was not elected until November—which meant that the diocese was effectively leaderless during the months of discussion preceding the formation of the Protestant Episcopal Church of the Confederate States of America. Smith was present as an observer in July 1861 as delegates of several dioceses met in Montgomery to launch the new national church.[35]

## Polity of Slavery

However, neither changes in church government nor the war affected Smith's initial assignments, which probably were typical for an able-bodied priest in an undermanned diocese. From 1859 to 1867 he was missionary to Autauga County, assigned to St. Matthew's, Autaugaville, and to Prattville, near the site of Daniel Pratt's manufacturing enterprises. During most of this time he was rector of St. Paul's, Lowndesboro, where his charges included planters and their slaves.[36] Working with skill and energy, he encountered obstacles as varied as his congregations.

Smith was at first excited to find a growing interest in the Episcopal Church in Autauga County; this was especially so in Prattville, where the number of his communicants tripled from 1859 to 1861. He hoped that he could establish a "self-supporting parish," but soon he was complaining that "the distracted state of the country" was holding back further progress. Like other clergymen, Smith was facing the consequences of Confederate mobilization. Soldiers, managers, and mechanics were much in demand, and his congregation was not the only one to suffer.[37]

In Lowndes County, the heart of the Black Belt, Smith enjoyed a notable success catechizing and preaching to black folk. In one year (1861–1862) he baptized thirty-six persons, thirty-five of whom were black, and presented twelve candidates for confirmation, including nine slaves. Bishop Wilmer, who had made missionary work among slaves a priority, must have been delighted.[38] Yet it was difficult for any priest to keep slave parishioners. Owners moved their slaves or sold them, and the slaves often showed a strong desire to worship free of white control. In 1865 Smith reported only one African American communicant at St. Paul's, possibly as an indirect consequence of the invasion of the area by Federal troops in April.[39]

After the Confederacy's collapse, Alabama's un-Reconstructed bishop courted trouble by recommending that his clergymen omit the prayer for those in authority conventionally said during worship. The result was that Federal authorities, overreacting to the implied slight, banned Episcopal services for several months. For Smith and other priests, this affair was the culmination of a number of maddening disruptions. They had little choice, though, but to rally behind Wilmer. In 1866 Smith joined his fellows, who resolved that they would persevere despite "the interruptions of travel, the irregularity of the mails, the interference of military authorities," and the failure of many parishes to respond.[40]

Overall, the Alabama clergy were exhausted and discouraged. Though many of them had opposed war and secession, they had been loyal Confederates. For four years they had preached, consoled, raised money for wounded soldiers and destitute families—while shortages, currency inflation, and defeats mocked their efforts. Their own families had suffered because most of them lacked the time, means, or the blessing of society to make money through conventional channels. For years, subscriptions for ministers had typically been a few hundred dollars. But by the latter part of the war, the *Church Intelligencer* estimated that an income of five thousand dollars was necessary to support a family of six.[41] That figure might as well have been determined with Smith's family in mind—but how was he to manage his lands, or teach, while doing justice to three congregations? Under such circumstances, church work must sooner or later be secondary to survival, and the more conscientious the priest, the more depressed he would be.

## Breakdown and New Beginnings

Smith had hoped that the Protestant Episcopal Church would be a unifying force among Christians and a solid base for his own career. His nadir came in the years following the war, when it seemed that he could neither earn a living nor find a stable congregation. He began serving as a missionary to Snowdoun in rural Montgomery County in late 1865, a time when Federal troops barred him from meeting most of his other appointments. Though there were few communicants there, he stated in 1867 that a parish could be launched "provided the necessary labor and zeal could be bestowed." He made no report the following year, and in 1869 explained that he had been teaching school, which left him little time for visiting the flocks. He complained of bad weather and the state of the roads, which prevented his congregation from assembling. "How much of the want of success is due to my own unfaithfulness," he somberly offered, "it is not expected of me to say. May God have mercy on priest and people."[42]

In August 1868, he had taken on a mission at Mt. Meigs, also in Montgomery County. There his charges were relatively well-to-do and able to raise a substantial building fund, but their loyalty was to St. John's in the nearby city. In a mood of humility Smith reported that the drawing power of his services was less than that of "one of the most popular of the denominations," which held its meeting on the same day.[43] Clearly he had begun to doubt his ministerial talents, while his poverty must have been a nagging distraction. Just prior to the war he had been comfortably well-off, but five years after the peace, his properties were worth little more than five thousand dollars.[44]

Wilmer was a man of stern will, with the look of an Old Testament patriarch. But he understood Smith's troubles and, far from punishing him, decided to give him a change of scenery and a fresh challenge. In north-central Alabama there were several fledgling congregations with no priest to serve them. The climate was healthy and several of the towns were accessible by railroad. By the spring of 1870, Smith was the Episcopal Church's evangelist in the area, based in the town of Talladega, and serving Talladega and surrounding counties.[45] Supported by his church and a strong-minded wife, Smith pulled himself together and entered into the life of town and country.

Talladega in 1870 was a community of about two thousand souls. For decades it had been the county seat and trading center for a society of middling planters and yeomen farmers. As early as the 1850s, the tone of town life was influenced by a Whiggish elite—merchants, planters, entrepreneurs, and politicians who built beautiful homes, patronized specialty shops, and in general were willing to spend money in order to enjoy a more cosmopolitan atmosphere. Schools and learning flourished in these circumstances, despite the war. In addition, parents of sufficient means could choose among several private schools, including a female seminary run by the Reverend Thomas A. Cooke, an Episcopal priest.[46]

The presence of high-grade ore in the hills nearby, with ready access to transport (the Alabama and Tennessee Rivers Railroad) seemed to justify the optimism of local developers. However, the town needed rebuilding, and the people were not reunified. Union raiders had burned the center of town twice during the war. Subsequently townsfolk took sides in bitter disputes typical of the Reconstruction era. The old Whiggish elite, still a cultural and economic force, was fading into political oblivion or (much the same thing) Republicanism. Shortly after the Smiths arrived, a new Democratic elite of merchants and professional men consolidated their power, a state of affairs that more or less coincided with the Democratic "Redemption" of the state from Republican rule in 1874.[47]

Life in town had never included a stable Episcopal congregation. Local religious life was dominated by Methodists, Baptists, and Presbyterians; apparently there was considerable local prejudice against Episcopalians. Prodded by Cobbs, Cooke had held services for a few communicants, but plans for a parish were thrown into confusion by war. For a time, services were provided by the Reverend Joseph Nicholson, chaplain at a nearby conscript camp. Nicholson was a high churchman, a proponent of episcopacy whose views may have aggravated local prejudices.[48] The image of the Episcopal Church may also have suffered because a number of Republicans were members, including the family of industrialist Arthur Bingham, said to be an intense political partisan.[49]

Smith understood that one of his tasks was to win a place for the Protestant Episcopal Church. But that result, he believed, would follow naturally if he worked to gain the attention and respect of upstanding folk in and near town. The Smiths took possession of a large house that they shared with their four children and two black servants and their children. Eventually they took in an assortment of students and other boarders. Holding services in his own parlor and in a rented upper room, Smith gathered an interesting congregation, including the family of a country physician and a mixture of professionals, businessmen, and their families.[50] Bringing to bear all of his unpretentious conviction, he showed by example that Episcopalians cherished scripture and "heart religion." Yet his pulpit style conveyed the sense of disciplined faith. A Talladega clergyman later wrote that James Smith was "the old-fashioned type who used to number the headings of his sermons. After 'tenthly' usually came 'and lastly,' after which came 'in conclusion.'"[51]

If Smith followed the path marked out by a contemporary book written to attract inquirers, he may have tried to explain several questions: how the Protestant Episcopal doctrine and practice resembled that of the Roman Catholic Church, and how it differed; why the interiors of Episcopal churches were different from those of other Protestant churches; why the Episcopal Church did not have revivals; and more generally, whether a liturgical church could meet the religious needs of ordinary folk.[52]

On the last two points Smith's answer would have been emphatic. Exhortation might be an important tool for missionaries, but he believed that liturgical worship offered the best means of attaining a Christian character. He must have agreed with the author of an article in an Alabama Episcopal magazine, *The Old Church Path,* who wrote that human beings are both imitative and creatures of habit. Early in life, said the writer, men seize upon models of behavior, and what better model than the life of Jesus Christ, whose words and deeds are presented week after week in the liturgy of the Protestant Episcopal Church? The effect is "to chisel out . . . upon our rough humanity, a form and character as near as can be to the perfect pattern."[53] If such was the effect of Episcopal worship, one can imagine Smith saying, what else do the people need?

Smith never devoted himself to Talladega alone. Over the years he would serve congregations in Elyton, Jacksonville, Anniston, Montevallo, and elsewhere.[54] Yet Talladega, where he lived for almost all of the rest of his life, was the scene of his most concentrated labors. In the spring of 1871, he reported a confirmation class of thirteen and stated that he was serving thirty-four communicants (up ten from the previous year) and forty-six other baptized persons. In addition he presided over a Sunday school with two teachers and fifteen scholars. The next year there was a confirmation class of seven, with an overall flock of forty-five communicants and fifty-five other baptized persons. During that spring of 1872, Smith and his parishioners were awaiting completion of a chapel that (with its fixtures) would cost more than a thousand dollars. The new church would be called St. Peter's.[55]

Even as he described these successes, Smith remarked: "The harvest truly is great—but O that we had the laborers!" In the mid-1870s—economically troubled times—he found it hard to maintain the pace of parish growth. He managed to hold his ground despite the hard times and persistent anti-Episcopal sentiment, and in 1880, he reported a congregation made up of sixty communicants and sixty baptized non-communicants. With some pride, he concluded that "Sectarian prejudice, though somewhat abated, [is] still very strong. But one thing can be safely affirmed: the church is *respected* where it is not admired."[56]

The truth was that Smith, with his version of evangelical Anglicanism, had accomplished a great deal. In round figures there were ten times as many Episcopalians in town as there had been when he arrived. The 120 churchgoers of 1880 represented about ten percent of Talladega's white population. Most of the remaining nine-tenths were comfortable within the Methodist, Baptist, or Presbyterian churches. There is no evidence that Smith performed systematic work among Talladega's African American population. He was not expected to, and his efforts might not have been welcome; the religious lives of most black churchgoers were vigorous and separate.[57]

From 1880 to 1884 the number of parishioners at St. Peter's grew only slightly. Smith continued as rector but devoted a goodly portion of his attention to missionary work. For two years he lived in Jacksonville, working to build up nearby rural congregations and attempting to halt a decline in the membership of St. Luke's, the local parish.[58] In December 1884, though, he and his family returned to live in Talladega, where economic and political changes presented him with further opportunities to advance the role of the Protestant Episcopal Church in community life.[59]

That New South Religion?

By the mid-1880s a tremendous industrial development was underway in the nearby cities of Birmingham and Anniston, and Talladega was beginning to share in the excitement and prosperity. The Binghams had established the Eagle Works, a sawmill and factory for wooden products. Another Episcopalian, George W. Chambers, had begun a career of land speculation that would make him a leading developer of timber and minerals. A decade before, men like Chambers and Arthur Bingham would have been doubly outside the normal life of town leaders—both as capitalists and as Episcopalians. Now it seemed that there were would-be industrialists in all the churches.[60] Besides, new people—businessmen and clerks, railroad officers and hands, factory hands and craftsmen, lawyers and other professionals—were flowing with their families into the area, lending Talladega and other communities a brisker, more businesslike air. Now seemingly liberated from the destruction of war and the doldrums of Reconstruction, Talladega boasted dozens of business establishments. Two new narrow-gauge railroads (constructed with a mixture of local and outside capital) carried iron ore and timber, goods and people. Before the end of the decade, Talladega's population would approach four thousand.[61]

The 1880s was a time in which young men, having come of age politically, offered a challenge to the rule of the Civil War generation. The local exemplar of this new era was William H. Skaggs (1861–1947), a real estate speculator who in 1885 was elected mayor over the opposition of the merchant-elite old guard. Unlike his cautious predecessors, Skaggs viewed government as a tool for shaping the future. Supported by a coalition of old and new residents, he accomplished wonders. His three administrations (1885–1891) brought paved streets, public education, modern water and sewerage systems, and improved police and fire departments to the town. To say the least, Talladegans learned to cope with fast-paced material progress![62]

As Talladega grew more crowded, matters of behavior, order, and safety began to occupy a prominent place in public discussions. The town had always had its share of drunkenness and rowdy behavior, but in the 1880s many residents decided that the town square was an unacceptably rough place. By day or night, crowds of young men and boys loitered in front of the town's several saloons or clustered on corners, from which they hailed passersby. Bad language, fights, even gunplay were common results of these gatherings.[63]

In response, preachers warned against a whole catalog of sins, including several which were affronts to holiness and to decorum. The liquor trade was one of their particular targets and, for that matter, of reformist organizations such as the Women's Christian Temperance Union. All agreed with revivalist Sam Jones that liquor was "a good thing in its place, but its place is in hell." In fact, Talladega prohibitionists engaged in persistent campaigns against the saloons (to say nothing of the town's houses of ill repute); but not until 1907 were they able to win the political and legal battles necessary to close such profitable and well-patronized enterprises. Frustrated, evangelicals fell back upon the always-reliable revivals and protracted meetings. There, they believed, the eloquence of preachers and the enthusiasm of the crowds would bring people out of sin and into the better-regulated life of the churches.[64]

Smith may well have denounced drunkenness and other sins from the pulpit. Yet overall, his response to the problems of boom times reflected a balance of sacred and secular considerations. Like his evangelical colleagues, he considered it his duty to uphold standards of decorum. But the Episcopal Church, while endorsing temperance, treated the consumption of alcohol as a matter of personal, not communal discipline.[65] Thus Smith was not a prisoner of the Demon Rum question. Besides, as an old teacher and missionary, he had trained himself to approach problems in terms of education—breaking through limitations, not setting limits.

After spending his life in a world of rapid changes, Smith probably saw Talladega's future in terms of physical, cultural, and spiritual expansion. Certainly he was not the only citizen who worked to enlarge the role of the educated middle class and make their standards the norm; Skaggs and his supporters had ambitious plans for the educational life of the town. But Smith, more than many clergymen, was willing to mingle parish affairs with public affairs, broadly defined. Working with his congregation, he allowed them to raise funds through experiments in civic uplift.[66]

Southern women in the 1880s were on the verge of a movement of club work and civic activity that would, as noted above, be a quiet but pervasive contribution to Progressivism in Alabama.[67] Church benefit sales and parties were by no means new, but Smith's women parishioners entered into them with more than usual zest and imagination. In 1884, for example, the women of St. Peter's took over city hall and staged a "Japanese Tea Party" with a "Boston" art exhibit and cakewalk on the side. Two years later local Episcopalians sponsored a children's concert, which featured the singing and playing of children from the Alabama Institute for the Deaf and Blind.[68] However beneficial, such entertainments were not likely to attract large numbers of people. Yet soon Smith would give his approval to a more daring cultural enterprise.

Protestant clergymen had long regarded the theatre as an agency of worldly temptation. Smith, however, regarded drama as (potentially) a wholesome, moral form of entertainment—nor was he alone among late-nineteenth-century Episcopal clergy.[69] Whether Smith initiated the idea of staging plays for the benefit of St. Peter's is unknown; he may have been influenced by George W. Chambers, who would shortly build a public "opera house" where both amateur and professional companies were welcome.[70] In any case, benefit productions beginning with the play *Esmerelda* in 1886 helped to make theatre respectable in Talladega. Within two years local amateurs had organized the Talladega Dramatic Company and were performing melodramas to large audiences. An 1888 showing (for St. Peter's) of *Above the Clouds* featured such characters as a Country Gentleman, a Wronged Wife, and one Crazy Phil; the actor who played the latter offered "his pathetic picture of a wretched hearthstone." In addition to local people, the show attracted sixty patrons from nearby Anniston, who chartered a train for the trip.[71]

St. Peter's had helped to launch an activity that would offer young people recreation, even artistic opportunities—an alternative to street corners and saloons. In the process Smith and his parishioners had boosted civic pride and contributed to the spirit of cultural revival exemplified by Mayor Skaggs' new public school. Not surprisingly, the Protestant Episcopal Church in Talladega entered another period of growth. Spring 1886 saw Smith ministering to a total of 172 persons at St. Peter's.[72]

## Disorder v. Extra-Order

Meanwhile, Skaggs and his police force had been presenting young roughs with another alternative: behave or face punishment. Skaggs was willing to tolerate the saloons, whose taxes and fees helped underwrite civic improvements. But physical challenges to his regime were another matter. When a group of white delinquents repeatedly tried to "shoot up the square," he sentenced them to labor on the street gang, a punishment previously (and tacitly) reserved for black offenders. Public opinion was divided, in part because years of semi-frontier life had accustomed residents to slack or selective law enforcement. Some citizens saw Skaggs' response as overreaction—or even as a threat to that sacred totem, white supremacy. Others, more optimistic about the gains to be derived from the rule of law, were delighted. After a year of vigilance, Skaggs and his lawmen ruled the streets.[73] But the young mayor had not effected an overnight change in the collective psyche of Talladega youth.

In the summer of 1887, young people began committing acts of defiance in Talladega churches. The offenders were not drunken rowdies. Instead they were members of the group most likely to benefit from economic and cultural progress; they were children of "highly esteemed" parents. Judging by an article written by Baptist minister George A. Lofton, their rebellious acts included staring at worshippers; going in and out of church during services; talking, laughing, and smoking during worship; spitting on church floors; defacing hymnbooks, pews, and walls; and peeping into church windows while services were in progress. On at least one occasion the young people persisted after the minister had requested them to stop.[74]

Talladega ministers, like their counterparts elsewhere, were probably resigned to a certain amount of naughty behavior, but these youngsters presented a challenge to their elders.[75] Older Talladegans could doubtless remember how a similar problem had been solved a quarter century earlier, when drunken boors had annoyed ladies with "insolent utterances" spoken through church windows. Two of the leading laymen of the Methodist Church had run outside and caned the offenders—to the satisfaction of the historian who chronicled the incident.[76] Probably, most citizens expected that parents would administer whippings to the irreverent young folk of 1887.

Others, sympathetic to Mayor Skaggs' approach to discipline, would have preferred to resort to legal force. An individual signing himself "Order" wrote to the Talladega *Our Mountain Home* discussing the possibility of arrests unless the troubles ceased.[77] Order's attitude was sure to be offensive to clergymen, who naturally regarded the problem as falling within their jurisdiction. The seriousness of the situation—capped off by the threat of police intervention—moved Smith to address the public. Though in cultural affairs he had sometimes acted as a modernizer, he had scarcely forgotten the traditions that held the Protestant Episcopal Church together. Now he would argue that those traditions were superior to either frontier violence or state-regulated morality.

In a letter to the Talladega *Reporter and Watchtower*, Smith asked his neighbors to take a broad view of American religious practices. Surveying the nation's religious scenery, he declared that "the great mass of the people" had "drifted away from the primitive and scriptural idea that the chief business that a congregation has at the House of God is Worship." Part of the problem was inherent in the emphasis that many denominations placed upon preaching. "Now what do you hear of a Sunday morning?" he wrote. "One says I am going to hear the learned Dr. A *preach*, or the eloquent Dr. B., or the witty Mr. C., or the erratic Mr. D. All going to *preaching*, not to be instructed: not to be edified, but to be *entertained*." Raised with such expectations, Smith continued, young people naturally "set about entertaining themselves" when a preacher failed to engage their interest.[78]

Smith next turned to the recent disturbances, which he asserted were not the appropriate concern of law enforcement officials. Instead, he recommended Episcopal practices as preventative medicine. Parents, he declared, should put aside their prejudices against religious forms. Once they had trained their children "in the use of a solemn sound scriptural Liturgy, the trouble would be over," since piety and right behavior would long since have become habitual in the young.

Thus Smith, who had begun his career preaching to congregations that had broken away from central authority, made his plea for an "order" based upon liturgical discipline and conditioned reverence. At the same time he revealed that his hopes for the future lay in the direction of ecumenical movements. He quoted a Presbyterian minister who had advocated the adoption of a uniform liturgy among American Christians as a step toward "that organic unity . . . for which so many pious hearts are aching, throbbing." Of course, he noted, there was such a liturgy at hand—namely, that contained in the *Book of Common Prayer,* "that is, or ought to be the common heritage of all English-speaking Christians."[79]

Smith disclaimed any intention to offend, but he must have known that his version of "broad" religious views would draw fire from evangelicals. Hardly a week had passed before the Reverend George A. Lofton (whose sermons received considerable attention in *Our Mountain Home*) felt called upon to answer Smith in print. Citing St. Paul as his authority, Lofton dismissed Smith's liturgical leanings as "the bondage of old legal ceremonialism"; instead, he maintained that religion should be spontaneous. Christ, he reminded Smith, had established the institution of preaching and expected his followers to respect it. With one eye on Smith and another on church troubles, Lofton intoned that ministers should talk less of church and more of Christ. Yet he too believed that turning bothersome youngsters over to the police would be a "harsh," unwarranted action.[80]

This printed controversy—a brief recapitulation of a very old debate—ended after one exchange. As he had in fact been doing for decades, Smith politely challenged the religious practices of Talladega. It is a tribute to his reputation and accomplishments that he was not criticized more harshly (in the newspapers) in a community known for prejudice against ceremonial religion. As the fall came on, little more was heard from the youths, which must have made church people of all descriptions sigh with relief—especially the two clergymen who, whatever their differences, had agreed upon steering a middle course between anarchy and the extra-order of literal-minded Progressivism.

By the year's end Smith had retired from his rectorship to devote more time to missionary work. Still, he continued to exert an influence in St. Peter's parish life. In 1889 he was instrumental in reuniting the congregation after his heavy-handed successor, a ritualist, delivered one lecture too many on religious symbolism.[81] He continued intermittently to fill pulpits in Talladega and other communities, furthering his reputation as "the Episcopal Church's St. John, in Alabama."[82]

During the latter phases of his career, Smith had come to believe that clergymen should participate in the ordering of society. He was not precisely an advocate of what would soon be called the Social Gospel, but he was moving in that direction in a manner cautious and respectful of tradition. Perhaps, as he considered the changing face of north Alabama, he recalled a passage written years before in the *Church Intelligencer*: "The Christian minister is not merely the minister of the Church, he is the minister of the state, of society, and without the influences of which he is steward, every interest, every relation of man must suffer."[83]

Smith's health declined in the late 1890s. He was, compared to other establishment figures of his time (including the Bourbon reformers discussed in this book), a minor figure, but his reputation was such that when he died during a cold spell in February 1899, the Montgomery *Advertiser* took notice. Smith must have been happy that he lived to see the cornerstone laid for a new, stone St. Peter's.[84] Yet he regarded the work of the church as a matter of human lives and souls, not stone. Grounded in tradition, he had practiced a technique of reaching toward the future—a method, he was certain, by which a fallen humanity could pursue a destiny of knowledge and peace.

# 5
# Thomas Goode Jones
## The Personal Code of a Public Man

### Introduction

Students of legal history probably know that Thomas Goode Jones was the drafter of Alabama's 1887 Code of Ethics; if so, they also know that it was adopted by several states. It was an important influence upon the 1908 American Bar Association Canons of Ethics and upon subsequent efforts to regulate the ethics of the profession.[1] Students of political history are more likely to know Jones as a Confederate veteran and New South lawyer who achieved high office as Alabama's governor (1890–1894)[2] and as a federal judge (1901–1914).[3] Viewed in this light, Jones seems in many respects the perfect Bourbon: an advocate of limited government, a loyal servant of railroads and industry, and the beneficiary of a racist political system.[4]

Yet this friend of robber barons and disfranchisers was also an opponent of Alabama's convict lease system and the peonage that flourished under the state's contract labor laws. A confidante of Booker T. Washington and a determined foe of lynching, Jones may (to modern eyes) seem as much a reformer as a reactionary.[5] Certainly Jones' career was an exemplar of what a recent commentator has called the "dazzling incongruity of southern politics."[6]

Jones, in all probability, would have admitted no such contradictions. His papers and writings are focused and confident, conveying a determined sense of self. Like Washington and Tutwiler, whose careers of reform and improvement often ran parallel with his political ambitions, Jones accepted the racial realities of a post-slavery world dominated by former slaveholders. Within that world, he sought to follow scrupulously the letter of state and federal laws, to follow the oaths he had taken. Jones believed that obedience was a matter of honor. Otherwise, Jones was content to view race relations through the lens of old-time paternalism. For all his New South achievements, he sought to project an air of Old South gentility.

Such a theatrical approach to life can be wearing upon the psyche. Jones' early biographer, John Witherspoon DuBose, wrote that Jones was considered by some to be "self-conscious to the point of vanity of mind."[7] It is no great leap to argue that a man like Jones, self-absorbed but a devotee of duty and honor, must needs have a powerful ethical framework—one capable of guiding him through the contradictions of a convoluted life. In order to understand his ethics, it will first be useful to discuss his formative years, and next to identify unifying patterns of thought.

## Biographical Outline to 1887

Thomas Goode Jones was born November 26, 1844, near Macon, Georgia. He was the eldest son of Samuel Goode Jones and Martha Goode Jones, both descendants of old Virginia families. Samuel Goode Jones was a civil engineer, a graduate of Williams College who came south in 1839 and made a notable career as a railroad builder. He brought his family to Montgomery, Alabama, in the spring of 1850. A well-to-do planter and slaveholder,[8] a prominent citizen and successful lobbyist for his industry, he served during the Civil War as a Confederate railroad official and as captain of the Montgomery home guards.[9]

Politically, Samuel Goode Jones has been described as an "old line Whig,"[10] and he passed on to his son both a Whiggish faith in industrial development and a paternalistic sense of duty. Samuel Jones prepared his son for a gentleman's career, providing him with private tutors and sending him to schoolmasters in Montgomery and Virginia. By the fall of 1860, at age sixteen, Thomas Goode Jones was a cadet at Virginia Military Institute. Soon the Civil War would cut short his adolescence.

Jones' military career began soon after the outbreak of hostilities in Virginia, where he served under the command of Stonewall Jackson, his former VMI professor. By November 1862, Jones had enlisted in the 53rd Alabama and with this regiment saw action in Mississippi and Tennessee. In the spring of 1863, upon the recommendation of Confederate Attorney General Thomas H. Watts, an old Montgomery connection, he was assigned as aide to General John B. Gordon of the Army of Northern Virginia.[11] For the remainder of the war he carried messages for Gordon, a dangerous occupation that often brought him under fire. Wounded several times and promoted to the rank of major, he was commended by Robert E. Lee for braving a storm of Federal fire at Hare's Hill, near Petersburg. A few days later, Jones was one of the officers sent through the lines with a flag of truce prior to the surrender at Appomattox.[12]

Jones was marked for life by his experiences during the war, yet was not embittered by it, in part because of the lessons he learned from General

Gordon. Only twelve years older than Jones, Gordon had molded an "immature boy" into an officer.[13] An industrial promoter and lawyer before and after the war, Gordon was both an affirmation of Samuel Goode Jones' values and a pattern of determination in the face of defeat. The general and his aide remained on close terms; both carved out distinguished careers as Democratic politicians, railroad men, and Confederates devoted to a restored Union.[14]

Jones returned to Alabama and was soon engaged on several fronts, though his main ambition was to practice law. Proposing to live in pre-war style, he began to grow cotton in 1866 on a farm provided by his father, that same year marrying Georgena Caroline Bird of Montgomery. The marriage was a great success,[15] but the plantation venture was doomed by the instability of cotton markets and by Jones' inability, in those early post-emancipation days, to attract a sufficient number of farmhands. By the end of the decade he had lost his land and was encumbered with debts.[16]

Fortunately, his legal career was more promising. After studying under John A. Elmore (once William Lowndes Yancey's law partner) and Chief Justice A. J. Walker, he was admitted in 1868 to practice before the Alabama Supreme Court and the federal district court.[17] Within two years, Jones was appointed reporter of the supreme court, a move that indicated both the high esteem in which he was held and his ability to cross political lines.[18] At that time, Republicans controlled the high court. Its chief justice, the "scalawag" Elijah Wolsey Peck, had served as president of the Republican-dominated constitutional convention of 1867.[19] Walker had refused to administer the oath of office to Peck,[20] but Jones saw no reason to confuse law and partisanship. To the scandal of some Democrats, he even rode in a Fourth of July parade with the Republican justice.[21]

Jones served as reporter for about ten years,[22] during which time he established himself as a promising lawyer, working in partnership with former chief justice Samuel F. Rice, himself a scalawag Republican and railroad lawyer.[23] By the early 1880s, Jones was a lawyer for the powerful Louisville and Nashville Railroad,[24] one of the most important professional affiliations of his life. Simultaneously he was an active member of the Alabama State Bar Association (founded 1878), an organization that reflected the views of the profession's urban and corporate elite.[25] Like their counterparts in the American Bar Association, the leaders of the Alabama association favored uniform rules and procedures, and to this extent were reformist in their approach to law and the legal profession.[26] Jones' 1881 report as chairman of the Committee on Judicial Administration and Remedial Procedure—in which he called for adoption of a state ethics code—falls within this pattern.[27]

Politically, despite professional dealings and personal friendships with

Republicans, Jones was firmly identified with the Democratic Party and, therefore, with its racial politics.[28] He was a Democratic campaigner during the turbulent contests of 1874, when the election of gubernatorial candidate George S. Houston effectively broke the power of the Republicans.[29] Soon thereafter Jones began to move up the political ladder. From 1875 to 1884 he served as a Montgomery alderman, mastering the intricacies of local politics and making himself an expert on such technical matters as the law of quarantine—an expertise acquired as a result of the great yellow fever epidemic of 1878.[30] In 1884, the forty-year-old Jones was elected to the legislature. Reelected in 1886, he was chosen Speaker of the House.[31] Comfortable with the planters and businessmen whose representatives dominated the Democrats, he began to think about running for governor in his own right.[32]

Thus Jones established himself as a rising lawyer and politician, but he had never ceased to be a soldier. Indeed he had been an organizer of state troops as early as 1866, and he was one of Governor Houston's military advisors in 1874. Thereafter he served as captain of an elite company, the Montgomery Greys, before accepting command, in 1880, of the Second Regiment of state troops. As such, he was often in the public eye, and sometimes in personal danger, since the Second Regiment was used on several occasions to keep public order.[33] One of its most notable achievements was recorded on December 4, 1883, when Jones and his men prevented a Birmingham mob from killing a black prisoner. Jones' leadership—in this instance a combination of determination and tact—helped end the riot without bloodshed and contributed to his reputation as an expert on the lawful use of force.[34]

## Jones' Values and Ideals

Approaching middle age, Jones clung to the ideals of Old South paternalism: hierarchy, loyalty, duty, and honor.[35] Jones' exposure to antebellum society had convinced him that social hierarchies were a natural part of life.[36] His military experiences only reinforced the notion of hierarchy as an organizing principle. Professionally, he associated with elite lawyers at a time when the bar was increasingly specialized and stratified.[37] Certainly the legal business of the great regional railroads, notably that of the L&N, was conducted through what one historian has called a "hierarchical, federalized chain of firms and attorneys."[38]

Loyalty is both a military and a paternalistic virtue, and Jones displayed intense loyalty—not only to his former commanders, but also to persons who had been under his command. Who could forget, he asked at a meeting of Confederate veterans, the private soldier's "bright face, his tattered jacket and crownless hat," his "jests which tickled the very ribs of death," his "hope and faith and patience to the end"?[39] Like his mentor Gordon, Jones spoke often before veterans' encampments, urging his comrades to remember the glorious past but to put aside hatred.[40] Rejecting hate was not the same thing as abandoning shared beliefs. "Force," Jones would quote Gordon, "could not kill principle and truth, but altered conditions may require different applications of them."[41] Most notably in politics, the solidarity of Confederate veterans had helped achieve the Democratic victory of 1874—a quasi-military campaign—and Jones was one of many who embraced the soldiers of the Democratic Party as brothers in arms.[42]

In tandem with his affection for the band of Confederate brothers, Jones felt a patriarchal sense of obligation to Alabama's freedmen, who, in his opinion, had recently been thrust into civic responsibilities for which they were not ready. Indeed, he viewed it as the duty, as well as in the self-interest, of former slaveholders to provide black people with education and to recognize their new status as citizens.[43] In one of his most-quoted speeches Jones would spell out a vision of white men as the "custodians" of the African American, adding: "Let us make him feel that . . . we intend to be just to him, to be his friend, and that he ought to rely on us."[44] Old South racial doctrine was never more blandly set forth.[45]

For a man of such mingled authoritarian and benevolent impulses, the law was more than a respectable profession, more than a way to ally himself with a powerful corporation. In fact, law provided a system of belief in which Jones found roles consistent with his principles of honor. Mid-nineteenth-century legal thinkers viewed the courtroom as a place apart, ideally a realm of fair combat in which independent professionals fought fiercely (but without personal rancor) to protect their clients' interests. The operative word here is "fair," defined as taking place within the bounds of recognized procedures and traditions.[46]

Jones was inclined to describe chivalrous rivalry as a component of civilized behavior. At the Montgomery Confederate Memorial Day exercises of 1874, for example, he affirmed that "Honor to noble foes is the warrior's highest courage."[47] It seems certain that Jones polished his adversarial manners while working with Samuel F. Rice, a very successful attorney and judge who had survived a lifetime of legal and political controversy with reputation and independence intact. "First," Rice was quoted by his partner Ariosto A. Wiley, "We can differ and be honest. Second—We can differ and be friends. Third—We can differ and be patriots. Fourth—We can differ and be sincere worshippers of the same true and living God."[48] Jones' role models, from General Brown to Judge Rice, showed him how to fight hard without holding grudges. He determined for himself methods of preserving such ideals in the face of a rough and tumble practice.

## Jones and the Ethical Problems of Legal Practice

In court—whether in the nineteenth century or the twenty-first—the validity of the adversarial system depends upon the rulings of an impartial judge and the presence of a jury representing the people.[49] It also depends upon the integrity of lawyers, and Jones was well aware that many lawyers of his day had no intention of engaging in fair combat if they could help it. Complaints about "the law's delay" probably go back to the dawn of litigation.[50] But in Alabama the situation was aggravated by an unusually cumbersome system of pleading.[51] In addition it was a well-established custom for Alabama lawyers to disrupt trials with long "side-bar" remarks aimed at opposing counsel. Such speeches distracted juries and violated the unwritten rule that "attorneys should try the case and not one another." These abuses, Jones knew, were rooted within the profession itself.[52] Other ethical problems, however, had more to do with the impact of the outside world upon practitioners.

The explosive growth of railroads and heavy industry in the late nineteenth century touched off a revolution in law and practice. Railroad cases in particular influenced the development of new patterns in tort, negligence, labor relations, and other fields of law.[53] The sheer volume of claims against railroads promoted the creation of plaintiff and corporate defense factions within the bar.[54] Jones and most of his bar-association colleagues were among the latter, and as such were willing to criticize ambulance chasers and those who, in Jones' moderate language, "volunteer[ed] advice to bring a law suit."[55] Yet the real issue for Jones and like-minded lawyers was not merely the well being of their corporate clients, but the health of the profession. His overriding goal as a bar leader was to promote professional responsibility—certainly not to encourage money-grubbing, either in the wake of ambulances or in the offices of the robber barons.[56]

Powerful clients threatened the self-image of lawyers schooled in the old-fashioned ethic of independent judgment.[57] Railroads in particular were jealous mistresses, as Jones found in the late 1870s, when he paid a price for separating his professional and political personae. The North and South Alabama Railroad, a puppet of the L&N, was one of the chief clients of Jones' firm (Rice, Jones, and Wiley). Yet Alderman Jones, according to one account, took the lead in forcing the North and South to honor its contract to build a new depot in downtown Montgomery. When the railway threatened Judge Rice with the loss of its business, Jones resigned from the firm.[58]

As noted above, Jones was soon retained by the L&N itself. He may have viewed his new status as a reward for principled behavior, though apparently he was hired only after a change in the railroad's management.[59] In the future he would be sensitive to any implication that he was merely a paid spokesman. Early in 1887, for instance, Jones sent Alabama congressman Hilary A. Herbert a letter concerning possible difficulties in enforcing the Interstate Commerce Act. He wished to be discreet, since he believed that "many demagogues" would oppose any suggestion made by a railroad lawyer. In a follow-up letter he clarified this statement, insisting that he had written only as a public official (he was then Speaker of the House) concerned only with "the regulation of the people's business."[60]

In his own mind, Jones had achieved an ethical division of labor. When he was on duty as an officeholder, he was the people's lawyer. As such, he was bound to oppose any measure intended to limit basic rights—including the economic rights of black Alabamians, which, as Jones knew, were vulnerable to attack. Thus in the mid-1880s Jones successfully opposed the Wiley Contract Bill, which would have made it a misdemeanor for sharecroppers to break labor contracts. To Jones the bill proposed nothing less than a system of imprisonment for debt, which would have placed an unconstitutional lever of control in the hands of landlords.[61] Criticized by white constituents, he declared that he would "not represent my people if I had to do so with a padlock on my lips, or at the sacrifice of any honest conviction."[62] As the people's lawyer, it was Jones' duty to be independent-minded and forthright.

By the mid-1880s, Jones was at home in a complex ethical world, one drawn from elements of Old South chivalry and paternalism, military discipline, and industrial optimism—all tempered by an almost religious devotion to the traditions of the bar. Yoking together these principles and interests was not always easy, but Jones' personal code helped him resist the crassest impulses of racism, capitalism, and political partisanship. To that extent he was an inner-directed man. On the other hand, nothing in his ethics prevented him from thinking well of the state's ruling clique—the industrialists, Black Belt landowners, and supply merchants who controlled the Democratic Party. In this respect, like many successful lawyers of his or any other time, Jones was something of a pragmatist, ethically in tune with his culture.[63]

New South thought was simultaneously hopeful and nostalgic, tied to the cause of profits and to the Lost Cause,[64] and it should hardly surprise us that

Jones' 1887 ethics code reflects both the man and the era. A self-consciously reformist document intended to promote courtroom decorum, personal and fiscal integrity, scrupulous observance of due process, and professional concern for the "defenceless [sic] and oppressed," it proposed chiefly a return to well-established principles.[65] In public, moreover, Jones expressed a simplistic confidence in the integrity of his brethren at the bar. Once a proper code was in place, he predicted, "evil practices" would begin to disappear; such was the "moral power of the profession" when it spoke with one voice.[66] Like Julia Tutwiler and other reform-minded patricians, Jones truly believed in the power of reason to change behavior.

## Jones and the Ethos of Disfranchisement

Following his authorship of the ethics code, Jones was often in the public eye. As an officeholder, his objectivity as the people's lawyer was often strained by the pull of other forces. Serving as governor from 1890 to 1894 (during a long phase of deteriorating economic conditions), he faced the explosive political insurgency of farmers and their spokesmen.[67] In his 1892 reelection campaign he was challenged by a formidable agrarian, Reuben F. Kolb, who was supported by a large number of rebellious Democrats, as well as Populists and Republicans. In this extremity Jones resorted to racist appeals, asking voters to preserve "the walls of our civilization, which can be guarded only by a united white race."[68] His supporters revived the worst excesses of Reconstruction politics, complete with ballot box stuffing and intimidation of voters, especially in Black Belt counties. Jones, narrowly victorious, was so much disillusioned that he considered resigning and returning to work for the L&N.[69] Yet the following year he set his scruples firmly aside by signing the Sayre Act. This measure, a premonition of disfranchisement, was designed to make cheating unnecessary. Its method: to make the mechanics of voting more difficult for illiterates, while simultaneously increasing the power of appointed Democratic polling officials.[70]

By endorsing the Sayre Act, Jones came down firmly on the side of Democratic loyalists who feared the disruption of white solidarity and were determined to keep power by disfranchising the groups—blacks especially, but poor whites as well—most likely to vote against them.[71] The trend was regional; from 1890 to 1910, one southern state after another restricted its suffrage by means of devices including literacy, property, and residence requirements, and the enactment of white primaries. A chain of United States Supreme Court decisions (including the 1898 opinion in *Williams v. Mississippi*) had convinced some observers that constitution makers, so long as they avoided overtly racial language, could purge the voting rolls without provoking the intervention of the Federal government.[72]

Some disfranchisers were concerned mostly with the elimination of political enemies; others cherished hopes that suffrage limitation would purify politics; a number were bitter racists.[73] Jones shared something of the first two motives, but he would not have supported a movement that, to his knowledge, intended to employ the law as an engine of oppression. Indeed, he continued to view himself as a friend and mentor of black people. He had worked, as governor, to prevent lynching and to end the state's practice of leasing prisoners to corporations, each a practice that punished blacks and the poor.[74] In addition he had opposed constitutional maneuvers aimed at reducing appropriations for black education,[75] evidently persuading himself that the state's segregated school system offered blacks a reasonable chance to meet any literacy test imposed upon them.[76]

With a clear conscience Jones served as a delegate to Alabama's constitutional convention of July–August 1901. By that time, he and other conservative Democrats had ordered their priorities so that the security of well-to-do white men to determine public policy trumped everything else.[77] Jones believed that the new document's suffrage provisions should be formally colorblind, a feature that to him constituted a virtual promise of fair treatment. Yet some of his fellow delegates were neither so lawyerly nor so paternalistic. Indeed, many were willing to agree with delegate J. Thomas Heflin of Chambers County, for whom politics was essentially race war by other means.[78]

In the course of the convention Jones emerged as an opponent of one of the majority's proposed mechanisms of white control—a temporary "grandfather clause" intended to assist Confederate veterans and their descendants in registering to vote. With former governor William C. Oates and other Bourbons, Jones denounced the obvious racial favoritism behind the measure; in an eloquent speech he declared that the grandfather clause would be deemed a flagrant violation of the Fifteenth Amendment.[79] Such determined opposition—from a man who could not be dismissed as a rabble-rouser—had already provoked a remarkable incident. Jones had refused to yield the floor after a parliamentary ruling against him. During an exchange of angry words with convention chairman John B. Knox and other delegates, Jones kept speaking while Knox repeatedly commanded the sergeant at arms to remove him from the floor.[80]

The convention's final suffrage provisions, including the grandfather clause, were dizzyingly and intentionally complex.[81] Jones for his part was able to rebound from defeat, once more allowing his white supremacist voice to speak for his other mental compartments. He publicly supported the new constitution, which passed with the aid of stuffed ballot boxes in the Black Belt.[82] Anticipating the new order, Jones had reassured Booker T. Washington that the "permanent plan of suffrage will not in the end operate harshly on the [N]egro race; for coming up to its requirements will help to lift them up, and all deserving people can come up to the requirements."[83]

## Bourbon Reform in Action: Jones on the Bench

In the fall of 1901, former governor Jones was appointed (with Booker T. Washington's backing) federal judge of Alabama's Middle and Northern districts.[84] On the bench for the remainder of his career, he sought to be true to his legal values, especially those of fairness and due process. Though Jones remained complacent with the legal regime of suffrage limitation,[85] he grew increasingly determined to defend the economic rights of poor people. Most famously, he presided (1903–1904) over a series of peonage prosecutions, in the course of which he condemned the complicity of public officials and employers, and tried earnestly to convince public opinion that involuntary servitude was both unfair and socially destructive. Subsequently, Jones imposed lenient sentences upon convicted peon masters, perhaps intending to placate white public opinion, but primarily out of his lifelong assumption that a leader can, by means of good examples, change his followers' behavior.[86] From 1908 to 1911 he worked successfully behind the scenes (via elaborate mutual measures of secrecy) with Booker T. Washington and others to overturn a 1903 labor statute that had criminalized breeches of labor contracts.[87]

Freed from the burden of seeking votes, Jones was willing to pursue his thoughts even to the point of constitutional innovation. Enraged by a 1904 episode in which a Huntsville mob lynched a black prisoner after setting fire to the jail, he determined to his own satisfaction that racially motivated lynching could be punished as a denial of federally protected civil rights.[88] The U.S. Supreme Court undermined his position by reaffirming, in a contemporary case from Arkansas, the doctrine that only states or their agents could violate the equal protection clause of the Fourteenth Amendment.[89] That did not stop Jones from setting forth his own interpretation, arguing that the Thirteenth and Fourteenth amendments made an absolute guarantee of civic equality to former slaves, an equality that lynch mobs denied by lawless force. In such cases, Jones asserted that federal courts could intervene when the states could not or would not enforce their own laws. Thereby the national government, far from encroaching on states' rights, would be "arrayed behind the power of the state."[90]

Throughout the evolution of his thought, Jones considered himself to be the man he had always been—sobered, perhaps, by the persistence of problems he had hoped could be settled. Yet his sense of inner peace would be sorely tested by the final great controversy of his career, involving his role as trial judge in the long-running (1907–1914) battle between Alabama railroads and the administration of Governor Braxton Bragg Comer. The L&N was prominent among the litigants challenging state regulations, and Jones, who issued a number of injunctions at the railroads' request, was widely perceived as a partisan judge.[91] In 1911, Comer lashed out at him as the "czar of our laws" and as a man "environed" by large corporations.[92] Jones responded by reading into the record a denunciation of Comer as a demagogue.[93]

This unseemly exchange was reported in the state's newspapers, whose readers might well have concluded that each man was right. Yet there was no mistaking Jones' shock that anyone would question his integrity. It was clear that over the course of a long career, he had never doubted his ability to subordinate personal interests to principles. A patrician survivor, he was now forced to confront his own obsolescence—to understand that in the New South, while old times may not have been forgotten, old-time virtue was largely irrelevant. Poignantly, in the midst of his defensive anger, he was at pains to sum up his ethical life. "The environment by which men's lives are shaped and their motives to be judged," he declared, "is found in their ideals of honor, fidelity to trust and unselfish devotion to duty, as exemplified in their daily lives."[94]

# 6
# Joseph C. Manning
## Defender of the Voteless

## Introduction

In November 1901 the voters of Alabama adopted a new constitution by an official count of 108,613 to 81,734. The document contained stringent poll tax and literacy requirements, and was unblushingly designed to disfranchise 99 percent of the state's black citizens. In addition, though future United States Senator J. Thomas Heflin and other pro-constitution spokesmen ostentatiously wrapped themselves in the mantle of white supremacy, it was no secret that the suffrage standards would disfranchise thousands of hill country yeomen.[1] The men whose voices were to be silenced, black and white, were almost entirely Republicans or Populists, members of the very groups which had repeatedly united, during the tumultuous 1890s, to challenge Democratic rule.[2]

The constitutional convention of 1901, dominated by planters, lien merchants, and representatives of New South Industrialism, had made a conscious decision to follow the lead of other southern states in discarding a long-practiced means of overcoming insurgency—namely, ballot box stuffing. But Democratic leaders made sure that the old methods went out in a blaze of glory. The November margin of victory was provided by returns from eleven Black Belt counties where, as Republican postmaster Joseph C. Manning observed, the great majority of African Americans apparently voted to disfranchise themselves. With a convincing show of force, the Democratic Party had delivered Alabama into the hands of a radically reshaped electorate—composed largely of reliable Democrats. Even before the 1901 convention was held, the black editor of the Huntsville *Journal* had cried out: "It is good bye with the poor white folks and niggers now," for "the train of disfranchisement is on the rail."[3]

## Looking Backward

The train of disfranchisement also stranded the Bourbon reformers, several of whom are featured in the preceding chapters. These individuals, together with their friends and coconspirators, had based their thoughts and actions on an organic view of society. In their reasonable world all citizens, however humble, had genuine rights; all were heirs, through hope and hard work, to a better life. This was the gospel of unthreatening race relations as preached by Booker T. Washington—whose autobiography *Up from Slavery* appeared in the very year of disfranchisement.[4] This was the rule of law as advocated by Thomas Goode Jones.[5] It was the social gospel as practiced by Julia Tutwiler in the prison camps, and soon, by Montgomery clergyman Edgar Gardner Murphy on behalf of child laborers.[6] These were strenuous efforts informed by laudable ideas, but all were left behind in a society that was lacking in cordial interconnections.

Like other southerners, Alabamians had been moving through economic and political crises since Reconstruction. Reconstruction in Alabama ended in 1874, when the Democratic Party put together a merger of antebellum Democrats and former Whigs under the banner of white supremacy. Politics thereafter became a species of race war, in which the Redeemer or Bourbon Democrats sought to hold together groups across lines of class and geography. What did small-producing white farmers in north Alabama or the Wiregrass have in common with Black Belt planters or New South developers? As it happened, they all faced certain fundamental economic facts, and many of them shared a pervasive cultural attitude. The former was simple— all were forced to cope with the post–Civil War economy, burdened with devastation and debt. The latter was more complex, but it boiled down to a deep-rooted fear, a prevalent aversion, even hatred of African Americans. This may or may not be the "central theme of southern history,"[7] but it provided a convenient political diversion for planters, supply merchants, and New South industrialists, who shared a need for cheap, compliant labor and the desire to control their economic environments.

The crop lien-tenant farming system (ubiquitous in hill country and Black Belt alike) was particularly destructive in the late nineteenth century, an era of crop overproduction and falling prices.[8] The situation afflicted planters and merchants, too. But as prices continued to fall they tended to gain economic (often personal) control over the farmers to whom they were advancing credit and supplies. The stage was set for unrest among white yeomen who saw their independence threatened. Yet whenever large numbers of white farmers came close to making the connection that they were, as agrarian orators liked to put it, in the same boat with black sharecroppers, Democratic spokesmen would issue stirring calls for white unity. Or as Postmaster Manning would write, early in the twentieth century, the planter-merchant "Oligarchy" employed the black man "as a political scapegoat, that he, in his unfortunate condition . . . [might] condone and cloak the political rascality of those who usurp the control of government from both white[s] and blacks."[9]

Many yeomen remained Democrats out of habit, racism, or retroactive loyalty to the Confederacy. Others, however, were moved by deep-rooted ideological convictions to leave the Democratic Party. Half a century before the political broils of the late nineteenth century, certain Jacksonian prejudices—against monopolies, financial institutions and arrangements that favor the rich—had been acquired by the small-producing masses and passed down as folk wisdom. These farmers valued personal independence above political loyalty, and by the end of the 1870s they were willing to vote in large numbers for politicians styling themselves "Independents" or "Greenbackers."[10]

To preserve what they perceived (correctly) as their diminishing independence, a growing number of farmers were willing to consider schemes that went beyond what Greenbackers or Independents offered—that would have abolished the agricultural capitalism of the period. The most remarkable generator of alternatives was the Farmers' Alliance, which spread across the south in the 1880s. Alliance leaders developed a program of inflationism, producer control of crops, cooperative purchase of supplies, government regulation of railroads, and political cooperation between farmers and workers. The Alliance had won over 120,000 converts in Alabama by 1889. Its political offspring, the People's Party, was a direct threat to the world that the Bourbon reformers strove to correct from within.[11] Joe Manning, the Republican postmaster cited above, had been an important agent of that threat.

## Enter a Political Evangel

In January 1901, when Joseph Columbus Manning took over as postmaster of Alexander City, a thriving central Alabama railroad town, he had behind him almost a decade of political activity. The slender Manning, sandy-haired and just thirty-one, was the son of a Clay County supply merchant; he had grown up as a child of (relative) privilege in a small hill-country town.[12] Yet he made his reputation as a founder and "evangel" of a biracial state People's Party. Alabama Populists worked in tandem with the Jeffersonian Democrats, a more numerous faction of Alliancemen fully committed to taking over the Democratic Party but less committed to radical agrarianism.

In the state elections of 1892 and 1894, Manning and his Populists supported the Jeffersonian gubernatorial candidate, former State Commissioner of Agriculture Reuben F. Kolb. The latter, a talented politician, was too conventional to break definitively with the Democrats but too tainted with agrarianism to be welcomed back to the fold—so long as Black Belt Bourbons like Thomas Goode Jones and William C. Oates (governor, 1894–1896) were in charge. Alabama Republicans also supported Kolb in hopes of exploiting the wedge that the Jeffersonians had driven into the Democratic Party. Such temporary alliances, referred to as "fusion" politics, were the stuff of Manning's political education.[13]

The consensus of historians is that Kolb won more votes than his opponents in the hill country, Wiregrass, and perhaps even the Black Belt. In each election, however, he was "counted out," as Democrats stuffed ballot boxes in the Black Belt.[14] Manning worked to keep a reformist coalition together during these years, in spite of Jeffersonian efforts to make peace with the Democrats on the basis of a "white primary." His strategy was to unite all anti-Bourbon parties and factions, and to invite Congress (particularly congressional Republicans) to investigate Alabama elections. He was able to prevent Kolb and his most fanatical partisans from attempting an armed insurrection. But his congressional strategy failed, though he was able to attract considerable attention to ballot fraud in the south. Even in adversity, fusion (or as Manning liked to call it, cooperation) worked well enough to elect and eventually to seat two Populist and two Republican congressmen from Alabama in the Fifty-fourth Congress.[15]

Throughout the stormy scenes of the early 1890s, Manning's style was typically that of a stump-speaking Populist; he was truly the evangel of his cause.[16] As failures piled up and he was increasingly tied down to the politics of fusion, his emphasis shifted. By 1893–1896, he and his allies campaigned almost exclusively for "a free ballot and a fair count"—for election reform, for simple justice at the ballot box. To Manning, this goal necessarily came before any others could be achieved. To achieve it he was willing to seek funds and assistance from Midwestern "Free Silver" men, from northern Republicans, and others whose idealism or self-interest might be turned against the Bourbon status quo. In 1895, Manning was the chief mover behind a short-lived Southern Ballot Rights League, some of whose members favored disfranchisement as a means of preventing ballot-box stuffing.[17] None of his plans for a unified front were viable, it seemed. Worse, by 1896, it was clear to Manning that the Free Silver movement, speedily taking over the national Democratic Party, would provide the means by which Kolb and many of the Jeffersonians would return to the "Party of the Fathers." After the national People's Party followed the Democrats in nominating William Jennings Bryan for president in 1896, Manning resigned from the ranks of Populists. He joined the Republican Party because it was the only party from which he could continue to wage war on the Democrats.[18]

## Interlude of Troubles

A prophet is notoriously without honor—close to home, anyway—and the post-Populist Manning is a case in point. Apparently he expected the Republicans to welcome him and to give him one of the patronage positions typically filled by Gilded Age political foot soldiers; early on, Manning sought aid and advice from Booker T. Washington.[19] But he received no office for almost four years, during which time he wearied of being politic and accumulated grievances against the state's reigning Republican bosses. The latter included GOP state chairman William Vaughn, a disciple of the Republican kingmaker Marc Hanna.[20] Vaughn and his allies had worked with the agrarians in recent elections, but they were political animals for whom principles were an optional feature. By their standards Manning was a newcomer who had to prove his loyalty—doubtless a formidable politician but too likely to pursue his own agenda.

The late 1890s were lean years for Manning and his wife Zoe Duncan Manning. They lived for seven months with her parents in Bartlett, Texas, where Manning attempted to found a Republican newspaper. Next they moved to Tallapoosa County, Alabama, where the Mannings lived on a tenant farm furnished by relatives. By the summer of 1898, however, things began to look up. Manning had re-emerged in politics, campaigning with the "black-and-tan" (African American) wing of the Tallapoosa County GOP. In December he took the opportunity of a presidential visit to Alabama to secure an interview with Postmaster General Charles Emory Smith, who encouraged him to apply for a central Alabama postmastership. Shortly after, he secured the Alabama bureau of the *New Orleans Daily Item,* an "independent Republican" newspaper.[21]

From his journalistic perch, Manning warred with the Hanna–Vaughn machine; his articles on federal auditor and patronage-broker William Youngblood exposed the brand of "boodle" politics that they practiced.[22] He likewise observed the politics of disfranchisement, cheering on Alabama's slippery governor, the "silverite" Joseph F. Johnston. The governor, head of a proto-Progressive faction, had favored a constitutional convention bill in the state elections of 1898; this measure was enacted in December. But Johnston changed his mind when he saw that the measure's supporters were Bourbons from the Black Belt, railroad men, and "Gold" Democrats—components of what would later be dubbed the "Big Mule" coalition. Johnston called a special session of the legislature in April 1899 and lobbied successfully for repeal of the convention act. Manning praised him as a man who sacrificed political advantage "to protect the dear people," meanwhile spreading the rumor that the pro-convention crowd had raised "$25,000 of New York capital" to buy up convention delegates. Manning may or may not have been a significant factor in this short-lived defeat of disfranchisement. But his Democratic hometown newspaper, the *Alexander City Outlook*, said as much. Its editor declared: "When two Joes get their heads together any old fake is imminent, by Joe!"[23]

The years 1900–1901 saw anti-disfranchisement forces in disarray. Governor Johnston ran for the U.S. Senate seat held by John Tyler Morgan, a wily Confederate hero who had significant Free Silver credentials and a firm understanding with pro-disfranchisement Democrats. Morgan swept the county primaries (Democratic legislators would subsequently vote unanimously to reelect him), and his friend William J. Samford was elected governor. Historian Sheldon Hackney commented that the "one certainty coming out of the election was that there would be a constitutional convention."[24] Anti-convention and anti-constitution forces were anemic in comparison; the Democrats of that persuasion did not even organize until October 1901, a month before the November 11 ratification election.[25] Conspicuous by his absence in these events was Postmaster Manning, who to all practical purposes sat out the ratification campaign. The staunchly pro-constitution *Alexander City Outlook* was pleased but puzzled. On November 1, it conceded: "No man has stronger convictions than Mr. Manning, and he has the courage to advocate what he believes is right." Two weeks later, the constitutional battle over, the *Outlook* admitted that Manning "had been looked upon as a fighting opponent of the Democracy," adding cryptically that "no act of his in politics would merit rebuke."[26] What happened to Manning?

Any politician, even a crusading reformer, may bow before personal misfortune, and Manning, a year before ratification, had been desperate for steady income. He had secured nomination for the postmastership of Alexander City. Yet his appointment was held up by the particular request of none other than Senator Morgan—who, as Manning wrote a Republican friend, was determined to exact revenge "for what I did in 1894–95–96." Morgan had finally allowed the appointment to go through in December 1900, but only after Manning had secured endorsements from a large number of local politicians, Republican and Democratic, including the Fifth District congressman, the Democrat Sidney J. Bowie.[27] At some point in this process Manning may have promised a season, at least, of political inactivity. It is also possible that Manning viewed civil service as properly apolitical—the *Outlook* would quote him in the fall of 1902 to the effect that "his position . . . will not admit any political activity on his part as he views it."[28]

Apart from his enforced silence, Manning may have hoped to derive some benefit for his cause from the new constitution. That cause, the destruction of Democratic rule, had not changed; though Manning now believed that an initial step should be the expulsion of old-time bosses from the GOP. He was hopeful that Theodore Roosevelt, who had become president in September in the wake of William McKinley's assassination, would see the possibility of building a southern Republican Party out of hill-country materials, former Populists. To this end he was prepared to sound like a "Lily White" Republican, even to make uncharacteristically racist comparisons. In a post-ratification interview with the Washington, D.C. *Times,* Manning said: "Heretofore a great many good citizens, who wanted to act with the Republicans, kept away from conventions and primaries because of the dislike they had for mixing with an ignorant rabble, mostly colored, that was in the party for the offices only." Perceiving that "the Democratic framers of the new organic law intended no benefit to our side," he continued, "I am certain that the Republican Party down our way will be in future more compact, better organized, and on a higher plane."[29]

Manning had been taken aback when, in September 1901, the president appointed Thomas Goode Jones as judge of Alabama's Middle District. Jones, he complained to a Republican friend, was a "Democrat . . . of the ballot box stuffing and bourbon type . . . who would never be with us."[30] Still, Manning was aware (for it was no secret) that Roosevelt had acted on Booker T. Washington's advice. On matters pertaining to the intersection of race and politics, Roosevelt was hard to read. Over the year following ratification, it seemed to Manning and others that Roosevelt, in the words of one historian, was "more inclined to racial inclusion" than the (pro-Hanna) Vaughn machine.[31]

Perhaps that latter perception explains how Manning, at an August 1902 conclave of Republicans in Montgomery, came to shake off his public racism. Disturbed that members of the Old Guard had barred black delegates, Manning refused to attend the meeting. Instead he and a group of anti-Vaughn Republicans met in a hotel room. There they planned to promote an "Alabama League of Republican Clubs," a biracial organization devoted to building support for Roosevelt. Before and after the meeting, Manning denounced the state's office-holding GOP with such hyperbolic language that one Republican thought that he had gone mad. In truth, Manning was merely exercising his considerable talent for creating a commotion. The adverse publicity of the Montgomery meeting, together with adroit political maneuvering by Washington and his local allies spelled the end of Vaughn's reign.[32] Manning probably thought that the reality of a long-desired goal had been worth the sacrifice of his consistency.[33]

## Acting Locally

Manning had avoided playing the race card during his Populist years. As early as 1893, as the Jeffersonians sought to sacrifice their black supporters to the political expediency of white primaries, he had reminded them: "The domination we have to fear is that of the man with a black heart, without special reference to 'hide.'"[34] The black-hearted men, to his mind, were the ones who sought special powers and privileges—advantages that gave them power over men and events. In this light, Manning's crusade for a free ballot and a fair count was a political byproduct of his Jacksonian instincts. Except for occasional backsliding, he was true to that ideology all his life; thus he could not help but sympathize (increasingly, empathize) with the world's underdogs. Since African Americans were the ultimate underdogs in the south of disfranchisement and Jim Crow, he resolved to help them through deeds as well as words. As for good-deed doing, he decided that the lobby of his own post office was a good place to begin.

When Manning took charge of the Alexander City post office, an unwritten rule was that black patrons would hang back if whites were present. Or as Manning later put it, they would "huddle in a corner until all whites were waited upon." This was a special privilege that he could meet head-on. So at some point he "went into the office lobby for two or three days, telling those who came for mail to get in line as they came—first come, first served, old or young, black or white." Manning had a commanding presence, and he was able to persuade the startled townsfolk to accept the new system. The white folks were *not* pleased, though, when he added a second component of equality, ordering the young white woman who was his clerk to begin calling black customers by their proper titles. He had, in fact, decided not to tolerate the standard practice of speaking to black men and women, ministers and school principals, as though they were children. "You can just drop the Molly, Mandy, Dick stuff," he told his employee. "You can treat all patrons alike." These instructions touched upon all the chords of racial and sexual paranoia prevalent among many of the "best people," and for a time there was, as Manning put it, an angry "yak-yak" around town. Eventually, overt opposition to the new reign of courtesy slacked off, particularly after the clerk's mother, a southern woman with democratic sensibilities of her own, told Manning that he was in the right. With the support of levelheaded white folks, he had won a small victory for fair treatment of human beings.[35]

With the passage of time, Joseph Manning became even more assertive, more willing to stand up for equal opportunity in Alexander City. Because he was prepared to act upon this principle, Manning served sometimes as an advocate for the town's black population. In 1902, for example, he had learned that local officials had placed only one African American on the voting lists, even though hundreds of black men were of voting age. One black leader was "repeatedly told that the registrars were not registering that day," Manning subsequently wrote, observing that many "Negroes of property and good standing were humiliated by the same treatment." Incensed, he gathered together a number of the applicants and, according to a testimonial drawn up at a meeting of black citizens, led them "to the registration officers and made personal plea for fair treatment." The upshot was a modest victory; about twenty African Americans were entered on the city rolls.[36]

On another occasion Manning encouraged two black men, one a veteran of the Spanish-American War and the other a land-owning farmer, in their aim of founding a general store. The white storekeepers of Alexander City were unhappy at the prospect of losing some of their black trade; nevertheless, the two men opened their business in a building secured from a sympathetic property owner, and Manning was one of their first customers. For his pains, he "caught the devil of criticism" from some of the supply merchants, staunch defenders of white solidarity and social segregation, whose monopoly control over black consumers was being threatened. Manning had personally crossed the color line to strike a blow for the economic independence of black people, an offense not to be forgotten.[37]

There is no doubt that Manning tried to become part of the social and civic life of his town. He was an active member of the Methodist Church, and a founder of the Industrial and Development Association of Alexander City. For a time he was responsible for the Association's autumn Street Fair and Farmers' Jubilee. After a disastrous fire in June 1902 destroyed more than thirty buildings, Postmaster Manning was the first to get to a working telegraph wire. Soon under his direction food and supplies were arriving from Birmingham and Montgomery. His devotion to duty earned him praise from the solid citizens of the community. One previously dubious businessman wrote that Manning "has been kind, accommodating . . . and has given us by far the best service we have ever had."[38]

Yet Joe Manning never felt secure in the esteem of his neighbors. Years later he stated that his civic heroics were among the "few things that held to me enough people to enable my living in Alexander City, in the fact of my views." Mere attempts to be evenhanded with members of both races were enough to raise angry protests. Sill, he simply could not forbear from criticizing the blatant legal persecutions that were part of life in the turn-of-the-century south. From his dealings with a variety of African Americans,

Manning knew that they were not a menace to civilization, as Democratic politicians and apologists claimed. Instead he knew that most blacks were striving "amid difficulties known only to God and them, to raise the standard of their people." Worse culprits, to his way of thinking, were the respectable citizens of Alabama and other states, middle class whites who, in the belief that African Americans (and poor whites) must be taught stern lessons, had allowed their judicial officers to disregard human rights and constitutional liberties. Gradually, through bitter experience, Manning perfected his understanding of the disfranchisement-era south. In the long run, his knowledge did not go to waste.[39]

## Words and Deeds

From 1901 to 1905, Manning continued to look for the political reformation of the south under the leadership of President Roosevelt and his chief Alabama lieutenant, Booker T. Washington. Manning supported both men in the aftermath of the October 1901 "dinner at the White House." When southern journalists denounced Roosevelt for committing the "damnable outrage" of inviting a black man to lunch, Manning praised Roosevelt for his recognition of Washington's leadership and standing. It seemed to the impatient postmaster that he could, with the help of such powerful friends, enlighten the nation concerning disfranchisement and "the results arising from its application."[40] It is sad (or perhaps bleakly ironic) that Manning, an apostle of individualism and political emancipation, should depend upon the patronage of one whose (public) stock in trade was paternalism, whose administrative instinct was hierarchy.[41]

Still, Manning's prayers seemed on the point of being answered in the spring of 1903, when Federal District Attorney Warren S. Reese Jr., an ex-Populist, brought peonage charges against more than a dozen central Alabama planters and sawmill operators. Using information uncovered by secret agents, Reese arrested members of a ring of convict lease slave drivers and corrupt county officials in Tallapoosa County and elsewhere. The New York *Evening Post* and other national journals, encouraged by Washington and Manning, covered the trials in sensational detail.

The northern public, though, was not profoundly moved by the revelation that guarded stockades and shackles were the lot of scores—doubtless hundreds—of black Alabamians. Even the news that some peons were white failed to spark a drive for a move thorough federal investigation. Judge Thomas Goode Jones, who presided over the trials in Alabama's Middle District, denounced peonage eloquently and sincerely from the bench. But Reese found that jurors were reluctant to convict white men for such crimes; in any event, Jones favored lenient sentences. President Roosevelt, already courting the votes of Bourbon Democrats for the next presidential election, was silent. Almost from the beginning of the trials, Tom Heflin and like-minded politicians were openly denouncing Reese and the peonage prosecutions.[42]

Understandably depressed, Manning was fearful that the Bourbons' assault on civil liberties had gained national credibility. Now he was compelled, he felt, to strike out on his own with an appeal to the country. The odds were against him, but if he could gain the attention of a sufficiently large audience, he might—with financial aid from such "Conscience" Republicans as Oswald Garrison Villard of the *Evening Post*—pressure Roosevelt to take a stronger civil rights stance. In September 1904, on the eve of Roosevelt's reelection, Manning published the fruits of his work and thought in pamphlet form, under the appropriate title, *The Rise and Reign of the Bourbon Oligarchy*.

*Rise and Reign* was not Manning's first published work, nor would it be his last. When he died in 1930, he had several books or pamphlets to his credit, in addition to many newspaper articles.[43] In all these writings, Manning emphasized one basic theme—that the leaders of the southern Democratic Party, the leaders of southern society and economic life, had systematically denied basic freedoms to members of the biracial lower class. Moreover, he accused the spokesmen of the ruling oligarchy of fomenting a double-edged race hatred among yeoman class whites, corrupting and distracting them and using them as instruments in "keeping down" the blacks. Thus "the hardships, sufferings and wrongs heaped upon the blacks . . . [under] the institution of chattel slavery" had operated "to bring about a condition by which the whites of the South have come to endure a yoke of political serfdom." More than any of Manning's other works, *Rise and Reign* makes a detailed and statistical proof of these charges. Manning was clearly acquainted with the census records for Alabama and other southern states, as well as congressional election returns from all over the nation. Certainly in 1904 (as in his Populist days), he was exchanging ideas and information with journalists, politicians, intellectuals, and activists, northern and southern, black and white. These factors, combined with its author's emotional intensity, made *Rise and Reign* an incisive and arresting polemic.[44]

Manning began by praising the white farmers of north Alabama in Jacksonian terms as basically "brave and patriotic men, who dared to aspire to a true democracy." Called upon to defend slavery, many of these freedom-loving people had opposed "the revolutionary and fiery movement of secession." During the agrarian revolt of the 1890s, correspondingly, white and black reformers united to insist "that real democracy means the people shall rule, and that a real democrat is one who" would place "a fair and honest ballot . . . inviolate" in the hands of the people. By their own accounts, Manning continued, the Bourbons and businessmen who wrote the constitution of 1901 did so in order to eliminate black voting power—supposedly for the benefit of white citizens. But this rationale, which many Populists had opposed, did not mean that the freedmen had ceased to play a part in Bourbon politics. Neither the constitution nor the racist propaganda accompanying it had altered the nature or location of power in Alabama, as Manning showed by citing a notorious fact: "The method by which the 'democratic' oligarchy fastens its hold upon the 'democratic' machine in Alabama, and the condition is the same in other Southern states, is the basing of the representation in the conventions of the party and in the Alabama legislature upon an apportionment embracing the disfranchised blacks in the Black Belt counties and thereby prohibiting control . . . by the white counties of the states."[45]

Perhaps it was not surprising that Democratic bosses in Alabama and across the south insisted that "the soul [sic] issue of paramount importance is the alleged race issue." Assertive and grandiloquent, the planter-politicians presumed to speak for the whole south, and did so with such assurance that few northerners doubted the fact of white unity and majority rule within the region. Based on his personal knowledge and recent studies, however, Manning had a different tale to tell.[46]

Using election returns from several 1902 contests, he revealed the limited extent of white "backing behind the oligarchy." South Carolina's seven-man congressional slate, he pointed out, had been elected after polling an aggregate of 29,343 out of 32,185 votes cast; yet there were 130,374 white men of voting age in the state. Turning to Mississippi, Manning noted that favorite son John Sharp Williams had been elected to Congress without opposition, and that Mississippi's entire delegation (all Democrats) had received a total of 18,058 votes, though 150,922 white men were old enough to vote. In Alabama, where the Republican Party was relatively vigorous and where the Democrats had made white supremacy a campaign issue, Democratic incumbent William D. Jelks had won the gubernatorial race by a count of 67,649 to 24,190; yet fewer than 100,000 of Alabama's 232, 294 adult white men had voted.

Plainly, the Democratic voters of these states were a minority of the potential white voting population, and it was logical to conclude that the majority of white men were either disfranchised outright by the state poll taxes and literacy tests, or rendered apathetic by the certainty of Democratic victory. Manning, characteristically, summed up the situation in strong words.

"The great mass of [white] voters in the South have been dashed back into sullen silence and into hopeless acquiescence and, under present conditions, they are as helpless as are the blacks upon whose necks the bourbon heel was long since pressed."[47]

Manning did not claim that white farmers were free from the taint of racism. For years, instead of discussing "issues really effecting [*sic*] the welfare of the southern people," the disfranchisers and their political ancestors had bombarded the white south with "an amazing tirade of abuse of the Negro." Considering the persistence of Tom Heflin and his ilk, it was no wonder that a growing number of the white people were "misused and aroused beyond reason" on the subject of race relations and, therefore, "inflamed to further subservience to the oligarchy." By 1904 Manning saw distinctly what some reformers had not seen in the 1890s: that political demagoguery, accompanied by related crimes of social "vengeance" directed against black people, all furthered the larger interests of the Democratic Party. He was willing to concede that some black men were criminals (though most of their offenses, he noted, were "of little moment as compared to the crimes of whites"), but he was utterly disgusted with the way that editors, clergymen, and educators condoned the speeches of bigots and the actions of mobs. He emphasized repeatedly that promoting racial conflict was to the advantage of the ruling class. "It is cruel, it is shameful, . . . it is infamous," he cried, "to so ingeniously work up the sentiment of lawlessness as against the colored race."[48]

One particular effect of Democratic Negrophobia, Manning knew, was the reinforcement of the old belief that black people, as a race, were prone to criminality. In order to counter this stereotype he examined the census records and found that in 1890, fewer than 25,000 of the nation's nine million blacks were sitting in prisons or working on chain gangs; on the average, too, black convicts were jailed for less serious crimes than those committed by their white counterparts. Obviously he noted, "Both races supply violators of law," and yet African Americans had not made "so bad a showing for a people out of bondage, with their poor opportunities and environments."

His personal conception of the black man's character, moreover, was comprehensive and to the point. "Beginning in ignorance and want," he asserted, the freedmen have "risen to education, to property, and to usefulness . . . Colored homes, colored farms, colored schools, colored churches, colored banks, colored stores, colored teachers, colored doctors, colored lawyers—this is evidence that this race has not been wholly in idleness and depravity!"[49] Thus Manning revealed himself as a strict environmentalist and instinctive egalitarian. Shaped by his principles and personality, *Rise and Reign* is a little-known classic of the early civil rights movement.

In his conclusion, Manning called upon the Congress and federal government to abandon their "let the South alone" policy. "Only national interference," he stated, "can restore and uplift the beaten-down nationality of the Southern citizen."[50] Unfortunately, though, he was never able to raise sufficient funds to distribute his pamphlet widely, and in any case there are indications that his message would not have found favor among the leaders of Roosevelt's second administration. Privately, indeed, Roosevelt railed against "these white men of the South who say that the negro is unfit to cast a vote, and who . . . are equally clamorous in insisting that his votes be counted as cast." But publicly from 1905 to 1908, Roosevelt sided with the ruling class of the south in a series of speeches in which he emphasized the "backwardness" of African Americans and claimed that law-abiding blacks had a special responsibility to root out rapists and criminals.[51] There was little sentiment in favor of a socio-political reform of the south, Manning found, within the Progressive wing of the party of Lincoln.

## North toward Home

Joseph Manning served as postmaster in Alexander City until 1909, when he was dismissed for having opposed—together with many black Republicans—Roosevelt's handpicked successor, William Howard Taft. During the last three years of his service he had published a newspaper, the *Southern American,* a weekly journal "of outspoken opinion with the right spirit of true Americanism." In its pages he continued to insist that the northern public, from the President down, was wrong to accept planter-class spokesmen at face value as defenders of white supremacy. "The Negro," he said, was "disfranchised because he was and is a Republican more than for the reason that he was and is a Negro." Manning expanded upon the theme of biracial class disfranchisement and degradation in a speech before the May 1909 National Negro Conference, a meeting that helped launch the National Association for the Advancement of Colored People. There, according to an observant W. E. B. DuBois, a "slight, angular, and bitter" Manning demonstrated "that the enslavement of the white workingman was already following the oppression of the black."[52]

Throughout the last twenty years of his life, Manning led a nomadic existence. Writing for black newspapers, lecturing for the NAACP or other black organizations, and writing letters to white philanthropists, he embarked on a one-man crusade. In the process he endured poverty and sorrow—Zoe Duncan Manning left him, presumably because he could not provide a stable home—but he refused to give up until his health failed in the mid-1920s.

Even when he lay dying of cancer, he tried to ensure, through a series of remarkable memoirs, that his experience and perspective would not die with him. A passage from his 1928 history, *The Fadeout of Populism,* illustrates the clarity and far-sightedness of his analysis: "The real, the actual and vital issue arising in the South is not any alleged Negro problem . . . That which confronts the people of the South . . . is whether or not the constitution shall be enforced and the liberty principles underlying the foundation of our free government upheld. It is equally as impossible for the constitution . . . to stand for one thing in the free states of the North . . . and for another in the South, where the War Amendments are annulled, as it was impossible for the nation to continue, in Lincoln's time, half slave and half free."[53]

Manning died in New York in May 1930, surrounded by a few friends who, like himself, were exiles from a system that denied them their freedom. As Joseph murmured that he had "no regrets" over the life he had led, some of them must have reflected that few men had ever bought freedom so dearly or used it so well.[54]

# 7
# Henry D. Clayton

## Plantation Progressive on the Federal Bench

### Introduction

Thomas Goode Jones' 1901 appointment as judge of Alabama's Middle and Northern districts was followed soon after by his role in crafting the state's new disfranchising constitution. True, Jones had opposed the document's "grandfather clause," but he was a firm supporter of disfranchisement. Democratic observers of all stripes may have thought that Jones would be a safe man on the bench, but they were mistaken. Jones demonstrated his independence most notably during a series of peonage trials but also by his advocacy of federal solutions for the problem of lynching. Then, having angered conservatives by questioning their racial policy, Jones infuriated Progressives with a series of pro-railroad rulings.[1] By the end of his tenure, Democrats of all stripes must have yearned to see a more predictable man on the bench in Montgomery. The answer to their prayers came in the shape of Henry D. Clayton, a veteran congressman whose consciousness stretched back to old times that definitely had not been forgotten.

Clayton was a man who, failing to achieve greatness by any of the canonical standards,[2] was often physically and psychically close to it during the long years from Grover Cleveland to Calvin Coolidge. Like some hero in historical fiction, Clayton knew everyone and went everywhere. Yet he lacked the heroic capacity sometimes displayed by his predecessor, Jones—and more consistently by radicals like Joe Manning or anarchists Jacob Abrams and Mollie Steimer. A Progressive with a profoundly conservative social sense, Clayton played many roles, often seeing himself as a reformer. As a lawyer, judge, and politician, he preferred to employ a humane approach, but he was capable of displaying an authoritarian side. As a congressman (1897–1914) and federal judge (1914–1929), Clayton participated in an activist government but came to fear what sociologists would soon call the law of "unanticipated consequences."[3]

This law was rampant from 1917 to 1920, when federal officials worked many of the people into a war frenzy—a state of mind that possessed its own dynamic and lasted well beyond the restoration of peace.[4] As a visiting judge in New York, Clayton would preside in a spirit of vengeance over the famous *Abrams* sedition trial. Post-war, however, he was one of the first white Alabamians to oppose a resurgent Ku Klux Klan. Were he alive today, Clayton would recognize the irony inherent in recent (post-9/11) efforts to juggle liberty and security.

The following essay does not seek to detail Clayton's lawmaking or political campaigns. Rather, concentrating on his fifteen judicial years, it attempts to trace the intellectual journey of an important secondary figure, one whose devotion to the rule of law guided him through the changes of a full life. Above all, this work shows that Clayton applied deeply felt convictions to a world as complex, as threatened without and within, as our own.

## Formative Years

Born in 1857, namesake son of a lawyer who rose to high rank in the Confederate army, Clayton spent much of his youth on his parents' Barbour County plantation.[5] There he was trained to view the plantation hierarchy as part of the natural order of things, and slaveholding as (arguably) an evil but certainly not a sin.[6] An 1878 law graduate of The University of Alabama, Clayton practiced his profession in Barbour County and served as federal attorney for the state's Middle District from 1893 to 1896, meanwhile taking an increasingly important part in Democratic politics.[7] Through it all he retained the trappings, paternalistic outlook, and acquisitive instincts of a Black Belt planter. Several years after he became a federal judge, Clayton summed up his management philosophy in a letter intended for his brother: "I am willing to do whatever is fair and right but no man, whether he be tenant or highwayman, shall ever hold me up if I can help myself."[8]

No doubt Clayton derived much of his political philosophy from his father, who, as a circuit judge, had opposed the type of night riding practiced by the Reconstruction-era Ku Klux Klan. The elder Clayton feared that violence would beget violence, plunging society into chaos—besides which, he felt that "brave warriors" should not demean themselves by terrorizing helpless people.[9] On the other hand, Clayton Sr., like many ex-Confederates, believed absolutely that the foundation of southern civilization was "white supremacy" administered by the Democratic Party. In political campaigns against Republicans, notably the "redemption" election of 1874, the Claytons were willing to let ends justify means in their quest to regain authority.[10]

Over the following quarter century, the Democrats faced challenges mounted by a biracial coalition of agrarian reformers and Republicans.[11] They barely kept power, but at the turn of the century a Democratic combination—Black Belt planters, New South industrialists, and aspiring bosses from the north Alabama hill country—sought to solve their problems by disfranchising the opposition.[12] A party loyalist, the younger Clayton took a leading part in the campaign to ratify the 1901 constitution, working with another rising politician, Birmingham's Oscar W. Underwood.[13] The Democrats carried the day using the ballot-stuffing tactics that had served them so well since Reconstruction. Within a few years, nearly all black voters and a significant number of lower-class white voters were purged from the voting lists.[14] For the foreseeable future, meaningful political quarrels in Alabama would take place within the Democratic Party.[15] Predictably, divisions that the Democrats had only partially suppressed soon came to the fore.

## Congressional Years: The Structures of Politics

Like many young southern politicians of his era, the future Judge Clayton cut his political teeth as a member of the soft-money wing of the Democratic Party. In 1896 he had been elected to Congress from the third district as a younger generation of Alabamians—many of them supporters of William Jennings Bryan—asserted themselves in Alabama.[16] In fact, a generational restructuring of Alabama's House delegation was underway, with six of the state's nine seats newly filled from 1896 to 1904 by men who would secure multiple reelections.[17] The same years saw the rise of a business-oriented Progressive movement led by Braxton Bragg Comer, a cotton-mill entrepreneur who like Clayton was also a Barbour County planter. Advocating a strong railroad commission, Comer challenged the resurgent "Bourbon" coalition and was elected governor in 1906. He was immediately caught up in a legislative and courtroom war against the state's railroads, though he soon opened a second front in the form of a campaign for statewide prohibition.[18]

In the meantime, members of the new congressional generation were proving themselves flexible enough to represent varied popular and corporate interests, and sufficiently agile to survive in-state conflicts among ultraconservatives and Progressives.[19] Nationally, several of the Alabama congressmen were part of a southern-western coalition that sought to curb the excesses of capitalism through lower tariffs; a managed banking and currency system; fair restraints on the activities of railroads, corporations, and trusts; and strict regulation of speculation.[20] Inheritors, in their own minds, of the classical political principles of Jefferson and Jackson,[21] Democrats of this school tended to favor sharply defined laws. They were inclined to doubt systems of continuous—to their minds, intrusive—regulation favored by Theodore Roosevelt and Republican Progressives.[22]

By length of tenure, Clayton and several of his colleagues came to enjoy a measure of independence and the freedom to approach politics from a national perspective. So long as Republicans controlled the White House, each of these men could pose, in the words of a perceptive scholar, as a "Patriarch of his people," a statesman in touch with his constituents' needs but necessarily detached from the distribution of patronage.[23] Given the committee-driven structure of the House, it is not surprising that such congressmen became experts identified with particular topics. John Lawson Burnett, who represented the Seventh District from 1899 to 1919, was a consistent proponent of immigration restriction.[24] J. Thomas Heflin, who represented the Fifth District from 1904 to 1920, was a critic of cotton speculators and a proponent of white supremacy and prohibition.[25] Spanish-American War hero Richmond P. Hobson, who served the Sixth District from 1907 to 1915, advocated prohibition, women's suffrage, expansion of the navy, and other causes.[26] Underwood, representing Birmingham and the Ninth District from 1897 to 1915, was a master of tariff policy and from 1911 to 1915, served as chairman of the Ways and Means Committee.[27]

## Congressman and Law Reformer

Like Underwood, Clayton rose to a high rank in the House, serving (1911–1914) as chairman of the Judiciary Committee, from which position he would draft bills that were the basis of his signature accomplishment, the Clayton Antitrust Act.[28] Despite this foray into antitrust he was best known for his interest in matters of judicial oversight and policy, reflecting both his background as a federal attorney and an interest in professional ethics that led him, twice, to serve as a House manager in impeachment trials.[29] In 1905, he and his colleagues had failed in their attempt to remove a controversial Republican judge, Charles Swayne of Florida's Northern District.[30] Seven years later Clayton helped secure the removal of Commerce Court judge Robert W. Archbald, charged with improper financial dealings with litigants.[31]

In pressing such cases, Clayton wanted both to remove bad or incompetent judges and to rescue the judiciary from critics such as Theodore Roosevelt, who advocated the Populistic device of recall elections as a check upon judicial power.[32] A constitutional conservative (like many Wilsonians), Clayton was opposed to all attempts to alter the checks and balances of government, and likewise anxious to show that the existing system could work. Some years later, he noted that Swayne's escape had given "comfort" to those who regarded impeachment as an ineffective remedy, but he added happily that "we have heard no more of the recall of judges" since Archbald's conviction.[33]

Similar attitudes led Clayton to support simplified legal procedure. For decades, legal reformers had been attempting to modernize and streamline pleadings,[34] partly to relieve the pressure of overcrowded dockets and partly to liberate lawyers and their clients from the arcane rules of common-law pleading.[35] In some states these efforts had been relatively successful, though not without difficulties of the sort that Clayton, an experienced Alabama practitioner, knew firsthand.[36] At the federal level, procedural reform had been thwarted by the Conformity Act of 1872, which required judges to follow state procedures.[37] The resulting lack of uniformity worsened the law's delay and eventually stimulated a new generation to work toward an enhancement of judicial discretion.[38]

As early as 1906, inspired by legal philosopher Roscoe Pound, the American Bar Association appointed a special Committee of Fifteen to investigate the question. Over the next few years, a number of elite lawyers—including President William Howard Taft—backed passage of an enabling act that would allow the Supreme Court to set uniform rules for federal courts.[39] As Judiciary Committee chairman, Clayton twice introduced such an act.[40] In addition he introduced other measures which fell within the agenda of the Committee of Fifteen, including a bill designed to reduce the impact of "technical" errors committed by federal judges and a bill to allow removal of cases from a court's equity docket to its law docket.[41] These innovations ran headfirst into walls of political and professional inertia; few of them won easy acceptance.[42] Still, Clayton soldiered on, even after he left Congress, convinced that procedural reform would promote both justice and efficiency.[43]

## Departure from Congress

Clayton's decision to leave the House had more to do with success than failure, flowing ironically from the negative consequences of a Democratic triumph. For most of Clayton's congressional career Republicans controlled the White House, and he had little patronage at his disposal. Yet he had dropped hints and promises among constituents (he was a talented raconteur) of the largesse that would flow from a friendly administration.[44] This tactic worked so well that after Wilson's victory in 1912, Clayton had to face friends and neighbors who, "starved for federal patronage," behaved in "piranha-like" fashion.[45] The resulting conflicts, especially a fight over the postmastership of Dothan, diminished his pleasure in holding elective office.

After an unsuccessful attempt to secure nomination as Wilson's attorney general, Clayton in 1913 prepared to run for a Senate seat that had been held by Joseph F. Johnston.[46] Congressmen Underwood and Hobson also intended to run, however, and when it became clear in October 1913 that President Wilson was backing Underwood, Clayton withdrew. He did so, letting it be known that Wilson wanted him to continue working on behalf of the administration's still-pending antitrust measure.[47] But Underwood's biographer believes that Wilson offered Clayton a judgeship as a reward for loyalty, and the two men did have a private meeting at the right time for such an offer.[48] In any case, Clayton cleared the way for his friend Underwood, a fellow Wilsonian and national Democrat, to take on the ultra-prohibitionist Hobson. The contest that resulted provided a strange preview of political events to come.

Almost immediately, the Hobson-Underwood race degenerated into a mudslinging match, during which the two men attacked each other personally and through surrogates. Hobson claimed that Underwood was a tool of Wall Street, the liquor interests, and the Roman Catholic Church; the latter charge was apparently based on nothing more than the fact that Underwood had spoken before a New York Catholic organization.[49] Underwood's followers characterized Hobson as an unstable man whose election would pose a threat to white supremacy. This accusation stemmed partly from Hobson's advocacy of women's suffrage (which Underwood and Clayton opposed, fearing the enfranchisement of black women), but mainly from Hobson's sympathy for black soldiers dismissed without proper hearings following the 1906 riots at Brownsville, Texas.[50]

Backed by Alabama's Democratic establishment, Underwood won handily in the April 1914 primary.[51] But the manner in which he obtained his victory demonstrated the fragility of peace among Progressive factions, the ease with which cultural bigotry could creep into public discourse and, above all, how dangerous it was to stray from the paths of white supremacy. Scholars with the benefit of hindsight can see that the phobias of the War to Make the World Safe for Democracy were operative in pre-war Alabama. Even without hindsight, Clayton must have realized that a Senate seat would be no refuge from politics.

In fact, he could no longer feel secure in the House. In the spring primary of 1914, he faced his own Democratic opponent, the future congressman Henry Steagall—a talented politician who "never missed an opportunity to pick at the raw wounds of disappointed office-seekers."[52] This challenge, moreover, was played out at a time when Clayton's antitrust bill was under attack, requiring Clayton's extended presence in Washington.[53] In the end he defeated Steagall by a decent margin.[54] But his frame of mind may be gauged by a Montgomery *Advertiser* headline: "Clayton Assured by Many Friends."[55] It is no wonder that, wearied by the politics of importunity and accusation, he gratefully accepted Wilson's offer of a judgeship.

## Settling in as a Federal Judge

Clayton would serve fifteen years on the bench, during which time he would need all of the insight he had acquired as a student of the judiciary. He was the sole judge of the Middle District and shared responsibility in the Northern District with one other judge.[56] In a typical year in the Middle District, Clayton faced a civil docket containing seventy or more private suits and a criminal docket of two hundred or more cases, in addition to a number of suits to which the United States was a party. Caseloads in the Northern District tended to be higher, explosively so from 1920 to 1926, the height of the federal experiment in prohibition, when the criminal docket swelled to more than a thousand cases per year.[57] Clayton was not pleased with such workloads and occasionally made noises to the effect that he would be willing to serve on the appellate bench. All without effect; evidently he lacked sufficient political capital.[58]

Overall, Clayton responded to the pressures of work by developing a style that was colorful and efficient. Commanding his courtroom with the confident manner of a politician, he told stories, made observations on human nature, and in general managed to evoke an earlier era of lawyers and judges who "could not tolerate drabness."[59] He was sympathetic to many of the accused persons who came before him, though chiefly (especially in the case of black defendants) to those whose behavior was submissive. One of his correspondents recalled Clayton telling a black preacher that "niggers did not have middle names" in his court.[60] His anger, like his humor and good will, was spontaneous. Lawyers soon learned that he would speak his mind about tactics of which he disapproved and that he would not tolerate delays.[61] Determined to keep his desk clear, he managed to keep up with the press of business. Little more than a month before his death, a sick man, he presided over a week's session of court in which he handled eighty-five criminal cases.[62]

Clayton was the first Alabama federal judge to begin his service under the 1911 Judicial Code. Partly a delayed reaction to the creation of circuit courts of appeal in 1891, this enactment abolished the old federal circuit courts and made district courts the venue of first (federal) resort. In some respects the 1911 code had little practical impact upon district judges, who as de facto circuit judges had presided over most federal trials, anyway.[63] Clayton and his compeers were more directly affected by provisions that allowed for temporary reassignments in response to overcrowded dockets.[64] Efficient and gregarious, he was an ideal candidate for such duty. Over the years he would hear cases in many districts, including the Western District of Texas, the Southern District of New York, the Canal Zone, and (often in the 1920s) the Southern District of Florida.[65]

## The World War: Mere Anarchy, Passionate Intensity

Clayton had been on the bench little more than three years when he was caught up in the swift changes and powerful emotions that marked the First World War. Clayton's view of public policy had been that of the pre-presidential Wilson, who in the words of his biographer "believed the federal power should be used only to sweep away special privileges and artificial barriers to the development of individual energies."[66] Yet by the time he sought reelection in 1916, Wilson had embraced a more interventionist style of governing. Though he campaigned as the man who had kept the peace, he had backed a significant military build-up. With the coming of war in 1917, he abandoned all but lip service to states' rights principles, working with congressional allies to secure government management of economic, social, political, and intellectual life.[67]

Like other southern Democrats, Clayton had misgivings about such a concentration of power,[68] but he warmly and in the end blindly supported the war effort. The conflict often came into his courtrooms; his published rulings show different aspects of his response.[69] In November 1917, Clayton denied the petition of Mrs. Henrietta Rush, who sought custody of her soldier grandson in order to save him from trial for desertion. Her argument was that the boy, whose guardian she was, had enlisted without her permission (therefore illegally) at age seventeen.[70] While the enlistment of minors who lied about their ages was a real problem,[71] Clayton had no hesitation in ruling for the government. Like other federal judges, he held that the contract between a minor and the military was valid unless parents or guardians acted in a timely fashion. Mrs. Rush had waited nearly a year.[72]

Deference to the government's war power was the deciding factor in Clayton's refusal to free Oscar Graber, a Croatian imprisoned as an enemy alien.[73] Southern Democrats tended to be suspicious of immigrants,[74] and Clayton was no exception. As a congressman he had favored literacy tests for new arrivals.[75] In 1916 he had told a federal grand jury in New York that he had "no sympathy with any naturalized citizen who is given to carping criticism of this Government."[76] Predictably, Clayton was unimpressed with Graber's argument that he had declared his intention of becoming a U.S. citizen. Instead the judge based his decision upon precedent, which held that the actions taken by a chief executive or his agents in putting down insurrection are "not subject to review in the courts."[77]

Clayton aired his views on the peremptory nature of war powers during drawn-out hearings involving the condemnation of land for military bases. In January 1918, federal officers began condemnation proceedings of property near Montgomery; in fact, they had been in possession for months.[78] During initial proceedings, landowner A. G. Forbes had made no objection to the taking of his property. But when he learned what the government offered to pay, he decided to appeal. In May 1918, his attorneys filed pleadings challenging both the necessity and the validity of the confiscation.[79] At this point the contest became a war of filings and procedure, which ended when Clayton granted a motion to strike Forbes' pleas—thereby sending the case to trial over the issue of compensation. In his ruling Clayton took pains to justify the government, observing that the 1917 act authorizing wartime takings had given discretion (to apply the rules of eminent domain) to the secretary of war, not to judges or jurors.[80]

By May 1918, Congress had given its officials the most peremptory power of all, that of silencing the expression of thoughts.[81] This law, known as the Sedition Act (an amendment to the Espionage Act of 1917), made it a crime for any person to "willfully utter, print, write, or publish" language critical of America's form of government or obstructive of the war effort, or "willfully advocate, teach, defend or suggest the doing" of any disloyal action.[82] The product of a propaganda-enhanced atmosphere, the Sedition Act was a potent weapon in the Wilson administration's home front war, which quickly developed into a campaign of suppression. Though a handful of influential politicians, a band of legal intellectuals, and a number of radicals criticized the Sedition Act as a fatal abridgement of free speech,[83] federal officials employed it without hesitation, in ways drearily familiar to modern readers. Clayton was one of many judges from the Supreme Court down who were willing to enforce the regime of conformity.[84]

In early June 1918, Clayton received word of an event that would further inflame his feelings toward Germany and its supposed American friends— namely, the death in France of his younger brother Bertram, killed by a bomb.[85] He was crushed by the news but did not cease to perform routine duties, including a trip to Washington to lobby Congress for judicial pay raises.[86] Upon returning, he lectured a Middle District grand jury about "vice" at Montgomery military bases, observing that bootleggers, prostitutes, and those who aid them "are doing all they can do, to aid the ferocious Germans now fighting our army in France"—adding that the man "who talks against our government and our prosecution of war does wrong, does exceeding great wrong, and we have provided for his punishment."[87] He spoke at a Fourth of July rally in Mobile,[88] and later occupied himself with a bit of reelection work for Senator John H. Bankhead.[89] Superficially he was in control of himself. Yet by September, when he arrived in New York to help clear dockets in that state's Southern District, he was primed to serve as an agent of retribution.[90]

It was Clayton's fate to be in the metropolis at a time when the nation's mood, like his own, was marked by a combination of passionate determination and angry confusion. Dozens of stories appeared in the newspapers every day under screaming headlines: tales of intense fighting, horrifying reports of casualties, and speculations upon the possibility of an armistice, illustrated with maps and photographs.[91] Federal authorities in New York, pulling out all stops to mobilize bodies and minds, utilized citizen volunteers in sweeps designed to capture "slackers," or draft evaders. These organized mobs showed so little regard for civil liberties that even a pro-administration newspaper complained of "Amateur Prussianism."[92] Clayton wrote to his farm manager that "a thousand real slackers" had been rounded up recently, adding with some understatement that "it is very interesting to be in New York at this time."[93]

By the summer of 1918, the government was also taking an interest in public discussion of the Russian Revolution—the more so since the leaders of that movement had shown little inclination to continue fighting the Germans. Newspaper accounts emphasized "Bolshevist atrocities," and in September the government's Committee on Public Information launched a press campaign designed to convince the public that Bolshevik leaders "were merely hired German agents."[94] Even in multiethnic New York this Orwellian goal was not difficult to achieve. "Barring the relatively few extreme anarchists and socialists," as Clayton declared in a letter, New Yorkers were "splendid in their devotion to our country."[95]

Anarchists and socialists were more numerous than Clayton knew, and they had been deeply angered by President Wilson's recent decision to send United States troops to Russia.[96] Such policies inspired the anarchist Jacob Abrams and a group of his friends to print and, on the morning of August 23, distribute two leaflets. These called Wilson a coward, denounced the "hypocrisy of the plutocratic gang in Washington," and called for a general strike to prevent production of "bullets, bayonets, cannon, to murder not only the Germans, but also your dearest, best, who are in Russia and are fighting for freedom."[97] Within hours Abrams and his colleagues were arrested, brutally interrogated, and charged with four counts of conspiracy in violation of the

Sedition Act.[98] As it happened, the Abrams case was one of several sedition cases assigned to Clayton.[99] This was a strange chance, since Clayton was less experienced in applying espionage laws than three judges already in the district.[100]

The prosecution and the press treated the case as important, and in the course of a long trial (October 14–23) Clayton gave them what they wanted. One of his chief contributions was to exclude testimony that would have supported a major contention of the defense—namely, that since the United States was not at war with Russia (and since the leaflets were not pro-German), the 1918 act did not apply. Clayton was so far from agreeing with the defendants on this point that his comments "made their anti-interventionist propaganda seem a crime in itself."[101] From the standpoint of judicial theatre Clayton truly dominated the proceedings. Never known for reticence on the bench, he took the lead in cross-examining defendants, ridiculing their Russian backgrounds and their trades. He shut off their efforts to make political statements, though he was not above exploring matters (such as defendant Mollie Steimer's liberated views of marriage and love) that were likely to prejudice the jury.[102]

Clayton's attitude, together with popular prejudice against what he would call "the hellishness of anarchy," helped secure convictions for Abrams, Steimer, and three of their compatriots.[103] On October 25, Clayton handed down harsh sentences, but first, he indulged himself in a review—a defense, really—of the prosecution's case. Of the Sedition Act itself, he argued that Congress had an inherent right to counter the "German deceit and trickery and criminality" that had been "at work in our midst." The defendants, in effect German agents, had "hatched" their evil work "in the darkness of night in the gloom of hidden rooms." Clayton expressed shock that defense attorney Harry Weinberger had compared the radicals to Thomas Jefferson and Abraham Lincoln, asking: "Did anybody ever hear such rot?" He was appalled, too, by defense claims that "Christ was himself an anarchist." He had listened patiently, he claimed, "because I did not wish by any act of mine to influence the jury." Finally, he had concluded that the defendants, for all their criticism of capitalists, were not themselves genuine producers: "The only thing they know how to raise is hell."[104]

Clayton's speeches from the bench, like his conduct of the trial, won both praise and blame.[105] As a man who took an interest in his public image, he could easily have rejoiced in what amounted to a publicity coup.[106] Instead, upon his return to Alabama, he sank into an irritable depression—"too many little annoyances here, and too many questions to answer 'right off the bat.'" Not even the Armistice could lift his spirits. In fact on November 21, he confessed to his wife Bettie that he had "too much bitterness in my heart" to be as thankful as he should be. "I wanted our army to trod German soil," he wrote. "I wanted the German army to be annihilated."[107] If the Abrams trial demonstrated the completeness of Clayton's commitment to Wilson's war, its aftermath revealed the psychological costs of the role he had played. Even so, his more judicious instincts were reasserting themselves. He was reading "Grotius on Jus Postliminium," a "very interesting subject now that . . . we are to consider what the victorious nations have the right to do in good conscience" in the cause of justice.[108]

Clayton could not afford to put the Abrams case behind him until November 1919,[109] when the U.S. Supreme Court upheld the defendants' convictions. Even then he had to endure Justice Holmes' dissenting observation that the anarchists were "made to suffer not for what the indictment alleges but for the creed that they avow," as well as Holmes' famous conclusion that "the ultimate good desired is better reached by free trade in ideas."[110] By that time Clayton was considering the world with what Zechariah Chafee called the "post-Armistice mind,"[111] and beginning a movement away from Progressivism.[112] The regulatory furor of the war years now seemed excessive and dangerous, a threat to cherished freedoms. Turning his thoughts homeward, the Alabama judge was inclined to agree with former president Taft's statement that "the overwhelming mass of ill-digested legislation" was one of the nation's most serious problems.[113]

## Rethinking Reform: Changes in Alabama

Clayton of course knew that the federal government, under guise of wartime patriotism, had forced sweeping changes upon post-war Alabama in the form of the Eighteenth (prohibition) and the Nineteenth (women's suffrage) amendments. The former, ratified in 1919 with the ardent support of recently elected governor Thomas E. Kilby, was the ultimate extension of a type of Progressive campaign for which Clayton had never had much enthusiasm.[114] The suffrage amendment, on the other hand, had seemed to Clayton "an invitation for the states to destroy themselves"—his concern being that any expansion of suffrage might threaten white supremacy.[115] Women's suffrage was never ratified by Alabama's legislature, but upon its national ratification Kilby worked with lawmakers to ensure that women could vote in the 1920 elections.[116] Nor was this the end of reform. Before Kilby's four-year term expired, the state had increased its support of education, child welfare, and public health,[117] further alarming conservatives and making Clayton wonder if the political bedrock had shifted permanently.

His grounding, of course, was the Democratic New South of disfranchisement, racial/class hierarchy, and endless insecurity. Political candidates might
be gentlemen—mostly. But white supremacy and its attendant fixations of
class and religion were never far from the surface of politics, as the Hobson-
Underwood fight had revealed.[118] Clayton had hoped that the 1901 constitution had settled questions of racial and cultural dominance, apart from the
rabble-rousing inseparable from politics. Within this framework he had been
willing to be considered a Progressive.[119] But not now—not when the impact
of reform seemed to threaten the underlying system. Clayton and his friends
now had to face the prospect that a rising generation of leaders, shouting
the same reformist slogans they had shouted, might bring their world to
smash.[120]

Apart from racial preoccupations, Clayton and likeminded friends had every reason to ponder the changing impact of cultural prejudice. In the xeno-
phobic climate of the years spanning World War I, it was unlikely that the
"foreign" population of Birmingham and other cities—fairly small but highly
visible—would escape calumny.[121] This was especially the fate of Roman
Catholics, long viewed with suspicion by evangelical Protestants,[122] now an
easy target because they tended to resist efforts to close saloons or tighten enforcement of Blue Laws.[123] As early as 1910 the Georgia propagandist Tom
Watson had launched a campaign to portray Catholicism as the center of a
sinister conspiracy, publishing lurid diatribes in his widely read and region-
ally influential *Watson's Weekly Jeffersonian*.[124]

Six years later, before cheering crowds in Birmingham, Florida governor
Sidney J. Catts—an Alabama native who had based his career on a strange
mixture of reformism and religious bigotry—would describe Catholicism as
"an insidious force which threatened to tear down American institutions."[125]
Even the Progressive reformer Kilby owed his gubernatorial victory, according to one contemporary, to the fact that he had "induced voters to believe
that he was a stauncher foe of Catholicism than his opponents."[126] The intersection of nativism, patriotism, prohibitionism, and religious paranoia fueled such organizations as the True Americans, a ferociously anti-Catholic
group that wielded great political influence in Birmingham during and after
the war.[127]

To be sure, the greatest post-war vehicle of white Protestant tribalism was
the second Ku Klux Klan. Revived in Georgia in 1915, the Klan spread into
Alabama and other states in the guise of a fraternal order with psychic ties
to the past—a past symbolized by the mounted Klansmen who appeared
in D. W. Griffith's film *Birth of a Nation*.[128] Praised initially by spokesmen
of the old regime,[129] the Klan began to grow rapidly as its leaders appealed

to the transplanted rural white Protestants who had thronged to Alabama's cities and towns, and to whom "modernism" in all its forms was both threatening and tantalizing.[130] This new incarnation of the hooded order combined elements of boosterism with the more repressive aspects of wartime Americanism—overlaid with charitable and educational programs derived from Progressivism and prohibitionism.[131] Among its members, who eventually numbered more than one hundred thousand in Alabama,[132] were individuals ready to wage war "against Catholics, Jews, Negroes, aliens, strikers, boot-leggers, immoral women and miscellaneous sinners."[133]

As Klan membership swelled, its leaders condoned raids on businesses, beatings, kidnappings, and other lawless acts that mirrored the paramilitary violence of contemporary European fascists.[134] This vigilantism was puzzling and infuriating to a man like Clayton, who after all shared the Klansmen's patriotism and suspicion of foreigners. What he could not understand was their motive for violence. To his mind, the original Klan had been fighting for the southern way of life against an occupying force, a fact that somewhat justified its methods.[135] Why should the new edition of the order, at a time "of peace in our land, with orderly government functioning everywhere," seek to impose its will in secrecy and by force?[136] As a lawyer and judge, Clayton was wedded to an ethic of procedure and accountability, imperfect in operation but much preferable to lynch law administered by masked men.[137] An opponent of excessive government, Clayton was nonetheless devoted to the respectful preservation of government's traditional powers.

Therefore, Clayton must have read with approval a Montgomery *Advertiser* editorial of October 1, 1919, published after a day of racial unrest culminating in three lynchings. The "industrious and well-behaved negro," it proclaimed, should be "made secure from any form of hoodlumism."[138] Shortly thereafter Clayton's counterpart, state judge Leon McCord of Montgomery, praised the old-time Klan but asserted that existing law enforcement could provide all the protection white citizens needed. In "this day when the court is open practically at all times," McCord told a grand jury, "there is no need for the Ku Klux."[139] It is possible that McCord and other patricians recognized the threat—that of depopulation—posed by the "great migration," a demographic shift in which thousands of blacks moved to northern states.[140] Even former governor Comer, a paternalist and defender of the old racial regime, conceded that "the Negro has really been treated so bad and for so long that . . . he is suspicious all the time."[141] Such men had every reason to fear that Klan violence might contribute to the disruption of existing social and economic relations.[142]

In the early 1920s, Clayton and other old-time Democrats watched nervously as "a legion of aspiring politicians"—many of them in revolt against Bourbon and corporate power within the party—identified themselves with the Klan.[143] In 1920, the Klan had entered U.S. senatorial politics, backing prohibitionist Lycurgus B. Musgrove's strong challenge to Oscar Underwood and aiding Thomas Heflin's successful bid to replace the recently deceased John H. Bankhead.[144] At the same time, rank-and-file Klansmen seemed confident of their freedom to employ violence with impunity, probably because many policemen, sheriffs, and even state judges had joined the order.[145] Perhaps the most notorious accusation of Klan infiltration of the justice system concerned the 1921 Birmingham trial of E. L. Stephenson, a part-time Methodist minister, for the murder of James Coyle, a Catholic priest. Most historians of the case believe that the judge, defense lawyers (led by future Supreme Court justice Hugo L. Black), and a majority of jurors were Klan members or sympathizers. The acquittal was virtually automatic and, as former governor Emmet O'Neal put it, "made an open season in Alabama for the killing of Catholics."[146]

Among establishment figures O'Neal was unusual for his willingness to protest the Stephenson verdict. Clayton, Underwood, and their cohorts were well aware that Catholicism was political dynamite.[147] Moreover, the Stephenson case had not been a simple Klan killing. Father Coyle, the day he was murdered, had presided over the marriage of Stephenson's daughter Ruth, a recent convert to Catholicism, to Pedro Guzman, a native of Puerto Rico. In considering the case, most white Alabamians thought Guzman was black, an attitude fully exploited by the defense at Stephenson's trial.[148] It "was common talk on the streets of Birmingham," B. B. Comer summed up, "that Father Coyle had been guilty of improperly interfering" with Stephenson's family—an analysis that linked old fears of miscegenation to newer religious anxieties.[149] As late as the fall of 1921, Alabama patricians lacked sufficient moral outrage to take on the Klan.

Their reticence vanished with the May 17, 1922, abduction and flogging of J. D. Dowling of Birmingham—a well-connected physician whose mistake, apparently, was that he had strictly enforced state dairy regulations. Elite Alabamians were appalled that one of their own had suffered Klan-style justice, and major newspapers withdrew their support of the Klan.[150] Led by former U.S. Senator Frank S. White, the Birmingham Bar Association lobbied for anti-masking ordinances, protesting Klan-backed deprivations of citizens' constitutional rights and noting that the Klan had unleashed "prejudice, one of the elemental passions of the human race." With unconscious irony they charged that the Klan had thus worked to undermine the Democratic Party and its racial regime.[151] Earlier that month Clayton had written

White, observing that the Klan was the type of organization "productive of disorder in the beginning, and flagrant outrages are the culmination."[152]

## Long Distance Combat: Clayton Takes on the Klan

By this point Clayton was beginning to consider how he could inject himself into the Ku Klux Klan debate. He had never been much constrained by his judicial role. In the post-war years he had seized various opportunities to enter the public arena, including addresses that he gave before the California bar on procedural reform and the Mississippi bar on electric power.[153] At this time his ideas were running parallel to those of former U.S. Senator Leroy Percy and his friends, who were leading opponents of the Klan in that state.[154]

Clayton's anti-Klan stars came into alignment in mid-June 1922, when he agreed to address the Florida State Bar Association at its Orlando convention. He was asked on short notice but the logistics were simple, since he was then holding court in Jacksonville.[155] It was a relaxed situation for Clayton, since he knew many Florida lawyers.[156] He knew also that the Klan, already a presence in Jacksonville, Orlando, and Tampa, would be a topic of interest.[157]

On June 16, when Clayton stood up to address the Floridians,[158] it was clear that he had been considering possible reasons for the Klan's success. He began by noting as a contributing factor that the legal profession had failed to shape (even to attempt to shape) community opinion. Too many lawyers were money-grubbers—or else men who overspecialized, spending their days chasing after mastery of case law. Young attorneys were often poorly grounded in general law and government. Others had simply forgotten that the true purpose of government is the protection of life, liberty, and property. This last was not surprising, he said, since many political scientists assumed that "the main objects of organized society are sanitation, road building, public schools, and the like." He urged lawyers to assert themselves, "teach the principles of orderly government, and insist that lawful methods and none other should be relied on in any case or contingency."[159]

With recent events on his mind, Clayton then set forth the major points of his talk. First, he maintained that secret societies cannot be allowed to "assume the right to administer corrective or punitive justice"; and next, that such organizations, whatever their motives, are "conspiracies against law and government" that "offend the very spirit of the law."[160] He was willing to cast a tolerant glance in the direction of the old-time Klan or the vigilantes of early California, groups that he implied had been useful in chaotic times.[161] Yet he charged their modern counterparts with hiding at night under "shrouds and behind masks"—"inherent evidences of cowardice"—and declared that their methods of law enforcement "are un-American and inevitably lead the way to atrocities." If the Klan went unopposed, he predicted, government would lose its legitimacy and society might degenerate into "armed cliques."[162]

After these bursts of bold rhetoric, Clayton turned again to the role of Progressivism in the rise of the Klan. As one who regarded himself as a sadder but wiser survivor of the war years, he understood Klansmen's yearning for a simpler society. Freely criticizing "proponents of modernism" who viewed government as a pragmatic tool, he argued that they had contributed to an atmosphere in which every aspect of life was subject to oversight.[163] Clayton was well aware that many members of the Klan disliked the new regime of commissions and inspectors; he told his audience the story of Dowling's abduction and also described recent Klan-style violence against the northern-born city manager of Columbus, Georgia. His thought echoing issues surrounding the Abrams case, he charged that Klansmen were imitating those who had "squelched" their opponents and taught the people to snoop and interfere—"to talk and think violently about personal habits and customs."[164]

Thus Clayton lumped together Progressivism and wartime super-patriotism, while ignoring the decades of violence incited by southern racial propaganda. In truth he displayed little concern over the Klan's racial attitudes and ignored its religious bigotry.[165] Instead the erosion of constituted authority provoked Clayton's passion. His intention was to defend the very bones of the status quo, the system that underpinned many arrangements he cherished—including rule by well-placed white Protestants. He lamented the tragic circumstances by which so many native-born Americans were "guilty of the inexcusable self-deception of believing that they may do wrong and that thereby good will follow." A politician by nature and training, Clayton was willing to credit Klansmen with good intentions, even as he urged Florida lawyers to follow the anti-Klan examples of Frank White and Leroy Percy.[166]

Perhaps his emphasis upon "usurpation" was an effort to identify a theme upon which opponents of the Klan could unite. If Clayton hoped to inspire an audience, he was disappointed. The Florida lawyers listened politely—but the convention spent its energy discussing such issues as control over bar admissions and methods of choosing judges.[167] The Jacksonville *Florida Times-Union* and the Orlando *Morning Sentinel* reported the speech briefly, as did the Montgomery *Advertiser*.[168] Alabama's daily newspapers, Clayton later recalled, refused to print his speech;[169] perhaps for this reason Clayton, for a time, showed little inclination to make further denunciations of the Klan in

Alabama. Shortly after his Orlando speech he turned down an invitation to address the Birmingham Bar Association, citing the pressure of judicial duties.[170] Private (signed) responses to the Orlando speech were bland. Clayton received a handful of congratulations and several mildly critical letters—one of which blamed the rise of the Klan upon "the failures of the court[s] to deal adequately with crime, particularly social crime."[171]

It is hard to say to what extent Clayton viewed himself as a possible target of retaliation, but the thought must have crossed his mind. In the months after his Orlando appearance he received several anonymous letters from Ku Kluxers.[172] The most notable of these communications was from "A Klansman," whose five-page letter (dated June 28, 1922) was written on the stationery of an Orlando hotel. With smug hostility, this man charged that Clayton was ignorant of the Klan's true nature, assuring him that many of the lawyers at Orlando had been Klansmen who laughed inwardly at his speech. The Klan, said the writer, was much like the Methodists or Masons. Its members were law-abiding, though they had "taken in hand" situations the law could not handle. Klansmen, he said, were the best men of their communities, and membership was swelling. Having set the judge straight, "A Klansman" asked him to repent and join the hooded order.[173] The judge did not accept the offer.

For all that his speech had been ineffectual, Clayton remained proud of it—and rightly so, for his opposition to the Invisible Empire was one of the defining actions of his career.[174] He had already shed his ties to Progressivism. He was no longer ruled by the wartime paranoia that had marred his performance in 1918. What remained were the lawyer-jurist, willing to stand up for due process and open justice, and the patrician, convinced that he and his friends were the natural leaders of society.[175] It took some courage to say what Clayton had said—what he would continue to say—in the face of "A Klansman" and other masked thugs.[176]

## Post-Oratoria: The Old Guard Soldiers On

After the passage of arms in Orlando, Clayton resumed his busy career. He continued to be a welcome visiting judge, winning praise for his work. In 1923, for example, he presided over a complicated Florida case *(St. Paul Savings Bank v. American Clearing Company)* involving special arrangements made to facilitate "stumping" and clearing land. Before he was through he had considered issues of taxation, imminent domain, bonded indebtedness, and the constitutional laws of the United States and Florida. His opinion, in which he sought to shield individuals from the careless or overzealous extension of state power,[177] was subsequently cited by a fellow judge as "well-considered and learned."[178] He continued to handle the caseload of his home districts, where his decisions and decrees withstood scrutiny at least as well as those of his Northern District colleague William I. Grubb and his Southern District neighbor Robert T. Ervin.[179]

In the meantime, under the leadership of lawyer and promotional genius James W. Esdale, the Klan had continued to be a factor in Alabama politics,[180] and conservatives continued their resistance. Oscar Underwood, a presidential candidate in 1924, touched off a debate within the national Democratic convention by proposing an anti-Klan plank—a measure supported unanimously by the Alabama delegation, though not without serious reservations among Comer-style Progressives.[181] Underwood's ability to control the delegation may indicate that the party's old-guard coalition was far from dead or at least that opposition to the Klan was still perceived as a viable rallying point.[182] But in the wake of Underwood's failure to win the presidential nomination, the Klan made its own statement by holding his political "funeral," an event attended by thousands at Birmingham's Rickwood Field.[183] When he came up for reelection two years later, the veteran senator hesitated but decided not to run.[184]

That year, Esdale's Klan benefited from a generational shift. As the old guard faltered,[185] the war-made men stepped forward, led by Hugo L. Black and Bibb Graves,[186] Klansmen whose political instincts were attuned to coalition-building and to whom the hooded order was only one of several means to an end.[187] Historians may debate the Klan's impact upon the 1926 state elections,[188] but it is true that the Klan backed winners: Black for the U.S. Senate, Graves for governor, and Charles McCall for attorney general.[189] After those triumphs, a euphoric Esdale celebrated with the victors at a statewide meeting in Birmingham. Subsequently, he conceived "a grandiose scheme to bring every Alabama jury and every state legislator under the Klan's thumb."[190] Yet Esdale's dreams would prove to be illusory, in part because the rebellious impulse of the times encompassed more than the Klan's agenda. If anything, 1920s reformism in Alabama was the product of long-simmering animosity to what one historian has called "the balanced power-sharing arrangements . . . erected at the Constitutional Convention of 1901."[191] Some of the men who sought to disrupt that political order, notably Black and Graves, were also capable of growing into their roles—capable of exchanging the Klan's worldview for that of the New Deal.[192]

A second reason for Esdale's disappointment was that his organization possessed an Achilles' heel: namely, that a number of its members were addicted to lawless violence. In the year following the 1926 elections, Klansmen engaged in a frenzy of floggings, kidnappings, extortions, and other acts of terrorism. Their victims included a number of white women,[193] and while Clayton and his friends were disgusted at the prospect of "gangs of hooded demons flogging women and children," they welcomed the chance to condemn Klansmen for violating one of the most cherished principles of southern manhood. To their way of thinking, Klansmen could no longer claim to be the guardians of civilization. Rather they were bringing about what Clayton understood to be "the Rise of Barbarism in Alabama."[194]

Anxious to exploit the Klan's vulnerability, the leaders of the old guard launched a coordinated attack via the Montgomery *Advertiser*, Birmingham *News*, and Birmingham *Age-Herald*—all owned by journalistic mogul Victor Hanson, who promised to "identify the Klan . . . with brutality and outrage."[195] Of all Hanson's editors the most passionate and effective was the *Advertiser*'s Grover Hall,[196] who would subject the Klan to the type of publicity recently employed against German militarists and Bolshevists, printing every scrap of news unfavorable to the order. No stranger to a war of words, Clayton made an early entry into the lists. In a letter published on August 10, 1927, he praised Hall as "truthful, just, fearless and virile," declaring that the *Advertiser* and Hanson's other newspapers were the "chiefest contributors" to a changing climate of opinion.[197]

As the above makes clear, Clayton was near the center of the Bourbon counterattack. Writing and receiving letters, dispensing advice on legislative matters (such as an "anti-masking" bill aimed at the Klan), he was both a cheerleader and an effective spokesman for his side.[198] For him, the high point of the campaign was the publication in the Birmingham *News* and *Age-Herald* of an edited version of his Orlando speech. A front-page story on Sunday, August 14, 1927, it carried to tens of thousands of homes his message—that the Klan was unnecessary, a threat to constituted government, and if unchecked, fatal to all expectations of peace and fair play. The headline—"Good Men in Klan Garb Should Quit"—struck a conciliatory note that softened the article's effect.[199] For Clayton, who liked to remind friends that he had been one of the Klan's earliest foes,[200] the reprint represented a vindication five years delayed.

By the late summer and fall of 1927, the Hanson papers had created an atmosphere of crisis around the Klan. Having found his range, Hall gave *Advertiser* readers full coverage of a dramatic series of flogging trials in which Attorney General Charles McCall, elected with Klan backing but rapidly undergoing a change of heart, dueled with the order's talented defense attorney, Horace Wilkinson.[201] McCall's resignation from the Klan on October 20 has been described by historian Glenn Feldman as a "bombshell" that led 150 Tuscaloosa Klansmen to resign.[202] A few days later, when future U.S. Senator John Hollis Bankhead II demanded that Bibb Graves disband the Klan, the *Advertiser* covered the event with headlines of the type normally reserved for declarations of war.[203]

One of Clayton's last public acts in the war against the Klan was an address, summarized in the October 28 Montgomery *Advertiser,* in which he told federal grand jurors to go "back home, counsel your people, be law-abiding, and above all see that this masking business is stopped." Reprising his earlier writings and speeches, Clayton pilloried the Klan as a threat to order and "a disgrace" to the state. "What could be more cowardly," he asked, "than masked men whipping helpless women and girls?" He concluded: "There is no place for the Klan in Alabama now," and like Bankhead he called for the order to be disbanded.[204] Clayton, Bankhead, and other patrician crusaders intended to strike body blows against the Klan, and in truth they assisted in defeating Esdale's tawdry empire, which suffered precipitous declines in official membership.[205]

Clayton was an engaged spectator of the 1928 presidential election campaign, which was the next battlefield of Klan-backed and old-guard politicos. The pressure of judicial business kept him from attending the Democratic National Convention in Houston, but he was an enthusiastic supporter of the nominee, Al Smith of New York. To Clayton, Smith was an "ideal" candidate, a man of honor and experienced wisdom.[206] Even before the convention Clayton had been confident that Smith would carry Alabama, despite the New Yorker's well-known opposition to prohibition.[207] For their part, the state's Klansmen and prohibitionists, representing a large number of politically active Alabamians, were "united in their opposition" to Smith.[208] Some of their leaders (notably Hugo Black) were quiescent during the summer and fall—fearful of the vengeance that might follow a bolt. Tom Heflin went a step further by openly repudiating Smith.[209]

As the Klan and its political friends attacked Smith with the most strident anti-Catholic, anti-wet propaganda, Democratic loyalists swung into action. Editorialists and orators showered the electorate with well-rehearsed appeals to tradition, regional solidarity, and race hatred.[210] For some Bourbons these may have been mechanical performances, but for men like Clayton, for whom political loyalty was a quasi-religious principle, such occasions required no artifice. "I know you will do as you please and as your conscience and your judgment dictates," he wrote to a friend who must have been wavering. "I think I know," he continued, that "the only hope and safeguard of the civilization of the South lies in the Democratic organization, and in the solidarity of the white man's party." Referring to his friend as "a tower of strength," Clayton begged him to stay within the fold.[211]

It is likely that this man was one of thousands of white Alabamians who would cast their first Republican votes that fall. Yet when the dust had cleared, Clayton's side had carried Alabama for Smith—by a margin of only seven thousand votes.[212] Clayton's correspondence files show little or no involvement in the subsequent drama, in which (after complicated maneuvering and by a final vote of twenty-seven to twenty-one) the state Democratic committee expelled Tom Heflin and other prominent turncoats, keeping them from participating in the 1930 primaries.[213] Those events were played out in the final months of 1929, the time when Clayton's political and judicial careers were flickering out.

## Conclusions

In 1928 Clayton was seventy-one years old. He continued to be a model of energy and involvement, supervising his personal affairs, managing his courtroom, keeping an eye on politics and making himself available for ceremonial affairs. One of the latter, in 1924–1925, had been his acceptance (as surrogate for his deceased brother) of membership in France's Legion of Honor.[214] In the summer of 1929, however, he was stricken by "pernicious anemia" and liver cancer. Transfusions in November briefly improved his condition and allowed him to continue working, but within a month he had suffered a further deterioration that forced him to step down. Clayton applied for retirement just a week prior to his death on December 21.[215]

To his friends Clayton had seemed an irrepressible free spirit.[216] Anyone considering the phases of his public life—his years as disfranchiser, Progressive, and legal reformer, his role in wartime red-baiting, his subsequent work against the Ku Klux Klan—might be excused for concluding that he was an inconsistent man in inconsistent times. Yet with his whole career in perspective, it is clear that Clayton's lodestone was the value system of the nineteenth-century Black Belt—the paternal instincts, the racial and economic hierarchies that survived from his parents' time, and (perhaps above all) the political order cobbled together in 1901.[217]

Yet Clayton's respect for the totems of his class was reinforced by a professional discipline that prized due process, deliberation, and the refereed conflicts in the courts. His acceptance of the common-law viewpoint helps to explain both his advocacy of federal procedural reforms (intended to enhance justice within the established order) and his contempt for mob rule. Apart from the vagaries inevitable in a long, politically conditioned life, Clayton's mind worked consistently. His words, whether judicial or political, high-spirited or indignant, often conveyed a sense of transparent conviction.

How does Clayton fit into the historical patterns of Alabama's federal judiciary? Like Thomas Goode Jones he was both an authoritative judge and a political activist. It was his fate, as it was Jones', to antagonize influential Alabamians who thought of themselves as reformers but were impatient of due process. To some extent, therefore, Jones and Clayton prefigure Frank M. Johnson Jr.,[218] the Middle District's most celebrated judge. After all, Johnson's constitutional faith would antagonize—to put it mildly—George C. Wallace,[219] the state's great twentieth-century boss and pseudo-reformer. At decisive moments in their careers, all three judges placed human rights and legal values above the will of the electorate.

Even to mention these incidents, however, is to invoke the world inhabited by all three men, in which race was commonly the text—and always the subtext—of public affairs. Indeed, to set forth the history of Clayton's time is to prove that times change but things remain the same. When Clayton died more than seventy-five years ago, Alabama was governed by its 1901 disfranchisement constitution and neither the state nor the United States had achieved consensus concerning the racial, social, and economic problems that were legacies of slavery and the Civil War. To these had been added questions arising from World War I. How far should the government impose moral standards on its citizens? In seeking to protect society, how far should it limit civil liberties? Is it ever acceptable for citizens, in response to private or public wrongs, to take the law into their own hands? If Clayton and his cohorts could take part in political discussions today, they would be on familiar ground.

# Afterword

It is unlikely that anyone will mistake this book of essays for an Alabama version of Carl N. Degler's classic *The Other South*. Still it is worthwhile to remember that 1974 work, written to demonstrate that white southerners had not always been a "solid" body of racists. One would think that the point had been made long before that—by Virginius Dabney's *Liberalism in the South* (1932), C. Vann Woodward's *Strange Career of Jim Crow* (1955 and later editions), and several other books.[1] Yet even in the late twentieth century the image conjured by W. J. Cash of savage white southerners—gothic figures whipped into self-destructive frenzies—lingered on. It has not completely vanished today.[2]

Several Alabama histories, however, have pointed us away from this simplistic approach. Malcolm C. McMillan's *Constitutional Development in Alabama* (1955 and later editions), William Warren Rogers' *One-Gallused Rebellion* (1970), J. Mills Thornton's *Politics and Power in a Slave Society* (1978), and Wayne Flynt's *Poor But Proud* (1989) lead readers into a complex, often ambiguous world, where violence, prejudice, idealism, good intentions, and raw self-interest jostle each other, with various results.[3] The subjects of the essays in this book inhabit that world.

The cast of this book also consists, as Guy Hubbs points out in his introduction, largely of persons deeply influenced by Whiggish values and goals. Simply put, the Whigs believed that institutions can and should be structured to promote reason and enlightenment. Specifically, they believed that governments should assist by providing an environment in which the people can prosper and improve themselves. In Alabama, to Whig leaders like Benjamin F. Porter, Henry W. Hilliard, and Thomas H. Watts, the promotion of industry and transportation, the construction of schools, and the maintenance of such "eleemosynary" institutions as a penitentiary and an insane asylum all pointed toward civilization and away from frontier crudities. The Whig political faith lent itself to a paternalistic approach to politics, unpopular in the boisterous Jacksonian era. But in such persons as Henry and

Julia Tutwiler, it coincided with something close to a premodern view of social responsibilities—shaped and warped by slavery and racist assumptions,
to be sure—but productive both of personal kindness and corporate good.

Whiggish attitudes can be detected in the saintly Tutwilers and in earnest clergymen like James F. Smith. But they are also apparent in complex,
conflicted men like Porter and Thomas Goode Jones, and even in persons
whose personalities, however complex, revealed authoritarian tendencies—
like Henry D. Clayton or Booker T. Washington. All these Whiggish persons (some of whom, ironically, were New South Democrats) were dubious
about the directions in which Alabama society seemed to be heading. Their
solution, in generalized terms, was to tame the state, to guide its citizens toward those social and institutional structures most likely to promote peace,
reason, responsibility, and humane dealings. Most of them were openly reformist at one time or another, though all hoped that the existing "system"
could be made to work fairly. It is both appropriate and pleasantly amusing to
use the term "Bourbon reformers" to describe them.[4]

On the other hand, some reformers were not Whiggish by any definition. Joseph C. Manning is the chief representative in this volume of persons whose object, politically, was to restore the people to unfettered political freedom. Such people were certain that any political combination of
well-to-do persons, even those that set out to do good, would eventually use
power to protect their wealth. Like Whiggish politicians operating in the
post–Civil War Democratic Party, persistent Jacksonians cropped up in odd
places. Robert McKee, journalist and secretary to Bourbon-era governors,
was essentially a Jacksonian intellectual. In the 1880s he campaigned against a
profiteering "'state penitentiary ring.'" In the 1890s, furious with Democratic
ballot box stuffing, he supported the agrarian candidate Reuben F. Kolb.[5]
Joseph C. Manning, for his part, made his entrance into politics as a Populist
firebrand, but as noted above, he spent much of his career as a Republican.
Both men understood that the chief issue of the times was simple ballot
freedom—the ability of ordinary voters to cast ballots and to see those ballots
honestly counted.

One brutal lesson contained in this book is that both branches of reformers
failed. The Whiggish patricians and the Bourbon reformers failed to nudge
society toward reasoned humanity, failed to insure that institutions worked
fairly. The Jacksonians-turned-agrarians were unable to translate their economic values into law and failed just as badly in their efforts to prevent corrupt men from controlling elections. The reformers failed because their goals
ran counter to the great currents of the age—that is the concentration of
economic resources, particularly of industrial resources, accompanied by so-

cial stratification along economic lines. The men who benefited economically and politically from this concentration in Alabama were the leaders of the Democratic faction known in the twentieth century as the Black Belt–"Big Mule" coalition. They made use of racism to divide the laboring classes but were not above outright fraud—when, for example, they saw to the ratification of the 1901 constitution. From the time the disfranchisement regime was clamped down upon African Americans and poor whites, the reformist impulses known collectively as Progressivism played out as little more than family squabbles. Governor Braxton Bragg Comer's "war" against the railroads is perhaps the best instance of this.[6]

Within this twentieth-century world, with its limited electorate and circumscribed possibilities, demagoguery became a way of attracting attention among politicians who wanted to excite constituents and insure their own reelection, or (as in the case of J. Thomas Heflin) who simply enjoyed theatrics.[7] For politicians who wanted to reshape the Democratic power structure, like Hugo Black and Bibb Graves, theatrics and advertising/propaganda techniques perfected during the First World War came in handy. Black was remarkable in that he benefitted from the ultimate rabble-rousing commotion of the day, the Ku Klux Klan, even as he prepared to abandon it. The fact that he outgrew the Klan makes a wonderful story, but viewed in historical perspective it marked a conjunction of good judgment (Black's) and good luck (for Alabamians).[8]

Good luck because the politics of disfranchisement was fueled by poverty, powerlessness, and deep frustrations; power could as easily (more easily) fall into the hands of bad men as good. To borrow a figure of speech from Robert Penn Warren's fictional boss Willie Stark, the "human business" of Alabama was like a bottle of water, stoppered with a cork and tossed into the stove. That cork's going to blow sooner or later, with quite a bang—and in Alabama the political prizes went to the fellows who could manage the excitement, then put the cork back in.[9] Within a generation after Black and Graves strode across the stage, it was clear that a self-possessed, remorseless demagogue—George C. Wallace—could establish a political dynasty, while an equally talented but self-destructive man like James Folsom was unable to hold his own.

It would be wrong to conclude, however, that the reformers lived in vain or that they are not worthy of study. To begin with, it is notable that several of them were lawyers, which is hardly surprising, for until the early twentieth-century lawyers (with journalists and a smattering of other professionals) dominated the public intellectual life of most southern states. But from the beginning, from the era in which Harry Toulmin kept peace by holding filibusterers to the letter of the law, reform-minded lawyers knew the one really effective method of thwarting great concentrations of power, prejudice, and selfishness.

That method, under the Anglo-American system of common law, is to insist on receiving due process: fair adversarial play, issues played out under the rules, scrupulously, with observance of rights proclaimed under the U.S. Constitution and its associated statutes and decisions. This system of vanquishing evils is slow; under it, a good cause can be stymied for the full term of the "law's delay."[10] But lawyers as far separated in time as Harry Toulmin and Henry D. Clayton shared the reformer's faith in the eventual triumph of a just cause, if it can be heard in an impartial forum. Men as widely separated in temperament and sympathies as Thomas Goode Jones and Joseph C. Manning both looked to the U.S. Constitution to rectify the evils of disfranchisement. It turns out that all of them were right; the overthrow of a disfranchised, dysfunctional system was brought about by legal means. In that sense, the line between Harry Toulmin and Frank M. Johnson Jr. is drawn fairly straight.

# Notes

The author sincerely thanks the editors, boards, and other authorities of *The Alabama Review*, *The Alabama Historical Quarterly*, *Anglican and Episcopal History*, *Gulf Coast Historical Review*, *LH&RB*, *Occasional Publications of the Bounds Law Library*, and *Southern Studies* for permission to reprint materials previously published.

## Preface and Acknowledgments

1. Paul M. Pruitt Jr., "Introduction to the 2004 Edition" in Anne Gary Pannell and Dorothea E. Wyatt, *Julia S. Tutwiler and Social Progress in Alabama* (Tuscaloosa: University of Alabama Press, 2004), xxiii–xxiv; and "Convict Lease System and Peonage" and "Tutwiler, Julia," in *New Encyclopedia of Southern Culture: Volume 10: Law and Politics*, ed. James W. Ely Jr. and Bradley G. Bond (Chapel Hill: University of North Carolina Press, 2008), 26–30, 136–37.

## Introduction

1. Harry Toulmin, *An Oration Delivered at the Celebration of American Independence at Frankfort, (K.) on the 4th of July, 1804* (Lexington, KY: Thomas Anderson, 1804), 6.

2. One exception to this is John W. Quist's *Restless Visionaries: The Social Roots of Antebellum Reform in Alabama and Michigan* (Baton Rouge: Louisiana State University Press, 1998). Quist demonstrates that, contrary to conventional wisdom, the reform impulse was as strong in the Old Southwest as the Old Northwest, with the obvious exception of the anti-slavery movement.

3. Benjamin F. Porter, *Reports of Cases Argued and Adjudged in the Supreme Court of Alabama, Commencing at the June Term, 1834*, vol. 6 (Tuscaloosa: Printed at the Intelligencer and Expositor Office, 1835), v–vi.

## Chapter 1

1. Malcolm C. McMillan, *Constitutional Development in Alabama, 1798–1901: A Study in Politics, the Negro, and Sectionalism* (1955; repr. Spartanburg, South Carolina: The Reprint Company, 1978), 6–9. Created in 1800, Washington County was given its own judgeship in 1804. For Jefferson's first choice, who died after hold-

ing one term of court, see Thomas M. Owen, "Ephraim Kirby, First Superior Court Judge in What Is Now Alabama," in *Proceedings of the Twenty-Fourth Annual Meeting of the Alabama State Bar Association* (Montgomery: Brown Printing, 1901), 167–79. A judgeship for Madison County (Huntsville) would be approved in 1810; Obadiah Jones of Georgia filled it. See Clarence E. Carter, ed., *Territorial Papers of the United States: Volume V: The Territory of Mississippi* (Washington, D.C.: Government Printing Office, 1937), 320–21, 353–56, 370, 413–14; Carter, ed., *Territorial Papers: Volume VI*, 51–52; Paul M. Pruitt Jr. and David I. Durham, "Sources of Law in the Alabama Territory and the State of Alabama, 1798–1832: A Narrative Bibliography," and Kris Gilliland, "Mississippi, 1699–1817," in *Prestatehood Legal Materials: A Fifty-State Research Guide*, ed. Michael Chiorazzi and Marguerite Most (Binghamton, NY: Haworth Information Press, 2005), 1:1–29, 603–30. For short biographies of Toulmin, see Thomas M. Owen, *History of Alabama and Dictionary of Alabama Biography* (Chicago: S. J. Clarke, 1921), 7:1676–77; John Garraty and Mark C. Carnes, eds., *American National Biography* (New York: Oxford University Press, 1999), 21:768; and Dumas Malone, ed., *Dictionary of American Biography* (New York: Charles Scribner's Sons, 1936), vol. 9, pt. 2: 601–602.

2. See Johnson Jones Hooper, *Adventures of Captain Simon Suggs: Late of the Tallapoosa Volunteers; Together with "Taking the Census" and Other Alabama Sketches* (Philadelphia: T. B. Peterson, 1848); and Joseph Glover Baldwin, *The Flush Times of Alabama and Mississippi: A Series of Sketches* (New York: D. Appleton & Co., 1854).

3. The reference is to the master class as portrayed in Eugene Genovese, *The World the Slaveholders Made: Two Essays in Interpretation* (New York: Pantheon Books, 1969).

4. Leland L. Lengel, "Keeper of the Peace: Harry Toulmin in the West Florida Controversy, 1805–1813" (masters thesis, Duke University, 1962), 3–4.

5. Ibid., 5–7; and Marion Tinling and Godfrey Davies, eds., *The Western Country in 1793: Reports on Kentucky and Virginia by Harry Toulmin* (San Marino, California: Henry E. Huntington Library, 1948), v–viii. See also Craig Thompson Friend, "Inheriting Eden: The Creation of Society and Community in Early Kentucky, 1792–1812" (PhD dissertation, University of Kentucky, 1995), 10–56 passim.

6. Quoted in Tinling and Davies, *The Western Country in 1793*, viii–x (quoted passage on ix).

7. Lengel, "Keeper of the Peace," 8. Toulmin maintained his connection with Priestley, who emigrated in 1794 and settled in Philadelphia, continuing his work as a scientist and clergyman. For Priestley's activities see John Allen Macaulay, *Unitarianism in the Antebellum South: The Other Invisible Institution* (Tuscaloosa: University of Alabama Press, 2001) 21–27. As to Toulmin's family, he married his first wife, Ann Tremlett, in England; they had eight children. Toulmin's second wife was Martha Johnson, likewise an English woman. They were married in Washington County at an unknown date; together they had two children. See Owen, *History of Alabama and Dictionary of Alabama Biography*, 4:1677.

8. Lengel, "Keeper of the Peace," 8–10; Tinling and Davies, *The Western Country in 1793*, x–xiv; and Friend, "Inheriting Eden," 229–32, 233–38. A complicating factor for cerebral theologians, deists, and Presbyterians alike was the growing popularity

of emotional, revivalistic religion. Friend quotes Toulmin to the effect that Kentucky was home both to "unbelievers, who freely express their opinions" and "enthusiasts . . . who assemble in thousands in the woods, and continue night and day." Friend, "Inheriting Eden," 238.

9. Lengel notes of the Resolutions that "many supposed the young English liberal instrumental in the agitation which generated them." Lengel, "Keeper of the Peace," 10–11; and Julian P. Boyd, et al., eds., *The Papers of Thomas Jefferson*, vol. 30, *1 January 1798 to 31 January 1799* (Princeton: Princeton University Press, 2003), 550–56.

10. Harry Toulmin and James Blair, *A Review of the Criminal Law of the Commonwealth of Kentucky* (Frankfort, Kentucky: W. Hunter, 1804–1806), 1:ix. For information on Blair's subordinate role, see ibid., xii.

11. Benjamin Buford Williams, *A Literary History of Alabama: The Nineteenth Century* (Rutherford, New Jersey: Fairleigh Dickinson University Press, 1979), 24.

12. Compare the tables of contents in Toulmin and Blair, *A Review of the Criminal Law*, vol. 1, 2, and 3, with that in William Blackstone, *Commentaries on the Law of England* (1765; repr. Chicago: University of Chicago Press, 1979), vol. 4.

13. Toulmin and Blair, *Review of the Criminal Law*, 1:x, xi, xii.

14. Harry Toulmin, *The Clerk's Magazine and American Conveyancer's Assistant: Being a Collection Adapted to the United States of the Most Approved Precedents* (Philadelphia: Mathew Carey, 1806), i–v (quoted passages on i), xi–xxi. For Toulmin's sources, chiefly Blackstone, Frederic C. Jones' *Precedents in Conveying* (1794), and the statutes of the states listed above, see ibid., iv–v. Toulmin's book was issued in duodecimo; the title page declares that he was "Secretary of the State of Kentucky," which invites the inference that the book was begun before his appointment as a Mississippi territorial judge. The wily Carey also issued the volume under another title: *The American Attorney's Pocket Book*.

15. Lengel, "Keeper of the Peace," 11–13. One of Toulmin's motives for moving was a change of administration in Kentucky, where the newly elected governor, Christopher Greenup, would soon have "unhorsed him in favor of some political associate of the new regime" (ibid., 12).

16. Harry Toulmin, *An Oration Delivered at the Celebration of American Independence*, 1–8 (quoted passage on 6). Had Europeans colonized Louisiana, Toulmin argued that "in the course of a few years, that Territory would have been deluged with slaves from the coast of Africa." For the likely consequences, he advised listeners to consider "the dark & terrific scenes which have been exhibited in St. Domingo." Though Toulmin's attitude toward slavery is not a major concern of this study, the *Oration* leaves no doubt that he disapproved of the institution, congratulating Americans for their role in suppressing the international slave trade. Like many Jeffersonians he believed that slavery was doomed to fade before the advance of reason and enlightenment. Thus (with unconscious irony) he wrote that by the transfer of Louisiana to the United States, "instead of a new grave being opened for the children of captivity, there is a wide area thrown open to the sons of freedom." See ibid., 4. For the terror caused by slave revolts in Haiti and San Domingo, see Michael O'Brien, *Conjectures of Order: Intellectual Life in the American South* (Chapel Hill: University of North Carolina Press, 2004), 1:207–209.

17. Lengel, "Keeper of the Peace," 15–21. The seat of government in Washington County was St. Stephens, upstream on the Tombigbee from Fort Stoddart; as early as 1803 St. Stephens had been the location of a U.S. government "factory" for trade with Native Americans. The Mississippi Territory was eventually divided into the present-day states of Alabama and Mississippi. Reports (c. 1802) estimate the combined white and African American population of Washington County was between 750 and 1200. Rowland, *Mississippi*, 2:937. See William H. Brantley, *Three Capitals: A Book About the First Three Capitals of Alabama: St. Stephens, Huntsville, & Cahawba* (1947; repr. University: University of Alabama Press, 1976), 5–6. For Toulmin's activities in July 1805, see Isaac Joslin Cox, *The West Florida Controversy, 1799–1813: A Study in American Diplomacy* (Baltimore, Maryland: Johns Hopkins Press, 1918), 177.

18. Ephraim Kirby quoted in Aaron Welborn, "A Traitor in the Wilderness: The Arrest of Aaron Burr," *Alabama Heritage* 83 (Winter 2007), 14. For similar remarks made in 1803 by famous frontier preacher Lorenzo Dow, see Brantley, *Three Capitals*, 4–5

19. For an especially good summary of the Caller family, see Philip D. Beidler, *First Books: The Printed Word and Cultural Formation in Early Alabama* (Tuscaloosa: University of Alabama Press, 1999), 16–17.

20. The reference in the heading to "flush times," of course, is to a classic work that covers the same geography, revealing the same human failings that Toulmin would encounter. See Joseph Glover Baldwin, *The Flush Times of Alabama and Mississippi: A Series of Sketches* (New York: D. Appleton and Company, 1854).

21. David Lightner, "Private Land Claims in Alabama," *Alabama Review*, 20 (1967), 197; *American National Biography*, 21:768; For Toulmin's involvement in diplomatic matters as early as 1805, see *Debates and Proceedings of the Congress of the United States* (Washington, D.C.: Gales and Seaton, 1852), 15 (9th Congress, 1st Session), 1186–87, et seq. For Spanish fees and the 6 percent "tariff," see Lengel, "Keeper of the Peace," 31–32; Welborn gives the figure as 12 percent on goods going upstream or downstream, see "Traitor in the Wilderness," 14. For the perspective from Washington, D.C., see Frank Lawrence Owsley Jr. and Gene A. Smith, *Filibusters and Expansionists: Jeffersonian Manifest Destiny, 1800–1821* (Tuscaloosa: University of Alabama Press, 1997), 16–31.

22. Brewer, *Alabama: Her History*, 575; Owen, *History of Alabama and Dictionary of Alabama Biography*, 4:1677; and Winston Smith, *Days of Exile: The Story of the Vine and Olive Colony in Alabama* (1967; repr. Demopolis, Alabama: Marengo County Historical Society, 1978), 36. Toulmin's duties also involved arduous travel. For mention of an 1811 journey into the Territory of Orleans to swear in a group of public officials, see Dunbar Rowland, ed., *Official Letterbooks of W. C. C. Claiborne, 1801–1816* (Jackson, Mississippi: State Department of Archives and History, 1917), 5: 390–91.

23. John D.W. Guice, "The Cement of Society: Law in the Mississippi Territory," *Gulf Coast Historical Review*, 1 (Spring 1986), 77; William Baskerville Hamilton, *Anglo-American Law on the Frontier: Thomas Rodney and His Territorial Cases* (Durham, North Carolina: Duke University Press, 1953), 212–13 (quoted passage). For information about the possibility that Toulmin was improperly involved in one potentially rich claim, see David Lightner, "Private Land Claims in Alabama," 196–98;

for additional claims against Toulmin and evidence of lengthy litigation over land, see Edwin Lewis to Governor William Wyatt Bibb, 19 August 1818, in Carter, ed., *Territorial Papers: Volume XVIII*, 401–405.

24. Harry Toulmin, comp., *The Statutes of the Mississippi Territory, Revised and Digested By the Authority of the General Assembly* (Natchez: Samuel Terrell, 1807), 84–304. For frivolous demurrers, see ibid., 170–71; for attorney regulations, see ibid., 226–29. It seems noteworthy that Toulmin reprinted the Northwest Ordinance, though that famous federal enactment did not control the legislature of Mississippi (ibid., 467–77). However, the ordinance includes an article that guarantees "judicial proceedings according to the course of the common law" (ibid., 473).

25. For territorial criminal law, see ibid., 305–86; for federal land laws, see ibid., 486–546; for federal criminal law, see ibid., 547–87. See also Dunbar Rowland, *Mississippi: Comprising Sketches of Counties, Towns, Events, Institutions, and Persons* (1907; repr. Spartanburg, South Carolina: The Reprint Company, 1976), 2:794–95.

26. James Willard Hurst, *The Growth of American Law: The Law Makers* (Boston: Little, Brown and Company, 1950), 147–49; and John A. Conley, "Doing It By the Book: Justice of the Peace Manuals and English Law in Eighteenth-Century America," *Journal of Legal History*, 6 (1985), 272 (quoted passage), 257–98.

27. Harry Toulmin, *The Magistrate's Assistant: Being an Alphabetical Illustration of Sundry Legal Principles and Usages, Accompanied with a Variety of Necessary Forms, Compiled for the Use of the Justices of the Peace in the Mississippi Territory* (Natchez, Mississippi: Samuel Terrell, 1807).

28. Conley, "Doing It By the Book," 262. See Toulmin, *Magistrate's Assistant*, 5, 15, 17, 90, 126. For cites to the English legal gods and for an historical treatment of assize, general gaol delivery, oyer and terminer, nisi prius, and commission of the peace, see ibid., 31–32. For Toulmin's definition and proposed etymology of the term *felony*, see ibid., 102–103

29. Toulmin, *Magistrate's Assistant*, 3–5, 5–7, 7–29 (quoted passage on 25), 29–30, 31–32.

30. Frederick Jackson Turner, *The Frontier in American History* (New York: Henry Holt, 1947), 1–38, passim. Further study of Toulmin's frontier judgeship might cast light on the celebrated (and controversial) "Turner Thesis," by which American democracy is said to have grown organically from the restless energy, self-reliance, and egalitarian social outlook that marked frontier settlers.

31. Toulmin, *Magistrate's Assistant*, 14–18, 67–74, 79–96, 186–92 (quoted passage on 189).

32. Richard Peters, ed. *The Public Statutes at Large of the United States of America* (Boston: Charles C. Little and James Brown, 1850) 2:338, cited in Hamilton, *Anglo-American Law on the Frontier*, 94–95. See also Erwin C. Surrency, *History of the Federal Courts* (New York: Oceana Publications, Inc., 1987), 352. For more on territorial judges, see Kermit L. Hall, "Hacks and Derelicts Revisited: America's Territorial Judiciary, 1789–1959," *Western Historical Quarterly*, 12, no. 3 (1981), 273–89.

33. Toulmin, *Magistrate's Assistant*, title page. For another example of Toulmin as an agent of the federal government, see H. S. Halbert and T. H. Ball, *The Creek War of 1813 and 1814*, ed. Frank L. Owsley Jr. (1895; repr. Tuscaloosa: University of Ala-

bama Press, 1995), 212–13. For additional information on Toulmin and the admiralty, see Hamilton, *Anglo-American Law on the Frontier,* 98n27.

34. For an example of Toulmin's careful approach to the legal issues raised by Burr and his confederates, see Harry Toulmin to James Madison, 14 April 1807, in James Madison Papers, Library of Congress, Manuscript Division [microfilm], Series 1—General Correspondence, Reel 9. For Toulmin's role in these murky affairs, see Lengel, "Keeper of the Peace," 33–47; Hamilton, *Anglo-American Law on the Frontier,* 78–83; Albert James Pickett, *History of Alabama and Incidentally of Georgia and Mississippi, from the Earliest Period* (1851; repr. Birmingham: Birmingham Book and Magazine Company, 1962), 488–502; Thomas Perkins Abernethy, *The Burr Conspiracy* (New York: Oxford University Press, 1954), 198–226, especially 223–25; and Welborn, "Traitor in the Wilderness," 10–19. In justice to Mississippi adventurers in general, it should be pointed out that the U.S. Congress had in February 1804 passed the Mobile Act, asserting American "annexation of all navigable rivers and streams . . . that flowed into the Gulf of Mexico." Owsley and Smith, *Filibusters and Expansionists,* 23, 62. It was the practice of the Jefferson and Madison administrations to assert rights they had little intention of enforcing immediately—but that might come in handy later.

35. Lengel, "Keeper of the Peace," 57–93, especially 74–77, 84–88, 92–93. See also Isaac Joslin Cox, *The West Florida Controversy, 1798–1813: A Study in American Diplomacy* (Baltimore: Johns Hopkins Press, 1918).

36. Lengel, "Keeper of the Peace," 91–125; Pickett, *History of Alabama,* 481–87, 505–509; and Cox, *West Florida Controversy,* 482–85. J. C. A. Stagg, ed., *The Papers of James Madison: Presidential Series,* vol. 2 (Charlottesville: University Press of Virginia, 1992), 447–53, 606–609; Stagg, ed., *Papers of James Madison: Presidential Series,* vol. 3 (Charlottesville: University Press of Virginia, 1996), 3–4, 22–24, 36–39, 56–57, 68–70 (quoted passage on 68–69).

37. Alfred Tennyson, "Ulysses," lines 3–4.

38. Madison had assigned the present-day "Florida Parishes" of Louisiana to the Territory of Orleans as far east as the Perdido River; he would have been happy to see the Spanish surrender Mobile and the remainder of West Florida (and East Florida, for that matter) but was unwilling to seize them by force, unprovoked. See Pruitt and Durham, "Sources of Law in the Alabama Territory," 3; McMillan, *Constitutional Development,* 17–18; Cox, *West Florida Controversy,* 487–516, especially 490, 514–16; Lengel, "Keeper of the Peace," 111–19; and Owsley and Smith, *Filibusters and Expansionists,* 62–66, 67–81. The federal troops in question were supported by militia units packed with Kemper's men.

39. Stagg, ed., *Papers of James Madison: Presidential Series,* vol. 4 (Charlottesville: University Press of Virginia, 1999), 190–91. Toulmin thought that plots against his reputation, even his life, had been planned as early as 1807. See Cox, *West Florida Controversy,* 515–17; and Lengel, "Keeper of the Peace," 54–55, 80, 98, 114–17, 125–33.

40. For events surrounding Toulmin's impeachment, see Stagg, *Papers of James Madison: Presidential Series,* vol. 3, 110–16, 129–31, 153–54, 192–93, 201–204, 221, 302–304; Stagg, *Papers of James Madison: Presidential Series,* vol. 4, 28–29, 180–86, 190–91, 220–22; and *American State Papers: Miscellaneous* (Washington, D.C.: Gales and

Seaton, 1834), II: 162, 184 (quoted passage).There is evidence of further charges filed as late as 1817. See *American State Papers*, 443. See also Lengel, "Keeper of the Peace," 128–41.

41. Brantley, *Three Capitals*, 8, 11. For an 1816 estimate of a territory-wide population of 45,000 free people and 30,000 slaves, see ibid., 21. By 1819, the combined population of Alabama alone would grow to approximately 125,000; see Pruitt and Durham, "Sources of Law in the Alabama Territory," 17. For the origins of the various towns see Owen, *History of Alabama and Dictionary of Alabama Biography*, 1:186–88, 718–19; 2:1037–38, 1237, 1333; Nancy M. Rohr, ed., *Incidents of the War: The Civil War Journal of Mary Jane Chadick* (Huntsville, Alabama: Huntsville Madison County Historical Society, 2005), 4.; and H. S. Halbert and T. H. Ball, *The Creek War of 1813 and 1814*, ed. Frank L. Owsley Jr. (Tuscaloosa: University of Alabama Press, 1995), 307–12.

42. This phrase was used in the mid-twentieth century by Harry E. Rogers of Greenville, Alabama, to describe the life of south Alabama—a society based on agriculture and small towns.

43. Halbert and Ball, *Creek War of 1813 and 1814*, 93. See ibid., 94–97 for more about the divisions among the Creeks.

44. Ibid., 85, 87. For a survey see Owsley, *Filibusters and Expansionists*, 82–102.

45. Halbert and Ball, *Creek War of 1813 and 1814*, 88–90, 91–93, 129 (quoted passage), 143–76, 296–300. The Fort Mims dead have been recorded as 250 or more. Owsley, *Filibusters and Expansionists*, 95.

46. Halbert and Ball, *Creek War of 1813 and 1814*, 125–42, 241–78. Of course Caller, who died in 1819, did not cease plotting and scheming, but he was handicapped by the circulation of a mock-heroic poem satirizing his military pretensions. Beidler, *First Books*, 14–22.

47. Toulmin to President James Madison, 2 June 1813, Carter, ed., *Territorial Papers: Volume VI*, 371–72.

48. Pruitt and Durham, "Sources of Law in the Alabama Territory," 6–7; Guice, "The Cement of Society," 78–80.

49. Hamilton, *Anglo-American Law on the Frontier*, 94–95, 98–99.

50. Toulmin to William Lattimore, 18 December 1815, Carter, ed., *Territorial Papers: Volume VI*, 618–22; "Decision by Judge Toulmin" (Superior Court of Mobile County, April term 1815), *Territorial Papers: Volume VI*, 516–25 (quoted passage on 525). For analogous information on judicial matters in the territory of Florida, see Kermit L. Hall and Eric W. Rise, *From Local Courts to National Tribunals: The Federal District Courts of Florida, 1821–1990* (Brooklyn: Carlson Publishing, Inc., 1991), 5–20.

51. Brantley, *Three Capitals*, 17–24 (quoted passage on 18).

52. Carter, *Territorial Papers: Volume XVIII*, 54–55, 238–39, 570–71, 666–68; Owen, *History of Alabama and Dictionary of Alabama Biography*, 4:1716–17, 1738. For indications that lower territorial courts continued to handle federal matters including a suit against a federal officer tried first in Mobile and a case involving the importation of slaves, see Carter, *Territorial Papers: Volume XVIII*, 563, 575–76, 637–38. For cases of various kinds over which Toulmin presided in the late Mississippi or Alabama territorial years, see Records Group 21, Records of the District Courts of the United

States, U.S. District and Other Courts in Alabama, National Archives and Records Administration, Southeastern Region (Atlanta), Cases 54, 56, 57, 58, 59, 60, 62, 63, 64, 65, 66, 67, 68, 70, et al. Of these, No. 59, *U.S. v. Negro Slave, Ben* is of interest because it shows the practical application of laws against the international slave trade. These documents are difficult to read; some are apparently fragmentary. One of them excerpts an (arguably) anti-slavery jury charge made by Toulmin in October 1816.

53. Between 1808 and 1819, Toulmin's old judicial territory had been subdivided into twenty-two counties. He was elected as the delegate of Baldwin County, created from Washington County in 1809. For the 1819 convention members and their counties, see Brantley, *Three Capitals*, 44; for county dates, see McMillan, *Constitutional Development*, 22, 25n42.

54. McMillan sees a division between north and south Alabama at the convention; north Alabama, he said, had 28 votes to 16 for south Alabama. McMillan, *Constitutional Development*, 31–32.

55. The chief architects of the 1819 constitution were Committee of Fifteen chairman Clement Comer Clay of Madison County, committee members Henry Hitchcock of Washington County and William R. King of Dallas County, and territorial governor William Wyatt Bibb. The latter (also the first governor of the state) was not a member of the convention. Hitchcock, a youthful attorney who was Toulmin's friend, may have been a conduit for Toulmin's influence upon the document as drafted. Brantley, *Three Capitals*, 44–45.

56. Alabama's constitution similarly lacked such restrictions on office-holding. See McMillan, *Constitutional Development*, 35–36. For the 1819 constitution's tendency to confer power on the legislative branch see ibid., 38–39. See also Pruitt and Durham, "Sources of Law in the Alabama Territory," 14–16.

57. Under the 1819 constitution, however, the right to own slaves was guaranteed. See McMillan, *Constitutional Development*, 42–43. For Toulmin's attitude toward slavery, see note 16.

58. Ibid., 35 (quoted passage), 36–37, 39, 40. The Committee of Fifteen had proposed that Alabama follow the U.S. Constitution in counting each slave as a three-fifths person for apportionment purposes, but this was struck down in a vote that pitted the more generally slave-owning south Alabamians against spokesmen of the small-scale farmers of north Alabama.

59. See Thomas Perkins Abernethy, *The Formative Period in Alabama, 1815–1828*, intro. by David T. Morgan (1922, repr. Tuscaloosa: University of Alabama Press, 1990), especially 120–51.

60. Brantley, *Three Capitals*, 57. For Lipscomb's long history as a judge, see Brewer, *Alabama, Her History*, 405–406.

61. Brantley, *Three Capitals*, 100–101, 100n2, 118–19 (quoted passages).

62. Edward Turner, *Statutes of the Mississippi Territory: The Constitution of the United States, . . . and Such Acts of Congress as Relate to the Mississippi Territory* (Natchez, Mississippi: P. Isler, 1816).

63. Brantley, *Three Capitals*, 119 (quoted passages). And see Harry Toulmin, *A Digest of the Laws of the State of Alabama: Containing the Statutes and Resolutions in Force at the End of the General Assembly in January, 1823* (Catawba: Ginn and Curtis, 1823).

64. Toulmin, *Digest of the Laws of the State of Alabama*, iii–xxxiv. For more information about Toulmin's editing and the index produced by Henry Hitchcock after Toulmin's death, see Brantley, *Three Capitals*, 118, 120n2.

65. Toulmin, *Digest of the Laws of the State of Alabama*, 261–66, 627–46. Readers should not imagine that early Alabama racial statutes were lenient. Emancipated slaves were officially required to leave the state, and the January 1823 act "to carry into effect" federal laws against the international slave trade provided that contraband slaves should labor for the state.

66. Ibid., 387–442.

67. Brantley, *Three Capitals*, 119, 120. Isaac J. Cox says that Toulmin died on 11 November 1823; see Malone, ed., *Dictionary of American Biography*, vol. 9, pt. 2, 601.

68. Readers who detect a respectful parody of Romans 8: 38–39 are quite right.

# Chapter 2

1. For recent commentary on the slave-obsessed south, see J. Mills Thornton III, *Politics and Power in a Slave Society: Alabama, 1800–1860* (Baton Rouge: Louisiana State University Press, 1978), xviii–xix, 312–15; William J. Cooper Jr., *Liberty and Slavery: Southern Politics to 1860* (New York: Knopf, 1983), 170–73, 174, 177, 178–81, 219–20, 248–49; and Bertram Wyatt-Brown, *Southern Honor: Ethics and Behavior in the Old South* (New York: Oxford University Press, 1983), xii, xv–xvii, 369, 402–34. For earlier versions, see Clement Eaton, *A History of the Old South*, 2nd edition (New York: McMillan, 1966), 252–55, 343–45, 350–55, 421–22, 431–34; and W. J. Cash, *The Mind of the Old South* (New York: Vintage Books, 1941), 90–97. On the beginnings of southern penitentiaries, see Edward L. Ayers, *Vengeance and Justice: Crime and Punishment in the Nineteenth-Century American South* (New York: Oxford University Press, 1984), 34–73.

2. "Hon. Benjamin F. Porter," *American Review*, 9 (May 1849), 447–48; John Buckner Little, *The History of Butler County, Alabama, from 1815–1885* (Cincinnati: Elm St. Printing Co., 1885), 114; John Belton O'Neall, *Biographical Sketches of the Bench and Bar of South Carolina* (Charleston: S. G. Courtenay & Co., 1859), 2:549; [Ina Marie Porter Ockenden], "Benjamin Faneuil Porter," ms. in the B. F. Porter Papers, Auburn University Archives (hereinafter cited as AU). Ockenden says that Porter was apprenticed to a Dr. Geddings. See also William Garrett, *Reminiscences of Public Men in Alabama, for Thirty Years* (Atlanta: Plantation Pub. Co., 1872), 310–11.

3. "Hon. Benjamin F. Porter," *American Review*, 448; Little, *History of Butler County*, 114–15; and O'Neall, *Biographical Sketches of the Bench and Bar*, 2:603.

4. Little, *History of Butler County*, 115; O'Neall, *Biographical Sketches of the Bench and Bar*, 2:549–50; "Hon. Benjamin F. Porter," *American Review*, 447. On the better prospects for green attorneys in Alabama, see Joseph Glover Baldwin, *The Flush Times of Alabama and Mississippi* (1853; repr. Gloucester, MA: Peter Smith, 1974), 34–35.

5. Benjamin F. Porter, *Reminiscences of Men and Things in Alabama*, ed. Sara Walls (Tuscaloosa: Portals Press, 1983), 29–32.

6. Ibid., 33, 38–39; O'Neall, *Biographical Sketches of the Bench and Bar*, 2:550. For

examples of the Dellet-Porter practice, see Benjamin F. Porter to James Dellet, 2 and 12 December 1831, 23 April 1832, 1 December 1832, 11 October 1834, 11 December 1834 (photocopy) in the James Dellet Papers, Alabama Department of Archives and History (hereinafter cited as Dellet Papers, ADAH). In letter citations, Porter will hereinafter be noted as BFP.

7. Garrett, *Reminiscences of Public Men*, 311; Governor John Gayle to BFP, 20 January 1832, Porter Papers, AU (certificate of Porter's election as county judge); BFP to Dellet, 26 November 1832, Dellet Papers, ADAH (quoted passages).

8. "Hon. Benjamin F. Porter," American Review, 449, 451; *Journal of the House of Representatives of the State of Alabama, Begun and Held at the Town of Tuscaloosa, on the Third Monday in November, 1832* (Tuscaloosa: E. Walker, 1833), 41, 84–85, 94 (cited hereinafter as *House Journal* [1832–1833]; other legislative journals cited analogously); *House Journal* (1833–1834), 33, 126, 137, 205–206, 208; BFP to James Dellet, 5 June 1834, Dellet Papers, ADAH; Porter, *Reminiscences of Men and Things*, 41–43. On the states' rights crisis, see Albert B. Moore, *History of Alabama* (Tuscaloosa: University Supply Store, 1951), 163–71; and Thornton, *Politics and Power*, 27–30.

9. Porter, *Reminiscences of Men and Things*, 40.

10. *House Journal* (1833–1834), 34, 120–21, 210; *House Journal* (1834–1835), 75–76, 81, 90, 99, 110, 116, 190. During these years there was discussion of eliminating state taxation altogether. Porter protested a proposed measure in 1834 by resigning from the Ways and Means Committee. See Porter, *Reminiscences of Men and Things*, 85.

11. BFP to Dellet, 31 June [sic] 1934, 2 December 1834, Dellet Papers, ADAH; Thornton, *Politics and Power*, 50–55. See also Lawrence Frederick Kohl, *The Politics of Individualism: Parties and the American Character in the Jacksonian Era* (New York: Oxford University Press, 1989), 63–65, 68, 70, 74–75, 79, 83; and Thomas Brown, *Politics and Statesmanship: Essays on the American Whig Party* (New York: Columbia University Press, 1985), 156–86.

12. For sarcastic comments on politics and the legislature, see BFP to James Dellet, 8 August 1835, 16 [10?] October 1835, Dellet Papers, ADAH.

13. For Porter on slavery, see [Benjamin F. Porter], "The Mission of America," *DeBow's Review*, 4 (September 1847), 117–18; and *House Journal* (1838–1839), 52, 106.

14. *House Journal* (1833–1834), 26–27; *House Journal* (1834–1835), 13, 22, 45, 99, 170, 177, 181–82; *House Journal* (1838–1839), 256–58; Porter, *Reminiscences of Men and Things*, 47, 103–104. Porter represented Monroe County in the 1832 special session, 1833–1834, and 1834–1835 legislatures; he represented Tuscaloosa County in the 1837 regular session, 1838–1839, 1839–1840, 1842–1843, 1845–1846, and 1847–1848 legislatures. See Owen, *History of Alabama and Dictionary of Alabama Biography*, 2:1035, 1338.

15. Little, *History of Butler County*, 115; Rufus Bealle, preface to *Reminiscences of Men and Things*, Porter, 17, 20; "Advertisement," in Benjamin F. Porter, *Reports of Cases Argued and Adjudged in the Supreme Court of Alabama, Commencing at the June Term, 1834*, vol. 1 (Tuscaloosa: Printed at the Intelligencer and Expositor Office, 1835), i. This and subsequent reports will be cited under "Bluebook" rules, in this instance, as 1 Porter. See also "To Bench and Bar," 2 Porter 3; and front matter in 3 Porter.

16. Preface, 6 Porter v–vi.

17. Bealle, preface to *Reminiscences of Men and Things*, Porter, 17, 20; "Hon

Benjamin F. Porter," *American Review*, 448; Willis G. Clark, *History of Education in Alabama, 1702–1889* (Washington, D.C.: Government Printing Office, 1889), 45–46; and see BFP to James Dellet, 31 June 1834 [sic], 4 December 1834, Dellet Papers, ADAH.

18. See cases at 3 Porter 112, 389, 442; 5 Porter 54, 88, 169, 213; 6 Porter 9, 184, 352; 7 Porter 9, 47, 187. For an example of Porter's legal reasoning see O'Neall, *Biographical Sketches of the Bench and Bar*, 2:553–55; and "Hon. Benjamin F. Porter," *American Review*, 447–48.

19. O'Neall, *Biographical Sketches of the Bench and Bar*, 2:250–51; BFP to Dellet, 8 August 1835, 13 January 1936 (photocopy), 17 June 1936 (photocopy), 15 and 24 August 1836, 7 September 1836, 16 and 19 June 1837, Dellet Papers, ADAH; Garrett, *Reminiscences of Public Men*, 311. W. W. Screws says that Porter was editor, circa 1837–1838, of the *Tuscaloosa Independent Monitor*, a notable Whig newspaper. W. W. Screws, "Alabama Journalism," in *Memorial Record of Alabama* (Madison, Wisconsin: Brandt and Fuller, 1893), 2:174. A search of the paper's files has produced no evidence to support Screws' claim.

20. O'Neall, *Biographical Sketches of the Bench and Bar*, 2:552–53; "Hon. Benjamin F. Porter," *American Review*, 450; Tuscaloosa *Independent Monitor*, 11 June 1847; BFP to James Dellet, 16 June 1837, 14 October 1839, 30 April 1845, Dellet Papers, ADAH.

21. Little, *History of Butler County*, 120; Garrett, *Reminiscences of Public Men*, 313–14.

22. Benjamin F. Porter, "Address Delivered Before the Philomathic Society of the University of Alabama, on the Occasion of Its Fourth Anniversary" (Tuscaloosa: Published by Request, 1836), 17–20; Benjamin F. Porter, "The Past and the Present: A Discourse Delivered Before the Erosophic Society of the University of Alabama" (Tuscaloosa: 1845), 23, 25; and Benjamin F. Porter, *Argument of Benjamin F. Porter, in Support of a Bill, Introduced by Him, in the House of Representatives of Alabama, to Abrogate the Punishment of Death* (Tuscaloosa: 1846), 7, 15.

23. See the Tuscaloosa *Independent Monitor*, 28 December 1842, for a banquet given to novelist William Gilmore Simms by Porter, F. A. P. Barnard, A. B. Meek, and others. See also William Stanley Hoole, "Alabama and W. Gilmore Simms (Part 2)," *Alabama Review*, 16 (July 1963), 188–89; and Robert H. McKenzie, "Alexander Beaufort Meek: Pioneer Alabama Lawyer and Literary Figure" (unpublished paper, University of Alabama Center for Law and Service, 1983). For a scattering of perceptive observations on culture and intellect in Tuscaloosa and the antebellum southwest, see Michael O'Brien, *Conjectures of Order: Intellectual Life and the American South, 1810–1860* (Chapel Hill: University of North Carolina Press, 2004), 1:342–63; generally see William Warren Rogers, Robert David Ward, Leah Rawls Atkins, and Wayne Flynt, *Alabama: The History of a Deep South State* (Tuscaloosa: University of Alabama Press, 1994), 113–35.

24. Porter, "Address Delivered Before the Philomathic Society," 5–8; Tuscaloosa *Independent Monitor*, 16 October 1840; and Porter, *Past and the Present*, 5, 18–19.

25. Porter, *Past and the Present*, 33–34; See also Tuscaloosa *Independent Monitor*, 4 February 1846.

26. See Baldwin, *Flush Times;* Johnson Jones Hooper, *Some Adventures of Captain*

*Simon Suggs: Late of the Tallapoosa Volunteers,* ed. Johanna Nicol Shields (Tuscaloosa: University of Alabama Press, 1993); and John Gorman Barr, *Rowdy Tales from Early Alabama,* ed. G. Ward Hubbs (Tuscaloosa: University of Alabama Press, 1981).

27. Porter, *Reminiscences of Men and Things,* 62; and Tuscaloosa *Independent Monitor,* 27 March 1840.

28. See generally John W. Quist, *Restless Visionaries: The Social Roots of Antebellum Reform in Alabama and Michigan* (Baton Rouge: Louisiana State University Press, 1998).

29. For anti-crime activities, see Tuscaloosa *State Intelligencer and States Rights Expositor,* September 26, 1835; and Porter, *Reminiscences of Men and Things,* 49. For Porter as founder of schools, see Tuscaloosa *Independent Monitor,* 11 December 1844, 3 September 1845. For his temperance sentiments see Benjamin F. Porter, *Odd Fellowship and Its Purposes: The Substance of a Discourse Delivered Before the Tuscaloosa Lodge No. 7, Independent Order of Odd Fellows, and Other Citizens of Tuscaloosa, August 12, 1845* (Tuscaloosa: M. D. J. Slade, 1845), 17–18; and "O'Neall, *Biographical Sketches of the Bench and Bar,* 2:552.

30. For a connection between the common law and Alabama's criminal law, see John G. Aikin, *A Digest of the Laws of the State of Alabama, Containing All the Statutes of a Public and General Nature in Force at the Close of the Session of the General Assembly in January 1833* (Philadelphia: A. Towar, 1833), 107 (Sec. 35). (Hereinafter this work will be cited as *Aikin.*)

31. Ayers, *Vengeance and Justice,* 42–43; Louis P. Masur, *Rites of Execution: Capital Punishment and the Transformation of American Culture, 1776–1865* (New York: Oxford University Press, 1989), 3–4, 71–72.

32. *Aikin,* 102–106, especially 102 (Secs. 3–4, 7–9, 11–12), 103 (Sec. 19), and 105 (Sec. 25).

33. *Acts Passed at the Annual Session of the General Assembly of the State of Alabama, Begun and Held in the Town of Tuscaloosa, on the Third Monday in November, One Thousand Eight Hundred and Thirty Five* (Tuscaloosa: 1836), 50–51 (cited hereinafter as *Acts of Alabama* [1836]; other acts cited analogously).

34. Blackstone published his magnum opus from 1765–1769. For pertinent passages in a contemporary edition, see William Blackstone, *Commentaries on the Laws of England, in Four Books with an Analysis of the Work,* ed. W. N. Welsby, 21st edition (London: S. Sweet, 1844), 4: Chap. 1, 15–18 (Secs. 16–19).

35. Toulmin, *Digest of the Laws of the State of Alabama,* 929 (Sec. 19); *Aikin,* 102 (Sec. 1); 1819 Constitution, Art. VI, Sec. 19.

36. Edward Livingston, *A System of Penal Law for the United States of America, Consisting of a Code of Crimes and Punishments: A Code of Procedure in Criminal Cases: A Code of Prison Discipline and a Book of Definitions, Prepared and Presented to the House of Representatives of the United States* (Washington, D.C.: Gales & Seaton, 1828). Livingston subsequently authored *A System of Penal Law for the State of Louisiana: Consisting of a Code of Crimes and Punishments, a Code of Procedure, a Code of Evidence, a Code of Reform and Prison Discipline, a Book of Definitions: Prepared under the Authority of a Law of the Said State* (Philadelphia: James Kay, 1833), a celebrated work—but not adopted by Louisiana.

37. See Masur, *Rites of Execution,* 100–102, 108–10.

38. Ibid., 13, 21, 98–100, 106–109, 115; Ayers, *Vengeance and Justice*, 37–40, 44–45; Gustave De Beaumont and Alexis De Tocqueville, *On the Penitentiary System in the United States, and Its Application in France; with an Appendix on Penal Colonies, and Also, Statistical Notes*, trans. Francis Lieber (Philadelphia: Carey, Lea & Blanchard, 1833), 4–6, 20–27. And see generally David J. Rothman, *The Discovery of the Asylum: Social Order and Disorder in the New Republic* (Boston: Little, Brown, 1971).

39. *Alabama State Intelligencer* (Tuscaloosa), 1 June 1833.

40. Porter, *Argument . . . to Abrogate the Punishment of Death*, 13–14; Porter, "Address Delivered Before the Philomathic Society," 15; and Ayers, *Vengeance and Justice*, 43.

41. On relations among lawyers, see Baldwin, *Flush Times*, 34–45, 163–82; and Thornton, *Politics and Power*, 65–66, 73. Alabama's population nearly doubled in the 1830s (from about 309,000 to 590,000), which must have contributed to a sense of urgency about crime; see Owen, *History of Alabama and Dictionary of Alabama Biography*, 2:1133–34.

42. *Alabama State Intelligencer* (Tuscaloosa), 1 June 1833; *House Journal* (1833–1834), 10–11; *Acts of Alabama* (1833–1834), 26; Ayers, *Vengeance and Justice*, 38–39, 43–48, 49, 53, 57; Moore, *History of Alabama*, 814; and Beaumont and Tocqueville, *Penitentiary System*, xviii, xix, xxii–xxiii.

43. *Mobile Commercial Register and Patriot*, 6 August 1834; and Ayers, *Vengeance and Justice*, 49. For a recent interpretation of the penitentiary campaign in Alabama, see Robert David Ward and William Warren Rogers, *Alabama's Response to the Penitentiary Movement, 1829–1865* (Gainesville: University Press of Florida, 2003), 12–34.

44. *House Journal* (1833–1834), 190; *Acts of Alabama* (1833–1834), 47; Porter, *Reminiscences of Men and Things*, 46.

45. Porter, *Argument . . . to Abrogate the Punishment of Death*, 11; see also Eli N. Evans, *Judah P. Benjamin: The Jewish Confederate* (New York: Free Press, 1988), 9. For information on grass-roots reactions to Vesey's conspiracy (and others), see Sally E. Hadden, *Slave Patrols: Law and Violence in Virginia and the Carolinas* (Cambridge: Harvard University Press, 2001), 137–66.

46. *Mobile Commercial Register and Patriot*, 12–17 May 1834; *Mobile Daily Commercial Register and Patriot*, 22 and 29 November 1834, 21 February 1835; *Boyington v. The State*, 2 Porter 100–44 (1835); and Charles R. S. Boyington, *A Statement of the Trial of Charles R. S. Boyington, Who Was Indicted and Executed for the Murder of Nathaniel Frost: To Which Is Added a Number of Fugitive Pieces, in Verse* (Mobile: Printed at the Office of the *Mercantile Advertiser*, 1835). See generally Paul M. Pruitt Jr. and Robert Bond Higgins, "Crime and Punishment in Antebellum Mobile: The Long Story of Charles R. S. Boyington," *Gulf Coast Historical Review*, 11 (Spring 1996), 6–40.

47. Porter, *Argument . . . To Abrogate the Punishment of Death*, 10–11; Porter, *Reminiscences of Men and Things*, 65; and *The State of Alabama v. Middleton*, 5 Porter 484–97 (1837).

48. Quoted in John Bartlett, *Bartlett's Familiar Quotations*, ed. Justin Kaplan, 17th edition (Boston: Little, Brown & Co., 2002), 412. Story made the remark in an 1829 lecture on legal study.

49. Porter, "Address Before the Philomathic Society," 5, 6–13, 14–15, 17. It is probably impossible to know exactly which philosophical works contributed to Porter's

construct. Rousseau's notion of a virtuous natural society corrupted by civilization seems a likely candidate but so do the various political and legal philosophers (Grotius, Hobbes, Locke, Pufendorf, Jefferson) of the European and American Enlightenments, who posited that "the state was the outcome of a covenant or agreement among men," and that the purpose of the state is "the protection of those people to which it owed its being." See Maurice Cranston, "Introduction" in Jean Jacques Rousseau, *The Social Contract* (Harmondsworth, Middlesex, UK: Penguin Books, 1971), 26.

50. Porter, "Address Before the Philomathic Society," 7, 8–9, 12–14.

51. Ibid., 14–16, 16–17.

52. Ibid., 5–6, 18–20.

53. Porter, *Reminiscences of Men and Things*, 62.

54. Ibid., 62–63.

55. For Porter in the legislature see *House Journal* (1837), 7–8, 19, 25, 30, 35, 52–53, 83, 106–107, 116–17, 124–25, 157–59; for Porter's banking report, see Porter, *Reminiscences of Men and Things*, 103–104.

56. *House Journal* (1837), 135–36.

57. *House Journal* (1838–1839), 28, 256–58, 265–67; William Brantley, *Banking in Alabama, 1860–1816*, 2 volumes (Birmingham: Oxmoor Press, 1961–1967), 1:329–61, 2:30, 71–72, 108, 377.

58. Garrett, *Reminiscences of Public Men*, 71–78. For coverage of these issues, see *House Journal* (1838–1839), 7, 19–20, 25, 46, 55, 74, 95, 115, 178, 192, 198, 201–202, 223, 227. Common schools in Alabama derived most of their income from funds produced by sales of "sixteenth section" lands—most of which funds were deposited in poorly managed state banks; see Moore, *History of Alabama*, 321–25.

59. *House Journal* (1838–1839), 7, 23, 77, 141–42, 189, 252; *Acts of Alabama* (1838–1839), 80–81. Supposedly outlawed by the 1819 constitution, imprisonment for debt was still a matter of concern for constitution makers as late as 1868; see McMillan, *Constitutional Development in Alabama*, 35, 134.

60. *House Journal* (1838–1839), 3–4, 18. For biographies, see Owen, *History of Alabama and Dictionary of Alabama Biography*, 3:171, 174; 4:423, 1095, 1222–23, 1359, 1549, 1555, 1773–74, 1829; Garrett, *Reminiscences of Public Men*, 87–91, 97–99, 185, 199, 302–303; and David I. Durham, *A Southern Moderate in Radical Times: Henry W. Hilliard, 1808–1892* (Baton Rouge: Louisiana State University Press, 2008).

61. Ayers, *Vengeance and Justice*, 53–54.

62. Garrett, *Reminiscences of Public Men*, 67–68; and *Tuscaloosa Independent Monitor*, 1 December 1838.

63. *House Journal* (1838–1839), 15, 27, 40; see also 48, 61. See Ward and Rogers, *Alabama's Response to the Penitentiary Movement*, 38, 40–41. Bagby had opposed the penitentiary in 1834; Ward and Rogers note his 1838 desire to "terrify" evildoers with the certainty of punishment.

64. Thornton, *Politics and Power*, 95–96; *House Journal* (1838–1839), 61. Note that the text of bills was typically not given in House and Senate journals. A search in the "Bills and Reports" record series in the ADAH failed to turn up copies of this (or other) bills authored or submitted by Porter.

65. *House Journal* (1838–1839), 126, 151, 194–97, 213; *Senate Journal* (1838–1839), 146–47, 156; *Acts of Alabama* (1838–1839), 33–34; Ward and Rogers, *Alabama's Response to the Penitentiary Movement*, 42–44.

66. *Acts of Alabama* (1838–1839), 33–34; *House Journal* (1838–1839), 263–64; Ward and Rogers, *Alabama's Response to the Penitentiary Movement*, 45–46.

67. *House Journal* (1839–1840), 10, 30–31, 54–55, 195, 198, 206, 214, 257–58; *House Journal* (1841–1842), 14; *Tuscaloosa Independent Monitor*, 11 December 1840; Ward and Rogers, *Alabama's Response to the Penitentiary Movement*, 48, 51–57, 58–59.

68. *Acts of Alabama* (1840–1841), 103–92, especially 121–38; Ward and Rogers, *Alabama's Response to the Penitentiary Movement*, 58.

69. For information on Collier (Democrat), Ormond (Whig), and Goldthwaite (Democrat), see Owen, *History of Alabama and Dictionary of Alabama Biography*, 3:380, 675; 4:1303. For Porter's further role, see *House Journal* (1839–1849), 198, 214. William Marshall Inge, who argued eloquently against the death penalty and in favor of giving juries the option of imposing life sentences in capital cases, is one of the enigmas of Alabama politics. Born in 1802 in North Carolina, he served as a Democratic congressman from Tennessee (1833–1835) before moving to Sumter County, Alabama. Garrett, *Reminiscences of Public Men*, 183–84, says he was an outspoken Whig. There is some disagreement over the date of Inge's death but it is clear he died young of heart disease. See *Biographical Directory of the United States Congress, 1774–1989* (Washington, D.C.: Government Printing Office, 1989), 1243; and *Tuscaloosa Independent Monitor*, 11 January 1841.

70. For Phelan and for Porter's assignments, see *House Journal* (1839–1840), 4, 28, 37, 41, 52; and Porter, *Reminiscences of Men and Things*, 62, 86. For penitentiary issues, see *House Journal* (1839–1840), 10, 30–31, 42, 54–55, 91, 97, 133, 195, 198, 206, 214, 257–58, 288. For educational matters, including Porter on female education, see *House Journal* (1839–1840), 31, 63, 89, 94, 95, 97, 105, 162–63, 167–68, 254, 290. For banking issues see Brantley, *Banking in Alabama*, 2:108; and *House Journal* (1839–1840), 8, 31, 49, 140–41, 154–55, 174–75, 192–93, 202–203, 210, 225–31, 234–35, 239–42, 248–50, 275–84, 294–95, 374–76.

71. Garrett, *Reminiscences of Public Men*, 109–10; *House Journal* (1839–1840), 106, 143–48, 179–80, 223–24, 233.

72. Harriet Amos, *Cotton City: Urban Development in Antebellum Mobile* (University: University of Alabama Press, 1985), 124–25; Garrett, *Reminiscences of Public Men*, 107–108; *House Journal* (1839–1840), 6–7, 41, 142, 272.

73. BFP to James Dellet, 16 June 1837, Dellet papers, ADAH; see also BFP to William Phineas Brown [sic], 29 August 1840, 16 [10?] September 1840, in the William Phineas Browne Papers (hereinafter cited as Browne Papers), ADAH.

74. *House Journal* (1839–1840), 130, 260, 262; *Acts of Alabama* (1839–1840), 11–12; *Aikin*, xxxv; Constitution of Alabama, Art. 3, Sec. 25.

75. See *The State ex rel. the Attorney General v. Porter*, 1 *Alabama Reports* (1840), 689; *House Journal* (1839–1840), 262, 336–37; and *The State ex rel. the Attorney General v. Paul*, 5 Stewart and Porter (1833), 40–53.

76. *Tuscaloosa Independent Monitor*, 9 March 1840; Garrett, *Reminiscences of Public Men*, 311.

77. Garrett, *Reminiscences of Public Men*, 311; Porter, *Reminiscences of Men and Things*, 64–65; *Tuscaloosa Independent Monitor*, 14 August 1840.

78. *Tuscaloosa Independent Monitor*, 17 July 1840, 14 August 1840.

79. *The State ex rel. the Attorney General v. Porter*, 1 *Alabama Reports* (1840), 688–708; Garrett, *Reminiscences of Public Men*, 311–12; Porter, *Reminiscences of Men and Things*, 58.

80. BFP to William Phineas Brown [sic], 29 August, 16 [10?] September, 30 October 1840, Browne Papers, ADAH.

81. Milo B. Howard, "The General Ticket," *Alabama Review*, 19 (July 1966), 163–66; and *Tuscaloosa Independent Monitor*, 11 September 1840, 16 October 1840.

82. Howard, "General Ticket," 163–74.

83. Little, *History of Butler County*, 117; Garrett, *Reminiscences of Public Men*, 317. Porter was occasionally mentioned as a gubernatorial candidate; see *Tuscaloosa Independent Monitor*, 4 and 19 December 1840, 5 April 1843, 14 and 21 May 1845.

84. *Tuscaloosa Independent Monitor*, 19 October 1842, 26 February 1845, 12 March 1845, 9 April 1845; an advertisement in ibid., 26 March 1845, lists Porter as attorney for the Bank of Alabama.

85. *Tuscaloosa Independent Monitor*, 2 April 1845, 1 October 1845 (quoting the *Selma Free Press*), 22 October 1845, and 10 December 1845; Garrett, *Reminiscences of Public Men*, 317, 792; Little, *History of Butler County*, 115–16; and Paul M. Pruitt Jr., "The Life and Times of Legal Education in Alabama, 1819–1897: Bar Admissions, Law Schools, and the Profession," *Alabama Law Review*, 49 (Fall 1997), 286–88.

86. See Benjamin F. Porter, *The Office and Duties of Executives and Administrators, Being a Plain and Simple Treatise on the Rights, Responsibilities, and Duties of These Officers* . . . (Tuskaloosa [sic]: M. D. J. Slade, 1842); and Benjamin F. Porter, "The Law of Debtor and Creditor in Alabama," *Hunt's Merchants' Magazine*, 15 (December 1846), 580–82, continued in 16 (January 1847), 57–59; see also Little, *History of Butler County*, 115–16.

87. Pruitt, "Life and Times of Legal Education," 288; see also Clark, *History of Education*, 60; and James Benson Sellers, *History of the University of Alabama, 1818–1902* (University: University of Alabama Press, 1953), 160–61.

88. See Benjamin F. Porter, "Indian Mounds," *Hunt's Merchants' Magazine*, 15 (November 1846), 480–82; [Benjamin F. Porter], "The Mission of America: Influences of the Age in Law, Religion, Commerce, and the Arts," *DeBow's Review*, 4 (September 1847), 108–22; and Benjamin F. Porter, "A Memoir of Hon. John C. Calhoun," in O'Neall, *Biographical Sketches of the Bench and Bar*, 2:289–313. See also samples of Porter's travel writing and poetry in *Reminiscences of Men and Things*, 69–91. For his printed speeches, in addition to those already cited, see *Outlines of the Oration of Judge Porter Before the Republican Society and Other Citizens of Tuskaloosa [sic] County, at Hopewell, July 4, 1845* (Tuskaloosa [sic]: M. D. J. Slade, 1845). For the quoted passage, see Garrett, *Reminiscences of Public Men*, 313.

89. In the 1840s the law prescribed death for slaves convicted of rebellion or conspiracy, murder, attempted murder, or involuntary manslaughter of whites, rape of a white female (free blacks were also subject to this punishment), as well as robbery,

assault, burglary, or arson against whites. See C. C. Clay, *A Digest of the Laws of the State of Alabama: Containing All the Statutes of a Public and General Nature, in Force at the Close of the Session of the General Assembly, in February, 1843* . . . (Tuskaloosa [sic]: Marmaduke J. Slade, 1843) (hereinafter cited as *Clay*), 472 (Secs. 1–5). See also James Benson Sellers, *Slavery in Alabama* (University: University of Alabama Press, 1950), 244–51; and Ayers, *Vengeance and Justice*, 134–36. The question of slave executions was a complex issue. The 1840–1841 legislature passed an act providing for full restitution to owners of executed slaves (the previous standard had been compensation for half the slave's value). Governor Benjamin Fitzpatrick observed that the full compensation act would increase the difficulty of giving slaves fair trials, since the owners no longer had a "pecuniary" incentive to defend their slaves. The legislature of 1842–1843 restored the old system of half compensation, but they hid their work in a lengthy tax measure. See *Acts of Alabama* (1840–1841), 190 (Sec. 19); *House Journal* (1842–1843), 27–28, 339, 366–67; and *Acts of Alabama* (1842–1843), 9 (Sec. 23).

90. O'Neall, *Biographical Sketches of the Bench and Bar*, 2:553–55. For the inconsistency Porter spotted, see *Clay*, 472 (Sec. 4), and 474 (Sec. 18). The first section mandates death for slaves convicted of burglary or several other crimes. The latter seems, though the language is not altogether clear, to prescribe lashes and/or branding for slaves convicted of crimes for which a white person would be sent to the penitentiary. The inconsistency remained on the books, however; the 1845–1846 legislature saw an unsuccessful attempt by Representative B. B. Barker of Lauderdale County to amend the laws "in reference to the crime of burglary by slaves." See *House Journal* (1845–1846), 135, 293, 364. Barker would vote during this session for Porter's bill to abolish the death penalty altogether. Finally, see Wyatt-Brown, *Southern Honor*, 387–90.

91. *Acts of Alabama* (1840–1841), 150; and Porter, *Argument . . . to Abrogate the Punishment of Death*, 9.

92. Masur, *Rites of Execution*, 14, 50, 52–54, 62–63, 65–70, 73–76, 117–21. A survey of *The Hangman*, which was in 1845 the chief Massachusetts organ of the anticapital punishment movement, revealed little knowledge or information on southern affairs.

93. John L. O'Sullivan, *Report in Favor of the Abolition of the Punishment of Death by Law, Made to the Legislature of the State of New York, April 14, 1841* (New York: J. and H. G. Langley, 1841), "Preface," 3, 8–29, 30–38, 53–72, 72–76, 84–88, 89–93. See also Masur, *Rites of Execution*, 141–45; and Philip English Mackey, *Hanging in the Balance: The Anti-Capital Punishment Movement in New York State, 1776–1861* (New York: Garland Publishing, 1982). On the whole, Porter's *Argument . . . to Abrogate the Punishment of Death* contains many O'Sullivan-like approaches to the subject.

94. Garrett, *Reminiscences of Public Men*, 246–60, 278–79.

95. *House Journal* (1842–1843), 57, 63, 74, 88, 158, 306–309; *Tuscaloosa Independent Monitor*, 1 February 1843. Of the twenty-five men who voted with Porter against tabling, a majority was from the Black Belt or Tennessee Valley plantation districts, or from Mobile; several were from Tuscaloosa and surrounding counties; at least six were Whigs. See *House Journal* (1845–1846), 3–4, 50; Garrett, *Reminiscences of Public Men*, 167–68, 230–33, 283–85, 292, 294, 296–97, 305–306, 360–61, 558–62; and Owen, *History*

*of Alabama and Dictionary of Alabama Biography,* 3:283, 499; 4:1732. Not all of these men supported abolition of the death penalty. Many may have simply wanted to show Porter fair treatment.

96. *House Journal* (1842–1843), 307–309; *Tuscaloosa Independent Monitor,* 1 February 1843. Of all Porter's capital punishment writings, this is the only one that addresses biblical arguments.

97. *Acts of Alabama* (1845–1846), 9–13; *Tuscaloosa Independent Monitor,* 16 July 1845. On the problems and lease of the penitentiary, see Ward and Rogers, *Alabama's Response to the Penitentiary Movement,* 60, 64, 70–71, 74, 82–100.

98. *Tuscaloosa Independent Monitor,* 28 January 1846. For Porter's bill to secure part of a convict's earnings to his family, see *House Journal* (1845–1846), 25, 66, 207; for debate and maneuvers concerning the leasing bill, see *House Journal* (1845–1846), 228, 333–34, 337, 358, 397–98; and for Porter's answer to the charge that teaching crafts to convicts tended to degrade the status of artisans, see *House Journal* (1845–1846), 455–56. See also *Acts of Alabama* (1845–1846), 11–12, 23–24. This session followed popular votes to remove the state capital from Tuscaloosa and to initiate biennial sessions of the legislature.

99. *House Journal* (1845–1846), 30, 52, 155, 324; *Tuscaloosa Independent Monitor,* 10 and 17 December 1845.

100. Porter, *Argument . . . to Abrogate the Punishment of Death,* 8. It is difficult to tell from House records whether Porter delivered this speech, though most likely he did.

101. Ibid., 8–13, 15–18.

102. Ibid., 14, 19.

103. *House Journal* (1845–1846), 324.

104. The total of twenty individuals takes into account 6 allies of 1843 and 15 allies of 1846; one man supported him on both occasions. His fellow protesters of 1843 were Thomas B. Cooper, a Whig lawyer from Cherokee County; Charles Dear, a Whig lawyer-planter from Wilcox County; Josiah Jones from Covington County; John S. Kennedy, a (probably) Democratic lawyer from Lauderdale County; Greene P. Rice, a (probably) Democratic lawyer-clergyman from Morgan County; and Waddy Tate, possibly a physician, from Limestone County. Porter's 1846 friends were B. B. Barker of Lauderdale County; William Barnett of Russell County; Clement Billingslea, a planter-physician from Montgomery County; Clement Claiborne Clay, a Democratic lawyer from Madison County, a future U.S. Senator and Confederate Senator, and the son of former governor Clement Comer Clay; George W. Gayle, a states' rights Democrat from Dallas County, a lawyer and cousin of former Governor John Gayle; James Guild, a Democratic physician from Tuscaloosa County; Crawford Motley Jackson, a Democratic lawyer from Autauga County; P. W. Kittrell of Greene County; Felix G. Norman, a Franklin County lawyer, schoolteacher, and entrepreneur; Woodson Northcutt of Marion County; Greene T. Rice; Joseph C. Smith of Mobile County; John Steele, a Democratic merchant-planter of Autauga County; Milton J. Tarver of Macon County; and Joseph W. Taylor, a Whig lawyer-journalist from Greene County. Biographical details are not available for several of these men, but for the rest, see Owen, *History of Alabama and Dictionary of Alabama Biography,* 1:627; 2:671, 921, 944, 1027, 1049; 3:151, 341–42, 398, 475, 646, 711, 888, 965; 4:1285, 1432,

1617, 1651; Garrett, *Reminiscences of Public Men,* 167–68, 225, 435–37, 484; and Willis Brewer, *Alabama: Her History, Resources, War Record, and Public Men* (Montgomery: Barrett and Brown, 1872), 110, 190, 219, 267, 357–59, 486. It seems unlikely that there was even an informal reformist coalition in the House. Of the nineteen men who voted against leasing the penitentiary, for instance, only six voted for Porter's bill to abolish capital punishment; see *House Journal* (1845–1846), 398.

105. Garrett, *Reminiscences of Public Men,* 463; Benjamin F. Porter, *Argument of Benjamin F. Porter, in Support of a Bill Introduced By Him Into the House of Representatives, "For the Preservation of the Sixteenth Section Grants, and to Establish Permanently, in the State of Alabama, a Common School Fund . . ."* (Tuscaloosa: N.p., 1848). For Porter's committee assignments, see *House Journal* (1847–1848), 12. Alabama would not have a centrally managed state educational system until the 1850s; see Moore, *History of Alabama,* 331–33. For Porter's continued interest in the welfare of prisoners, see *House Journal* (1847–1848), 67, 85, 110, 138, 165–66, 218, 248–53, 253–56, 261–62, 280–81, 288–90, 305–308, 358, 374–76, 392.

106. Garrett, *Reminiscences of Public Men,* 317. In 1852 Porter supported Franklin Pearce over the Whig Winfield Scott, presumably because he was disgusted with the abolitionist element that had dominated Taylor's Whig administration.

107. BFP to James Dellet, 15 March 1844, Dellet Papers, ADAH; Invitation to the funeral of Mrs. Eliza Porter, 8 April 1846, Porter Papers, AU. In the fall of 1846, Porter thought of teaching at the "University of Louisiana"; see Recommendation by George D. Shortridge, 10 October 1846, Porter Papers, AU.

108. Garrett, *Reminiscences of Public Men,* 318. For Porter's exclusion, see Church Minutes, First Baptist Church, Tuscaloosa, Alabama, 15 April 1850, 13 May 1850; and see Basil Manly to BFP, 22 April 1850, in Manly Diary (Box 2, Diary 2, Volume 5, 131–33), Hoole Special Collections Library, University of Alabama. For an example of Porter's angry mood, see BFP to William Phineas Browne, 12 February 1848, Browne Papers, ADAH.

109. [Ockenden], "Benjamin Faneuil Porter," Porter Papers, AU; O'Neall, *Biographical Sketches of the Bench and Bar,* 2:551; Little, *History of Butler County,* 118; Garrett, *Reminiscences of Public Men,* 314; Porter, *Reminiscences of Men and Things,* 69–84; Charleston, S.C. *Evening News,* 29 July 1850. "Hon. Benjamin F. Porter," *American Review,* 450–51, notes that Porter had visited Charleston in 1846 and 1848.

110. Garrett, *Reminiscences of Public Men,* 314–16; O'Neall, *Biographical Sketches of the Bench and Bar,* 2:551. Porter contributed to the *Charleston Courier* as well as to the *Evening News;* see Benjamin Faneuil Porter Scrapbook, 1849–1850, South Carolina Library, University of South Carolina. At about this time, according to an undated clipping, Porter attempted to start a law school in Charleston (evidently with summer sessions in Rome, Georgia). Porter Papers, AU.

111. *Acts of Alabama* (1851–1852), 15–20; Porter, *Reminiscences of Men and Things,* 85, 96; Garrett, *Reminiscences of Public Men,* 316–17; Porter had long been a partisan of industrial development; see *Tuscaloosa Independent Monitor,* 12 February 1845, 25 June 1845, 27 August 1845, 12 November 1845, 24 December 1845.

112. Garrett, *Reminiscences of Public Men,* 313, 316; O'Neall, *Biographical Sketches of the Bench and Bar,* 2:551–52. For interesting glimpses of Porter as a literary man, see

BFP to T. and J. W. Johnson, 6, 8, and 18 January 1856, 29 July 1856, 3 February 1857, 24 March 1857, 29 September 1857, in the Simon Gratz Collection, Historical Society of Pennsylvania. And see Sara Walls, foreword to *Reminiscences of Men and Things*, Porter, 13–15; and William H. Brantley, "Our Law Books," *The Alabama Lawyer*, 3 (October 1942), 381–82.

113. Eighth Census (1860), Free Schedules, Alabama, Marshall County, Western District, Guntersville, 8:935; and Eighth Census (1860), Slave Schedules, Alabama, Marshall County, Western Division, 3: 417–18.

114. Little, *History of Butler County*, 119–20; Marilyn D. Hahn, comp., *Butler County in the Nineteenth Century* (Birmingham: Hahn, 1978), 158, 160–61; Bealle, preface to *Reminiscences of Men and Things*, Porter, 20; BFP to B. F. Perry, 8 and 31 May 1860, in the B. F. Perry Papers, ADAH. After the war, Porter helped found an organization to honor Alabama soldiers. See Owen, *History of Alabama and Dictionary of Alabama Biography*, 1:694–95; 4:1375–76; and see Michael J. Daniel, "The Secession Crisis in Butler County, Alabama, 1860–1861," *Alabama Review*, 42 (April 1989), 123.

115. "To the People of Alabama," broadside or clipping dated 9 January 1865, Scrapbook, Porter Papers, AU. See also Michael Jackson Daniel, "Red Hills and Piney Woods: A Political History of Butler County in the Nineteenth Century" (PhD dissertation, University of Alabama, 1985), 165–66.

116. BFP to J. F. McGogy, 7 September 1866, and BFP to Wager Swayne, 21 December 1866, in RG 105, Records of the Bureau of Refugees, Freedmen, and Abandoned Lands, 1865–1870, Records of the Assistant Commissioner for the State of Alabama, Letters received, 1866, National Archives and Records Administration.

117. Garrett, *Reminiscences of Public Men*, 317–18; Little, *History of Butler County*, 119; BFP to T. and J. W. Johnson, 30 May 1868, Gratz Collection, Historical Society of Pennsylvania; B.F. Porter's obituary clipping, Scrapbook, Porter Papers, AU. For the harsh fates of scalawags in Alabama see Sarah W. Wiggins, *The Scalawag in Alabama Politics, 1865–1881* (1977; repr. Tuscaloosa: University of Alabama Press, 1991), and William Warren Rogers Jr., *Black Belt Scalawag: Charles Hays and the Southern Republicans in the Age of Reconstruction* (Athens: University of Georgia Press, 1993).

# Chapter 3

1. Henry Tutwiler (1807–1884) was born in Virginia to a family of Swiss extraction. He attended the University of Virginia from 1825 to 1829 and received one of the first master's degrees awarded by that institution. From 1831 to 1837 he was professor of ancient languages at the University of Alabama. Thereafter he taught at Marion College and LaGrange College before founding (in 1847) the Greene Springs School near Havana, Greene County. In 1835 he married Julia Ashe, daughter of the University of Alabama's first steward. See Owen, *History of Alabama and Dictionary of Alabama Biography*, 1:671–72; 4:1694–95; William R. Smith Sr., *Reminiscences of a Long Life: Historical, Political, Personal, and Literary* (Washington, D.C.: W. R. Smith Sr., 1889), 227–33, 246; and Thomas Chalmers McCorvey, "Henry Tutwiler and the Influence of the University of Virginia on Education in Alabama," in *Transactions of the Alabama Historical Society* (Montgomery: Printed for the Society, 1906) 5: 83–106.

2. Eoline Wallace Moore, "Julia Tutwiler, Teacher," *Birmingham-Southern College Bulletin*, 27 (1934): 6–7; Anne Gary Pannell and Dorothea E. Wyatt, *Julia S. Tutwiler and Social Progress in Alabama*, introduction by Paul M. Pruitt Jr. (1961: repr. Tuscaloosa: University of Alabama Press, 2004). See also Julia S. Tutwiler, "Our Brother in Stripes, in the School Room," *National Educational Association Journal of Proceedings and Addresses, Session of the Year 1890*, 602–603.

3. Paul M. Pruitt Jr., introduction to *Julia S. Tutwiler and Social Progress*, by Pannell and Wyatt, xxi–xxiv. For a similar comparison between Tutwiler and Washington, see Kathryn Tucker Windham, *My Name Is Julia* (Birmingham: Birmingham Public Library Press, 1991), 17–18.

4. Moore, "Julia Tutwiler, Teacher," 10–11, 15–23; Helen Christine Bennett, "Julia Tutwiler, First Citizen of Alabama," *Pictorial Review* (April 1913); and *Montgomery Advertiser*, 9 June 1910. For the more complex realities of prison reform, see Mary Ellen Curtin, *Black Prisoners and Their World: Alabama, 1865–1900* (Charlottesville: University Press of Virginia, 2000).

5. Moore, "Julia Tutwiler, Teacher," 14.

6. Henry Lee Hargrove, *Julia S. Tutwiler of Alabama* (N.p, 1916), 6.

7. The standard work is Anne Gary Pannell and Dorthea E. Wyatt, *Julia S. Tutwiler and Social Progress in Alabama*, published in 1961 and reissued in 2004. Other biographical works include Clara L. Pitts, "Julia Strudwick Tutwiler" (EdD dissertation, George Washington University, 1942). See also Robert Raymond Kunkel, "A Rhetorical Analysis of Julia Strudwick Tutwiler's Reform Speeches, 1880–1900" (PhD dissertation, Louisiana State University, 1978). More than a decade ago, the current author published a two-part magazine biography. See Paul M. Pruitt Jr., "Julia S. Tutwiler: Years of Innocence," *Alabama Heritage* 22 (Fall 1991), 37–44; and "Julia S. Tutwiler: Years of Experience," *Alabama Heritage* 23 (Winter 1992), 31–39.

8. Owen, *History of Alabama and Dictionary of Alabama Biography*, 4:1694–95; McCorvey, "Henry Tutwiler," 100–103, 104–105. For the number of slaves, see G. Ward Hubbs, *Guarding Greensboro: A Confederate Company in the Making of a Southern Community* (Athens: University of Georgia Press, 2003), 65; and [Henry Tutwiler], "Address to the Freedmen of Alabama," in George Burke Johnston, *Thomas Chalmers McCorvey: Teacher, Poet, Historian* (Blacksburg, Virginia: White Rhinoceros Press, 1985), 237–38. For the number of students, see the *Greensboro Beacon*, 10 August 1850.

9. Anne Firor Scott, *The Southern Lady: From Pedestal to Politics, 1830–1930* (Chicago: University of Chicago Press, 1970), 4–7, 71; see also Thomas Woody, *A History of Women's Education in the United States* (New York: The Science Press, 1929), 2:227–28, 266–67.

10. Rebecca Latimer Felton, *Country Life in Georgia in the Days of My Youth* (Atlanta: Index Printing Company, 1919), 58–62. Felton (1835–1930) was in many respects Tutwiler's Georgia counterpart. The well-educated child of a Whig family, she taught school and involved herself in causes. Like Tutwiler she worked with the WCTU against the convict lease system; much earlier than Tutwiler, she advocated women's suffrage. In 1922 she served in the U.S. Senate for twenty-four hours (filling the vacancy caused by the death of Thomas E. Watson), thus becoming the first

woman U.S. Senator. See John E. Talmadge, *Rebecca Latimer Felton: Nine Stormy Decades* (Athens: University of Georgia Press, 1960).

11. One accomplished Alabama woman whose education was superficially deficient was Amelia Gayle Gorgas. See Sarah Woolfolk Wiggins, *Love and Duty: Amelia and Josiah Gorgas and Their Family* (Tuscaloosa: University of Alabama Press, 2005), 2–3. On the topic of women's education generally, see Michael O'Brien, *Conjectures of Order: Intellectual Life and the American South, 1810–1860* (Chapel Hill: University of North Carolina Press, 2004), 1:253–84.

12. Moore, "Julia Tutwiler, Teacher," 5; McCorvey, "Henry Tutwiler," 103; Porter quoted in Garrett, *Reminiscences of Public Men*, 314; and see Scott, *Southern Lady*, 67–71. The daughters of neighboring planters also attended the Greene Springs School. See Pannell and Wyatt, *Julia S. Tutwiler and Social Progress*, 9; and [Legrand Tutwiler], "Some Recollections of Legrand Tutwiler, Former Slave of Dr. Henry Tutwiler, of Greene Springs," [n.d.], Papers of Henry Tutwiler and Family, Manuscripts Department, Alderman Library, University of Virginia.

13. K.T.M. to Netta [Netta Tutwiler McCorvey], [circa 1916], Julia S. Tutwiler Papers, Hoole Special Collections Library, University of Alabama (hereinafter cited as Tutwiler Papers, UA). This letter is a memoir of Julia S. Tutwiler written by Katherine Tutwiler Meriwether.

14. McCorvey, "Henry Tutwiler," 100–102.

15. Julia S. Tutwiler to Ida Tutwiler, [n.d.], Ida Tutwiler Letters, Southern Historical Collection, University of North Carolina, Chapel Hill (hereinafter cited as Ida Tutwiler Letters, UNC).

16. [Henry Tutwiler], *Address Delivered Before the Erosophic Society at the University of Alabama, August 9, 1834, By Professor Tutwiler* (Tuscaloosa: Robinson and Davenport, Printers, 1834), 4–6, 10–11.

17. K.T.M. to Netta [Netta Tutwiler McCorvey], [circa 1916], Tutwiler Papers, UA. There is no direct evidence that Julia Tutwiler read the works of such feminists as the Grimke sisters or Margaret Fuller. On the other hand, Henry Tutwiler encouraged students to use his large, well-stocked library. For mid-century feminists, see Scott, *Southern Lady*, 51–55, 61–64; and Estelle B. Freedman, *Their Sisters' Keepers: Women's Prison Reform in America, 1830–1930* (Ann Arbor: University of Michigan Press, 1981), 30–31.

18. Pannell and Wyatt, *Julia S. Tutwiler and Social Progress*, 12–13. For a summary of the national Whig outlook, see Lawrence Frederick Kohl, *The Politics of Individualism: Parties and the American Character in the Jacksonian Era* (New York: Oxford University Press, 1989), 63–65, 68, 70, 72, 74–75, 79, 83.

19. For Alabama Whigs, see Thornton, *Politics and Power*, 87–89, 96, 294–95, 302. As noted in Chapter Two, Benjamin F. Porter was the most visibly reformist of the Alabama Whigs.

20. McCorvey, "Henry Tutwiler," 103.

21. [Legrand Tutwiler], "Some Recollections," 2–5; Moore, "Julia Tutwiler, Teacher," 5. See also Scott, *Southern Lady*, 28–37; and Kenneth R. Johnson, "White Married Women in Antebellum Alabama," *Alabama Review*, 43 (January 1990), 3–17.

22. For her interest in cloth, see Julia S. Tutwiler to "My dearest Netta," 4 October

1873, Tutwiler Papers, UA (this letter is part of a series that will be cited hereinafter as Julia Tutwiler to Netta). For her interest in gardening, see Kenneth R. Johnson, ed., "A Southern Student Describes the Inauguration of President James Buchanan," *Alabama Historical Quarterly*, 31 (Fall and Winter 1969), 240; for her hatred of housework, see K.T.M. to Netta, [1916], Tutwiler Papers, UA.

23. Elizabeth Fox-Genovese, *Within the Plantation Household: Black and White Women of the Old South* (Chapel Hill: University of North Carolina Press, 1988), 100–102.

24. Dwight L. Dumond, *Letters of James Gillespie Birney, 1831–1857* (2 volumes; New York: D. Appleton-Century, 1938), 17–18, 19 (quoted passage). See also Hubbs, *Guarding Greensboro*, 64–65. Birney was a Kentuckian who came to Alabama in 1817. In the 1820s and early 1830s he was a lawyer-politician with many philanthropic interests, including the American Colonization Society. He recruited Henry Tutwiler for the University of Alabama faculty. By the mid-1830s his antislavery views were too pronounced for white Alabamians, and he left the state. For mounting intolerance of antislavery ideas in the region, see Elizabeth Fox-Genovese and Eugene Genovese, *The Mind of the Master Class: History and Faith in the Southern Slaveholders' Worldview* (New York: Cambridge University Press, 2005), 229–40. For Tutwiler's personal slave code, see Johnston, *Thomas Chalmers McCorvey*, 6–7.

25. Affirmations of the slaves' basic humanity were, for antebellum Whigs, a coded way of saying that slaves possessed basic human rights. Such mild rhetoric, combined with occasional references to slavery as a doomed institution and perhaps even more occasional civil disobedience (teaching slaves to read, for example) marked the extent to which white antislavery Alabamians were willing to go. The current author has elsewhere referred to them as "crypto-abolitionists." See "Amicus Curiae: Henry W. Hilliard's View of Slavery," in David I. Durham and Paul M. Pruitt Jr., *A Journey in Brazil: Henry Washington Hilliard and the Brazilian Anti-Slavery Society* (Tuscaloosa: University of Alabama School of Law, 2008), 1–14. Durham quotes Hilliard on slavery as an institution opposed by the "civilized world"; Durham, *Southern Moderate in Radical Times*, 105.

26. Tutwiler, "Address to the Freedmen of Alabama," 237–38; Tutwiler, *Address Delivered Before the Erosophic Society*, 10–11; [Legrand Tutwiler], "Some Recollections," 1–2.

27. *Birmingham Age Herald*, 13 December 1898; K.T.M. to Netta, [1916], Tutwiler Papers, UA.

28. For the Tutwiler family's patriotism, see Pannell and Wyatt, *Julia S. Tutwiler and Social Progress*, 13. Julia Tutwiler's patriotism may have been influenced by the deaths of Greene Springs graduates, more than fifty of whom died in the war; one of these, Ruffin Ashe, was a relative. See *Resolutions in Memoriam and Roll of Honor of the Hermathenian Society of Greene Springs School* (Columbus, Mississippi: Mississippi Index Job Rooms, 1867), 6. For Julia Tutwiler on the trials of emancipation, see Tutwiler, "Our Brother in Stripes," 602; for a similar line of thought, see Hubbs, *Guarding Greensboro*, 66. For the residence of former slaves at Greene Springs, see Tutwiler, "Address to the Freedmen of Alabama," 238.

29. Tutwiler, "Address to the Freedmen of Alabama," 237–38.

30. Tutwiler, "Our Brother in Stripes," 601–602.

31. K.T.M. to Netta, [circa 1916], Tutwiler Papers, UA; Moore, "Julia Tutwiler, Teacher," 4–5; Pannell and Wyatt, *Julia S. Tutwiler and Social Progress*, 12, 132n6.

32. Steven M. Stowe, "The Not-So-Cloistered Academy: Elite Women's Education and Family Feeling in the Old South," in *The Web of Southern Social Relations: Women, Family, and Education*, ed. Walter J. Fraser Jr. et al. (Athens: University of Georgia Press, 1985), 93–94.

33. Tutwiler to Ida, [n.d.], Ida Tutwiler Letters, UNC.

34. Ibid.; K.T.M. to Netta, [circa 1916], Tutwiler Papers, UA; and Pannell and Wyatt, *Julia S, Tutwiler and Social Progress*, 13–16, 17–18.

35. Tutwiler to Ida, [n.d.], Ida Tutwiler Letters, UNC; K.T.M. to Netta, [circa 1916], Tutwiler Papers, UA; Pannell and Wyatt, *Julia S. Tutwiler and Social Progress*, 18–21, 132n1. K.T.M. recalled that "two young Mississippi men" had often visited Julia during her last stay at Madame Maroteau's school. Possibly her bitter memories stemmed from romantic disappointment, though it is just as likely that she suffered from that state of patriotic quasi-grief that afflicted so many southerners at the time.

36. K.T.M. to Netta, [circa 1916], Tutwiler Papers, UA.

37. Tutwiler to Ida, [n.d.], Ida Tutwiler Letters, UNC; and Pannell and Wyatt, *Julia S. Tutwiler and Social Progress*, 21–23. An incomplete manuscript in the Tutwiler Papers, UA, by Mrs. Kelly Meriwether (probably Julia's sister "K.T.M.") states that on at least one occasion during her Greene Springs years, Julia rode into the countryside, "taking one of her little brothers behind her," to give classes to poor children. Henry Tutwiler was probably as discontented during these years as his daughter. See George Long to Henry Tutwiler, 27 August 1868, in *Letters of George Long*, ed. Thomas Fitz-Hugh (Charlottesville: The Library, University of Virginia, 1917), 49–51.

38. Pannell and Wyatt, *Julia S. Tutwiler and Social Progress*, 224–33; Julia Tutwiler, "A Year in a German Model School," *National Educational Association Journal of Proceedings and Addresses, Session of the Year 1891* (Topeka: The Association, 1891), 161–63. See also "A History of Nursing: Kaiserswerth and the Deaconess Movement," [n.d.], typescript, 2–4, 5, 20–21, 27–29, Tutwiler Papers, UA.

39. Tutwiler, "A Year in a German Model School," 167; and see Julia S. Tutweiler [sic], "The Technical Education of Women," *Education: An International Magazine*, 3 (1883), 201–207. "Technical Education" began life as a paper delivered before the Alabama Educational Association in 1880, where a man read it. The association's leadership doubted the propriety of a woman speaking in public!

40. Tutwiler, "A Year in a German Model School," 164–67, 168.

41. Ibid., 163, 167; Pannell and Wyatt, *Julia S. Tutwiler and Social Progress*, 35–36, 109.

42. Pannell and Wyatt, *Julia S. Tutwiler and Social Progress*, 34–36, 109; Tutwiler, "A Year in a German Model School," 163, 167.

43. Julia Tutwiler to Netta, 4 December 1874, 15 February 1875, 27 March 1875, 10 April 1875, Tutwiler Papers, UA; Pannell and Wyatt, *Julia S. Tutwiler and Social Progress*, 38–39.

44. Julia Tutwiler to Netta, 27 March 1875, Tutwiler Papers, UA. For citations to

the works published during Tutwiler's sojourn abroad see Paul M. Pruitt Jr., "Julia Tutwiler," in *Research Guide to American Historical Biography*, ed. Suzanne Niemeyer (Washington, D.C.: Beacham Press, 1990), 2188–96.

45. Julia Tutwiler to Netta, 3 December 1874, 15 February 1875, 27 March 1875, Tutwiler Papers, UA. For a concise treatment of the end of Reconstruction, see Allen Johnston Going, *Bourbon Democracy in Alabama, 1874–1890* (1951; repr. Tuscaloosa: University of Alabama Press, 1992), 9–26.

46. Pannell and Wyatt, *Julia S. Tutwiler and Social Progress*, 53–54; see also Owen, *History of Alabama and Dictionary of Alabama Biography*, 3:808; and Saffold Berney, *Hand-Book of Alabama*, 2nd ed. (Birmingham: Roberts and Son, Printers, 1892) 217–20.

47. Julia S. Tutwiler to Robert McKee, 25 May 1878, in the Robert McKee Papers, Alabama Department of Archives and History.

48. Tutwiler, "Technical Education of Women," 201–206; see also Pannell and Wyatt, *Julia S. Tutwiler and Social Progress*, 56.

49. Julia S. Tutwiler, "The Charities of Paris, No. I: What One Woman Can Do," typescript (part of a longer manuscript of Julia Tutwiler's writings), 97–100, 101, 103, Tutwiler Papers, UA.

50. See Pitts, "Julia Strudwick Tutwiler," 190–91; Pannell and Wyatt, *Julia S. Tutwiler and Social Progress*, 108; and see [Julia S. Tutwiler], "A Primitive Lesson," typescript, 1, Tutwiler Papers, UA.

51. [Julia S. Tutwiler], "Alabama's Report at the International Historical Congress of Charities and Corrections," typescript, 7, Tutwiler Papers, UA.

52. See the Tuscaloosa Female Benevolent Society Papers, Hoole Special Collections Library, University of Alabama. These papers consist of notebooks, of which two, covering the period since the late 1860s, were missing at the time this essay was composed. See Pitts, "Julia Strudwick Tutwiler," 190–92; and Pannell and Wyatt, *Julia S. Tutwiler and Social Progress*, 1–109.

53. *Montgomery Advertiser*, 9 December 1880.

54. *Tuscaloosa Gazette*, 18 November 1880; Tutwiler, "Alabama's Report at the International Historical Congress of Charities and Corrections," 7.

55. *Montgomery Advertiser*, 9 December 1880; *Tuscaloosa Clarion*, 7 December 1880; *Tuscaloosa Gazette*, 18 November 1880.

56. *Eutaw Mirror* quoted in the *Tuscaloosa Gazette*, 18 November 1880.

57. *Senate Journal* (1880–1881), 3, 605–606; *House Journal* (1880–1881), 950; *Acts of Alabama* (1880–1881), 129–31.

58. See Julia S. Tutwiler to Colonel [A. C.] Hargrove, 8 February 1891, Tutwiler Papers, UA. For Tutwiler's relationship with Watts, see Pannell and Wyatt, *Julia S. Tutwiler and Social Progress*, 101, 139n6; for Watts' interest in "Woman's Law," see *Report of the Organization and of the First, Second, and Third Annual Meetings of the Alabama State Bar Association* (Montgomery: Barrett & Co., 1882), 55. Watts, a former Whig turned post-war Democrat, had been the last Confederate governor of Alabama.

59. *Senate Journal* (1880–1881), 14–15, 42. At least seven of the committee's nine members were from the Black Belt. For Troy, see Owen, *History of Alabama and Dic-*

*tionary of Alabama Biography,* 4:1685–86; for Seay see *Northern Alabama, Historical and Biographical* (Birmingham: Smith & De Land, 1888), 612. N. H. R. Dawson, Speaker of the House, was brother of R. H. Dawson, who would serve (1883–1897) as the reform-minded president of the Board of Inspectors of State Convicts. R. H. Dawson is extensively discussed in (in a sense, he is the protagonist of) Curtin's *Black Prisoners and Their World.*

60. See *Eutaw Whig and Observer,* 11 and 25 December 1879; or the article by "Humanus," see ibid., 22 January 1880.

61. See governor's message in *Senate Journal* (1880–1881), 33–35, 36–37. The legislature regulated "hard labor" sentencing; see *Acts of Alabama* (1880–1881), 37–38. In general the 1880–1881 legislature was sensitive to public concerns because the Democratic Party, in power since 1874, was under attack from Greenbackers and Independent Democrats who resented the government's inactivity in the face of persistent economic troubles. Spurred by Daniel S. Troy, the legislators created a state railroad commission, a more difficult undertaking than warming the jails. See Going, *Bourbon Democracy,* 54–60, 129–36.

62. Going, *Bourbon Democracy,* 171–72; see also William Warren Rogers and Robert David Ward, *Convicts, Coal, and the Banner Mine Tragedy* (Tuscaloosa: University of Alabama Press, 1987), 31–33, 33–50.

63. For Tutwiler's attitudes, see "Our Brother in Stripes," 603; and see *Proceedings of the Annual Sessions of the Women's Christian Temperance Union of the State of Alabama* (1884), 10. Tutwiler was chosen as superintendent of the department of "Influincing [sic] the Press." For Tutwiler's early advocacy of temperance, see Pannell and Wyatt, *Julia S. Tutwiler and Social Progress,* 119–20. And for the organization and achievements of Alabama clubwomen, see Mary Martha Thomas, *The New Woman in Alabama: Social Reforms and Suffrage, 1890–1920* (Tuscaloosa: University of Alabama Press, 1992).

64. Freedman, *Their Sisters' Keepers,* 30–33, 38–39, 42–45, 47, 49, 53–55, 61; Ruth Bordin, *Women and Temperance: The Quest for Power and Liberty, 1873–1900* (Philadelphia: Temple University Press, 1981), 96–97, 99–100.

65. Freedman, *Their Sisters' Keepers,* 24–25, 34, 39, 52, 55; and Thomas, *The New Woman in Alabama,* 17–18, 48.

66. Tutwiler, "Our Brother in Stripes," 603.

67. *Greensboro Southern Watchman,* 16 December 1880; Moore, "Julia Tutwiler, Teacher," 7.

# Chapter 4

1. *Memorial Record of Alabama* (Madison, Wisconsin: Brant and Fuller, 1893), 2:983; Seventh Census (1850), Free Schedules, Alabama, Autauga County, Huddleston Beat, 49–50; Seventh Census (1850), Slave Schedules, Alabama, Autauga County, Huddleston Beat, 55. All census citations are to microfilm editions of manuscript returns.

2. Owen, *History of Alabama and Dictionary of Alabama Biography,* 2:983; and Douglas R. Chandler, "The Formation of the Methodist Protestant Church," in *The*

*History of American Methodism in Three Volumes,* ed. Emory S. Buckle (New York: Abingdon Press, 1964), 1:636–99.

3. See Donald J. Mathews, *Religion in the Old South* (Chicago: University of Chicago Press, 1977), xiv–xv, xvii, 10–38.

4. Ibid., 19–21, 33–35; Anne C. Loveland, *Southern Evangelicals and the Social Order, 1800–1860* (Baton Rouge: Louisiana State University Press, 1980), 1–29, 65–90.

5. Loveland, *Southern Evangelicals,* 16–21; *Memorial Record,* 2:983.

6. Chandler, "Formation of the Methodist Protestant Church," 669–70.

7. *Memorial Record,* 2:983; Mathews, *Religion in the Old South,* 24–28.

8. Owen, *History of Alabama and Dictionary of Alabama Biography,* 2:983; Mathews, *Religion in the Old South,* 86–87.

9. Smith used his saddlebags as a Methodist circuit rider and as an Episcopal priest. See Randolph F. Blackford, "History of St. Peter's Church, Talladega" (mimeograph, n.d.; copies at St. Peter's, Talladega, and in author's possession), 6.

10. Chandler, "Formation of the Methodist Protestant Church," 660; Moore, *History of Alabama,* 149–52. For a more contemporary view, see the *Southern Aegis,* Ashville, Alabama, 27 March 1873.

11. Anson West, *A History of Methodism in Alabama* (Nashville: Publishing House, Methodist Episcopal Church, South, 1893), 741; Blackford, "History of St. Peter's," 6.

12. For a similar attitude, see Nicholas Hamner Cobbs to the Reverend Ethan Allen, 8 October 1846, in the Edwin A. Dalrymple Papers, Library of Congress.

13. *Memorial Record,* 2:984; and see Seventh Census (1850), Alabama, Lowndes County, Lowndes District, 224 (leaf 112).

14. Seventh Census (1850), Alabama, Lowndes County, Lowndes District, 224 (leaf 112n13); Marion Elias Lazenby, *History of Methodism in Alabama and West Florida* ([Nashville]: North Alabama Conference and Alabama West-Florida Conference of the Methodist Church, 1960), 318; Moore, *History of Alabama,* 272–73, 286–90.

15. Greenough White, *A Saint of the Southern Church: Memoir of the Right Reverend Nicholas Hamner Cobbs* (New York: James Potts and Company, 1897), 94.

16. Mathews, *Religion in the Old South,* 83–97, 136–84; Loveland, *Southern Evangelicals,* 186–256.

17. Smith may have been opposed to secession, as was his father, but opposing secession and opposing slavery were two different (if related) things. See *Memorial Record,* 2:983.

18. Eighth Census (1860), Alabama, Lowndes County, Northern District, 16; Smith's personal property was rated at $46,000, typically a clue to the extent of slave owning. James T. [sic] Smith was listed as owner of 46 slaves, roughly equivalent in value to Smith's chattel holdings. Ibid., 37–38.

19. A child, William B. Smith, is listed in the 1850 census but not in that of 1860. Other children may have been born and died without appearing in any census.

20. West, *History of Methodism,* 748–49.

21. Ibid., 749; Lazenby, *History of Methodism in Alabama and West Florida,* 316.

22. Lazenby, *History of Methodism in Alabama and West Florida,* 317–18; West, *History of Methodism,* 747–48. West puts Hall's original proposal in 1840. See also Mathews, *Religion in the Old South,* 81–83, 90.

23. Lazenby, *History of Methodism in Alabama and West Florida*, 316–17; Chandler, "Formation of the Methodist Protestant Church," 675, 679–82.

24. Mathew, *Religion in the Old South*, 82–97. For a discursive treatment of these same issues, see Michael O'Brien, *Conjectures of Order: Intellectual Life and the American South, 1810–1860* (Chapel Hill: University of North Carolina Press, 2004), 2:1093–98.

25. Owen, *History of Alabama and Dictionary of Alabama Biography*, 3:359; White, *Saint of the Southern Church*, 30–36.

26. Owen, *History of Alabama and Dictionary of Alabama Biography*, 1:536–38; Mattie Pegues Wood, *The Life of St. John's Parish, A History of St. John's Episcopal Church from 1834 to 1955* (Montgomery: The Paragon Press, 1955), 18–38. For parishes toward the end of Cobbs' tenure, see *Journal of the Proceedings of the Twenty-Sixth Annual Convention of the Protestant Episcopal Church in the Diocese of Alabama* (Mobile: Farrow & Dennett, 1857), 3. (This and other analogous books of proceedings cited hereinafter as *Journal of the Diocese*.)

27. For the Muhlenberg movement, see William Wilberforce Newton, *Dr. Muhlenberg* (Boston: Houghton Mifflin and Company, 1891), 121–71; William Wilson Manross, *A History of the American Episcopal Church* (New York: Morehouse-Gorman Company, 1950), 285–88; Donald Smith Armentrout, *James Hervey Otey, First Episcopal Bishop of Tennessee* (Knoxville and Memphis: The Episcopal Dioceses in Tennessee, 1984), 122–26.

28. Henry C. Lay, *Letters to a Man Bewildered Among Many Counselors, by a Presbyter of Alabama* (New York: Stanford and Swords, 1852), 18–22, 27–28; see also "The Episcopal Church and Slavery," *Raleigh Church Intelligencer*, 13 June 1860; and William Porcher DuBose, "Turning Points in My Life," in *William Porcher DuBose: Selected Writings*, ed. Jon Alexander (New York: Paulist Press, 1988), 71.

29. See Nicholas Hamner Cobbs, *An Answer to Some of the Popular Objections Against the Protestant Episcopal Church* (Tuscaloosa: J. W. Warres, Observer Office, 1849), 1–9; Lay, *Letters to a Man Bewildered*, 23, 25–27; Armentrout, *James Hervey Otey*, 54–55.

30. See Cobbs, *An Answer*, 1–3; Lay, *Letters to a Man Bewildered*, 29–32; Armentrout, *James Hervey Otey*, 53, 140; and Newton, *Dr. Muhlenberg*, 135.

31. West, *History of Methodism*, 741; *Memorial Record*, 2:983. See also Mildred Brewer Russell, *Lowndes Court House: A Chronicle of Hayneville, an Alabama Black Belt Village* (Montgomery: The Paragon Press, 1951) 23–24; and Lowndesboro Heritage Society, *Lowndesboro's Picturesque Legacies* (N.p., 1979), 58–59.

32. *Journal of the Diocese* (1858), 8, 27; *Journal of the Diocese* (1859), 6, 13, 39; *Journal of the Diocese* (1860), 10, 19; Armentrout, *James Hervey Otey*, 16–20.

33. *Raleigh Church Intelligencer*, 27 September 1860; the quotation is from the Authorized Edition of the Bible. See also Mathews, *Religion in the Old South*, 59–60, 114.

34. Owen, *History of Alabama and Dictionary of Alabama Biography*, 3:359; Wood, *Life of St. John's*, 42; White, *Saint of the Southern Church*, 98–99.

35. Joseph Blount Cheshire, *The Church in the Confederate States: A History of the Protestant Episcopal Church of the Confederate States* (New York: Longmans, Green, and Company, 1912), 35–37; Armentrout, *James Hervey Otey*, 86–88; *Proceedings of a Meeting of Bishops, Clergymen, and Laymen, of the Protestant Episcopal Church in the*

*Confederate States, at Montgomery, Alabama* (Montgomery: Barrett, Wimbish, and Company, 1861), 1–18.

36. See generally *Journals of the Diocese* (1859–1867).

37. *Journal of the Diocese* (1859), 39; *Journal of the Diocese* (1861), 38; *Journal of the Diocese* (1862), 38–43. On mobilization, see Raimondo Luraghi, *The Rise and Fall of the Plantation South* (New York: New Viewpoints, 1978), 112–32.

38. *Journal of the Diocese* (1863), 62, 94. The years 1861 to 1865 were a time of great interest in evangelizing to slaves; see Cheshire, *Church in the Confederate States*, 43, 61–63, 116–17, 127. For Smith's colleague William A. Stickney and his missionary work in west Alabama's Canebrake, see Harriet E. Amos, "Religious Reconstruction in Microcosm at Faunsdale Plantation," *Alabama Review*, 42 (October 1989), 244–56. For related experiences in other denominations, see the essays in John Boles, ed., *Masters and Slaves in the House of the Lord: Race and Religion in the American South, 1740–1870* (Lexington: University Press of Kentucky, 1988).

39. *Journal of the Diocese* (1865), 25. For the religious attitudes of African Americans following the Civil War, see Peter Kolchin, *First Freedom: The Responses of Alabama's Blacks to Emancipation and Reconstruction* (Westport: Greenwood Press, 1972), 107–22; and Amos, "Reconstruction in Microcosm," 257–89.

40. Cheshire, *Church in the Confederate States*, 178–201; Walter C. Whitaker, *Richard Hooker Wilmer, Second Bishop of Alabama* (Philadelphia: George W. Jacobs and Company, 1907), 122–48; Richard H. Wilmer to the Reverend Dr. Cushman, 16 June 1865, in the Richard Hooker Wilmer Papers, Manuscript Department, Duke University Library; *Journal of the Diocese* (1866), 25.

41. *Journal of the Diocese* (1863), 67; *Raleigh Church Intelligencer*, 27 November 1863; Gaines M. Foster, *Ghosts of the Confederacy: Defeat, the Lost Cause, and the Emergence of the New South* (New York: Oxford University Press, 1987), 13–14, 18, 23–24, 35.

42. *Journal of the Diocese* (1866), 20; *Journal of the Diocese* (1867), 27; *Journal of the Diocese* (1869), 26.

43. *Journal of the Diocese* (1869), 27.

44. Ninth Census (1870), Alabama, Talladega County, City of Talladega, Ward 1, 10.

45. *Journal of the Diocese* (1870), 2, 52, 53, 60.

46. E. Grace Jemison, *Historic Tales of Talladega* (1959; repr. [Huntsville]: The Strode Publishers, 1984), 105–14, 261–71, 279–80; Owen, *History of Alabama and Dictionary of Alabama Biography*, 2:1289; Jehu Wellington Vandiver, "Pioneer Talladega, Its Minutes and Memories," *Alabama Historical Quarterly*, 16 (Spring and Summer 1954), 95, 100, 101, 128–31, 134–35. Since 1861, Talladega had also been the home of the state school for the deaf; beginning in 1866, the school also instructed blind children.

47. Jemison, *Historic Tales*, 123–28, 137–60, 203–13; Vandiver, "Pioneer Talladega," 166–98; Rogers et al., *Alabama: History of a Deep South State*, 260–65. The Talladega City Council minutes, extant since 1874 (stored in Heritage Hall, Talladega, when this essay was originally published) provide plentiful evidence of the conservative or Bourbon attitudes of the aldermen.

48. Jemison, *Historic Tales*, 250–56, 261–62; Blackford, "History of St. Peter's," 2–5; *Raleigh Church Intelligencer*, 27 November 1863, 12 February 1864; *Journal of the Diocese* (1870), 60.

49. For Bingham's life, see Owen, *History of Alabama and Dictionary of Alabama Biography*, 3:150–51.

50. Ninth Census (1870), Alabama, Talladega County, City of Talladega, Ward 1, 10; Tenth Census (1880), Alabama, Talladega County, Talladega Town, Ward 4, 3; Jemison, *Historic Tales*, 254; *Journal of the Diocese* (1871), 71. The Smith family entry in the Ninth Census, cited above, has been altered in a handwriting different from that of the census taker, seemingly to indicate that one of Smith's children was a mulatto. At least one other family's entry was similarly altered. The son in question, Thomas, was "at school" in 1870, and he was listed as white in the Eighth Census. If Thomas was a mulatto, he was still Smith's child; Smith claims a son, Thomas, in *Memorial Record*, 2:984.

51. Blackford, "History of St. Peter's," 6.

52. The questions are paraphrased from George W. Shinn, *Questions About Our Church: Or, Words to Help People Who [Desire] Information Concerning the Episcopal Church* (New York: Thomas Whittaker, 1880), 5.

53. George N. James, "Influence of the Church's Liturgy in the Formation of Character," *The Old Church Path, A Monthly Magazine, Instructive and Practical*, I (December 1878), 15–17.

54. *Journal of the Diocese* (1870), 2, 52, 53, 60. See also subsequent *Journals of the Diocese;* Blackford, "History of St. Peter's," 7–8. In their history of Grace Church in Anniston, Carleton Lente and Louisa Nonemacher show Smith preaching from hotel porches, vacant lots, private homes, and a train station. Lente and Nonemacher, *Years of Grace* (N.p., 1948), 9.

55. *Journal of the Diocese* (1870), 60; *Journal of the Diocese* (1871), 71; *Journal of the Diocese* (1872), 62; Jemison, *Historic Tales*, 253–54.

56. *Journal of the Diocese* (1872), 62; *Journal of the Diocese* (1876), 61; *Journal of the Diocese* (1880), 53.

57. Owen gives the 1880 population of Talladega as 1233. The city limits were constricted in the 1870s for political reasons, but it is likely that at least two thousand people lived in Talladega and its surrounding neighborhoods, of whom one thousand or more were white. Owen, *History of Alabama and Dictionary of Alabama Biography*, 2:1289. "Candor" stated that there were 600 church members in Talladega, a figure that may not have included Episcopalians. *Talladega Our Mountain Home*, 18 April 1888. Jemison cites figures that place the number of Presbyterians at 330 in 1893, when the population was approximately 2,100. Jemison, *Historic Tales*, 246. For a white view of black religious attitudes, see William H. Skaggs, "Memorandum Relating to Certain Outstanding Events in the History of Talladega, Alabama, During the Administration of William H. Skaggs As Mayor, From April 1885 to April 1891," [circa 1920], copy, William H. Skaggs Collection, Alabama Department of Archives and History, 40–43. An Episcopal mission to Talladega's black community was begun in 1896. Blackford, "History of St. Peter's," 11.

58. *Journal of the Diocese* (1880), 51; *Journal of the Diocese* (1881), 49, 51, 53; *Journal of the Diocese* (1882), 3, 47, 48; *Journal of the Diocese* (1883), 3, 46–48, 50; *Journal of the Diocese* (1884), 3, 4, 52, 56, 57, 65.

59. *Talladega Our Mountain Home,* 17 December 1884; *Journal of the Diocese* (1880), 72; *Journal of the Diocese* (1885), 3, 31. In moving back to Talladega, Smith did not abandon his missionary duties; rather, he added assignments in Brierfield and Calera to existing assignments in Montevallo and Cross Plains (now Piedmont).

60. Jemison, *Historic Tales,* 161; *Northern Alabama, Historical and Biographical* (1888; repr. Spartanburg: The Reprint Company, 1976), 445–69; *Talladega Our Mountain Home,* 2 November 1881, 21 December 1881, 4 October 1882, 23 July 1884, and 26 May 1886.

61. *Northern Alabama,* 450–51; *Talladega Our Mountain Home,* 15 October 1879, 4 October 1882; Owen, *History of Alabama and Dictionary of Alabama Biography,* 2:1289.

62. *Memorial Record,* 2:982–83; Jemison, *Historic Tales,* 161–86; Skaggs, "Memorandum."

63. Skaggs, "Memorandum," 3–21; *Talladega Our Mountain Home,* 22 and 29 January 1879, 15 February 1882, 2 April 1884, 10 June 1885, 8 July 1885; *Talladega Reporter and Watchtower,* 8 April 1885.

64. H. C. Nixon, *Lower Piedmont Country: The Uplands of the Deep South* (1946; repr. Tuscaloosa: University of Alabama Press, 1984), 84; James Benson Sellers, *The Prohibition Movement in Alabama* (Chapel Hill: University of North Carolina Press, 1943), 63 72–73, 93–94, 113–14; *Talladega Our Mountain Home,* 27 July 1881, 10 and 24 August 1881, 22 July 1885, 5 and 19 August 1885, 28 October 1885, 23 December 1885, 10 March 1886, 11 April 1888, 24 October 1888; *Talladega Reporter and Watchtower,* 12 August 1885, 23 December 1885.

65. Sellers, *Prohibition Movement,* 15; Whitaker, *Richard Hooker Wilmer,* 183; Manross, *History of the American Episcopal Church,* 347.

66. For a similar vision of progress, see Whitaker, *Richard Hooker Wilmer,* 242–44. For Talladega public schools, see *Talladega Our Mountain Home,* 7 and 28 April 1886, 8 September 1886.

67. For women's reform movements in Alabama, see generally Thomas, *New Woman in Alabama.*

68. Vandiver, "Pioneer Talladega," 188, 217, 219; *Talladega Our Mountain Home,* 10 December 1884, 19 May 1886.

69. See George Wolfe Shinn, *The Stage as a Teacher: A Sermon . . .* (New York: N.p., 1900). For a famous clerical proponent of theatre as suitable entertainment (and occupation) for children, see Morton N. Cohen, *Lewis Carroll: A Biography* (New York: A. A. Knopf, 1995).

70. *Northern Alabama,* 466; Jemison, *Historic Tales,* 323–24. For an interesting intersection of Talladega civic life and professional theatre, see Paul M. Pruitt Jr., "Augustus Thomas and the Play *Alabama*: Contexts of a Late Nineteenth-Century Broadway Hit," *Markham Review,* 15 (1985–1986), 13–17.

71. *Talladega Our Mountain Home,* 15 December 1886, 8 February 1888, 7 and 21 March 1888, 4 and 18 April 1888. For earlier theatrical productions, see Vandiver, "Pioneer Talladega," 187, 219.

72. *Journal of the Diocese* (1886), see the entry for St. Peter's in the "Tabular Statement" foldout sheet.

73. Skaggs, "Memorandum," 3–23; perusal of Talladega City Council Minutes for the 1870s and 1880s will show that the liquor-related business was a mainstay of municipal income. For a published version of this story, see Paul M. Pruitt Jr., ed., "The Law Triumphs in Talladega: An Excerpt from William H. Skaggs' 'Memorandum,'" *Alabama Review*, 40 (April 1987), 133–48.

74. *Talladega Our Mountain Home*, 13 July 1887, 17 August 1887.

75. For misbehavior in a Talladega church, circa 1873, see Betsy Hamilton [Idora McClellan Moore], "Betsy's First Trip to Town," in Louisa Burke McCain, "Idora McClellan Moore: A Biographical Sketch, Including Selections from Her Writings" (M.S. thesis, Alabama Polytechnic Institute, 1934), 18–23; and the *Raleigh Church Intelligencer*, 25 April 1862.

76. West, *History of Methodism*, 691, 695.

77. *Talladega Our Mountain Home*, 13 July 1887. "Order" wrote another letter complaining about trains running on Sunday. Ibid., 17 April 1889.

78. *Talladega Reporter and Watchtower*, 27 July 1887.

79. Ibid.

80. *Talladega Our Mountain Home*, 3 August 1887.

81. Walter C. Whitaker, *History of the Protestant Episcopal Church in Alabama, 1763–1891* (Birmingham: Roberts and Sons, 1898), 277–78; *Talladega Our Mountain Home*, 5 and 26 June 1889, 31 July 1889, 14 August 1889, and 9 April 1890.

82. Blackford, "History of St. Peter's," 8; *Memorial Record*, 2:984; *Montgomery Advertiser* quoted in *Talladega Our Mountain Home*, 22 February 1899.

83. *Raleigh Church Intelligencer*, 19 July 1860. For the Episcopal Church and the Social Gospel, see Ferenc Morton Szasz, *The Divided Mind of Protestant America, 1880–1930* (University: University of Alabama Press, 1982), 49–52.

84. *Montgomery Advertiser* quoted in *Talladega Our Mountain Home*, 22 February 1899. Blackford says that the cornerstone was laid in 1896. Blackford, "History of St. Peter's," 11.

# Chapter 5

1. Walter B. Jones, "History of the Alabama Lawyer's Code of Ethics," *The Alabama Lawyer*, 17 (January 1956), 23–24.

2. Paul M. Pruitt Jr., "Thomas Goode Jones," in *Alabama Governors: A Political History of the State*, 116–21; and Carolyn Ruth Huggins, "Bourbonism and Radicalism in Alabama: The Gubernatorial Administration of Thomas Goode Jones, 1890–1894" (masters thesis, Auburn University, 1968).

3. Tony Freyer and Timothy Dixon, *Democracy and Judicial Independence: A History of the Federal Courts of Alabama, 1820–1994* (Brooklyn: Carlson Publishing, 1995), 63, 66, 68, 90, 93, 104, 111–16, 118–20, 274; Pete Daniel, *The Shadow of Slavery: Peonage in the South, 1901–1969* (Urbana: University of Illinois Press, 1990), 43–81; and Brent Jude Aucoin, *A "Rift in the Clouds": Race and the Southern Federal Judiciary, 1900–1910* (Fayetteville: University of Arkansas Press, 2007), 53–90.

4. William Warren Rogers, *The One-Gallused Rebellion: Agrarianism in Alabama, 1865–1896* (Baton Rouge: Louisiana State University Press, 1970), 118–20, 182–84, 198, 213–27, 274–75; and Sheldon Hackney, *Populism to Progressivism in Alabama* (Princeton: Princeton University Press, 1969), 59, 61–62, 202, 290–92, 296–98.

5. For a full exploration of this interpretation, see Brent Jude Aucoin, "Thomas Goode Jones, Redeemer and Reformer: The Racial Policies of a Conservative Democrat in Search of a 'New' South" (masters thesis, Miami University, 1993).

6. Burton D. Wechsler, "Black and White Disenfranchisement: Populism, Race, and Class," *American University Law Review*, 52 (October 2002), 51.

7. John Witherspoon DuBose, "A Historian's Tribute to Thomas Goode Jones," *The Alabama Lawyer*, 14 (January 1953), 47; this article was originally published in the *Birmingham Age-Herald*, 31 May 1914.

8. In 1860, Samuel Goode Jones claimed $50,000 in real estate and $119,500 in personal property; the latter included thirty-two slaves. See Eighth Census (1860), Free Schedules, Alabama, Montgomery and Morgan Counties, 19: 306; and Eighth Census (1860), Slave Schedules, Alabama, Mobile, Monroe, and Montgomery Counties, 4: 235. For Thomas Goode Jones' memories of slaves, see Thomas Goode Jones to Booker T. Washington, 20 September 1901, in *The Booker T. Washington Papers*, ed. Louis R. Harlan et al., vol. 6 (Urbana: University of Illinois Press, 1977), 214.

9. For Samuel G. Jones' career, see "Thomas Goode Jones" in *Northern Alabama: Historical and Biographical* (1888; repr. Spartanburg: Reprint Company, 1976), 600; Thomas M. Owen, *History of Alabama and Dictionary of Alabama Biography* (1921; repr. Spartanburg: Reprint Company, 1978), 3:941, 942; DuBose, "Historian's Tribute," 51; Malcolm Cook McMillan, "Thomas Goode Jones, 1844–1914: Warrior, Statesman, and Jurist," *The Alabama Lawyer*, 17 (October 1956), 376; and Ethel Armes, *The Story of Coal and Iron in Alabama* (1910; repr. Leeds, Alabama: Beechwood Books, 1987), 104, 109, 112.

10. Owen, *History of Alabama and Dictionary of Alabama Biography*, 3:941.

11. DuBose, "Historian's Tribute," 51–52; and McMillan, "Thomas Goode Jones, 1844–1914," 376–77.

12. Walter B. Jones, "Anecdotes About Governor Thomas Goode Jones," *The Alabama Lawyer*, 17 (July 1956), 289, 290–93; this article is partly based upon John Brown Gordon, *Reminiscences of the Civil War* (New York: Charles Scribner's Sons, 1903). For a personal account, see Thomas Goode Jones, *Last Days of the Army of Northern Virginia: An Address Delivered by Gov. Thos. G. Jones, Before the Virginia Division of the Association of the Army of Northern Virginia at the Annual Meeting, Richmond, Va., October 12, 1893* ([Richmond]: N.p., circa 1893).

13. Jones, "Anecdotes," 292.

14. See Thomas Goode Jones to General John B. Gordon, 28 December 1886, in Letterbook, 1886–1889 (leaf 3), Thomas Goode Jones Collection, Alabama State Department of Archives and History. This is one of several such letters, personal and official, exchanged by the two men in the mid-1880s. See also Thomas Goode Jones, *Resolutions and Address of Judge Thomas G. Jones: In Memory of Gen'l John B. Gordon, at Nashville, Tennessee, June 15, 1904* ([Nashville]: N.p., circa 1904), 13–16. For an over-

view of Brown's career see Robert Preston Brooks, "Gordon, John Brown," in *Dictionary of American Biography*, ed. Allen Johnson and Dumas Malone, vol. 4, bk. 1 (New York: Charles Scribner's Sons, 1960), 424–25.

15. DuBose, "Historian's Tribute," 54–55; and see *In Memoriam: Thomas Goode Jones, 1844–1914, Georgena Bird Jones, 1846–1921* (Montgomery: Thomas Goode Jones Camp, Sons of Confederate Veterans, 1956).

16. Dubose, "Historian's Tribute," 55; and McMillan, "Thomas Goode Jones, 1844–1914," 377. In 1868 Jones supplemented his income by editorial work for the Montgomery *Daily Picayune*, a short-lived newspaper remarkable (in McMillan's words) "for its sane approach to the problems of the period." Several issues are extant; see Montgomery *Daily Picayune*, 18, 23, and 24 June 1868.

17. DuBose, "Historian's Tribute," 54; McMillan, "Thomas Goode Jones, 1844–1914," 377; for John A. Elmore, William Lowndes Yancey, and Abram J. Walker, see William Garrett, *Reminiscences of Public Men in Alabama for Thirty Years* (1872; repr. Spartanburg: Reprint Company, 1975), 61–62, 454–55, 681–95.

18. DuBose, "Historian's Tribute," 57. DuBose states that Jones was unanimously recommended by the Montgomery bar.

19. For E. W. Peck, see *Northern Alabama*, 522–23; and Joel Kitchens, "E. W. Peck: Alabama's First Scalawag Chief Justice," *Alabama Review*, 54 (January 2001), 3–32.

20. William H. Brantley, *Chief Justice Stone of Alabama* (Birmingham: Birmingham Publishing Company, 1943), 215.

21. DuBose, "Historian's Tribute," 57.

22. "Thomas Goode Jones," *Northern Alabama*, 602. Jones' accomplishments as writer and digester can be followed in the *Alabama Reports*, volumes 42 to 62.

23. Jones practiced with the firm of Rice, Jones, and Wiley for much of the mid-1870s. For its other members, Samuel F. Rice and Ariosto A. Wiley, see *Northern Alabama*, 595–96, 607–608. For an example of Jones' railroad work, see *The South & North Alabama Railroad Co. v. Henlein & Burr*, 52 *Alabama Reports* (1875), 606–24. For the firm's defense of a black attorney who had been suspended from practice in the courts of Dallas County, see *Thomas v. The State, ex rel. Stepney*, 58 *Alabama Reports* (1877), 365–70.

24. J. H. Hubbell, *Hubbell's Legal Directory for Lawyers and Business Men* (New York: J. H. Hubbell and Company, 1883), 733. See also Jones to Russell Houston, 23 May 1887, Letterbook, 1886–1889, leaves 98–99, Jones Collection.

25. Freyer and Dixon, *Democracy and Judicial Independence*, 70–74; and Paul M. Pruitt Jr., "The Life and Times of Legal Education in Alabama, 1819–1897: Bar Admissions, Law Schools, and the Profession," *Alabama Law Review*, 49 (Fall 1997), 301–302, 304–305, 309–18.

26. Lawrence M. Friedman, *A History of American Law*, 2nd ed. (New York: Simon and Schuster, 1985), 407–408.

27. *Report of the Organization and of the First, Second, and Third Annual Meetings of the Alabama State Bar Association* (Montgomery: Smith and Armstrong, Printers, 1882), 224–41. For other members of the committee, see ibid., 164.

28. See Walter L. Fleming, *Civil War and Reconstruction in Alabama, with New Introduction by Sarah Woolfolk Wiggins* (1905; repr. Spartanburg, South Carolina: The

Reprint Company, 1978), 782–98. See also McMillan, *Constitutional Development in Alabama*, 175.

29. McMillan, "Thomas Goode Jones, 1844–1914," 378; DuBose, "Historian's Tribute," 56.

30. See Thomas G. Jones, "Some Observations on the Law of Quarantine," *Southern Law Journal and Reporter*, 1 (February 1880), 161–75; and Robert Partin, "Alabama's Yellow Fever Epidemic of 1878," *Alabama Review*, 10 (January 1957), 31–51.

31. "Thomas Goode Jones," *Northern Alabama*, 602.

32. Jones to My Dear Captain, 14 March 1888, Letterbook, 1886–1889, (leaf 249), Jones Collection.

33. McMillan, "Thomas Goode Jones, 1844–1914," 378; and "Thomas Goode Jones," *Northern Alabama*, 601 (quoted passage).

34. "Thomas Goode Jones," *Northern Alabama*, 601–602. For information on this riot, see *Posey v. The State*, 73 *Alabama Reports* (1883), 490–95. For a later case in which Jones and his regiment stopped a lynching, see *Hawes v. The State*, 88 *Alabama Reports* (1889), 37–73, especially 53; see also *Birmingham Evening News*, 10 December 1888, which contains Jones' warning to rioters. Jones sponsored a "Riot Act" in the legislature. McMillan, "Thomas Goode Jones, 1844–1914," 379. For one such act sponsored by Jones, see *Acts of Alabama* (1884–1885), 143–44. For the decade's main anti-riot legislation, passed after Jones left the legislature, see *Acts of Alabama* (1888–1889), 99–102.

35. On these themes, see Bertram Wyatt-Brown, *Southern Honor: Ethics and Behavior in the Old South*.

36. See Eugene Genovese, *The World the Slaveholders Made*, 99–102.

37. Friedman, *A History of American Law*, 632–54; and Samuel Haber, *The Quest for Authority and Honor in the American Professions, 1750–1900* (Chicago: University of Chicago Press, 1991), 206–39.

38. William G. Thomas, *Lawyering for the Railroad: Business, Law, and Power in the New South* (Baton Rouge: Louisiana State University Press, 1999), 39–44.

39. Jones, *Last Days of the Army of Northern Virginia*, 45.

40. DuBose, "Historian's Tribute," 61–62.

41. Jones, *Resolutions and Address of Judge Thomas G. Jones, in Memory of Gen'l John B. Gordon*, 12.

42. William Warren Rogers et al., *Alabama: The History of a Deep South State* (Tuscaloosa: University of Alabama Press, 1994), 259–64.

43. Jones made these points in his first gubernatorial address. See *Journal of the Senate of the State of Alabama* (1890–1891), 177–78.

44. These are passages from a speech Jones delivered to the Alabama Constitutional Convention of 1901; see *Official Proceedings of the Constitutional Convention of the State of Alabama, May 21st, 1901, to September 3rd, 1901* (Wetumpka, Alabama: Wetumpka Printing Company, 1940), 4: 4303–4304.

45. For a discussion of New South paternalism, see George M. Fredrickson, *The Black Image in the White Mind: The Debate on Afro-American Character and Destiny, 1817–1914* (1971; repr. Middletown, Connecticut: Wesleyan University Press, 1987), 198–227.

46. Haber, *Quest for Authority and Honor*, 206–209. For comparisons of Jones'

work with those of contemporary legal ethicists (such as David Hoffman and George Sharswood), see Carol Rice Andrews, "The Lasting Legacy of the 1887 Code of Ethics of the Alabama State Bar Association," in *Gilded Age Legal Ethics: Essays on Thomas Goode Jones' 1887 Code and the Regulation of the Profession*, ed. Carol Rice Andrews, Paul M. Pruitt Jr., and David I. Durham (Tuscaloosa: University of Alabama School of Law, 2003), 9–25. For a slightly earlier Alabama view, see Wade Keyes, "Introductory Lecture, Delivered March 1860, Before the Class of the Montgomery Law School," in *Wade Keyes' Introductory Lecture to the Montgomery Law School: Legal Education in Mid-Nineteenth Century Alabama*, ed. David I. Durham and Paul M. Pruitt Jr. (Tuscaloosa: University of Alabama School of Law, 2001), 29–32.

47. DuBose, "Historian's Tribute," 61. Jones, like his mentor General Gordon, participated in the "ring tournament" revival of the late 1860s and 1870s. These contests, inspired by Sir Walter Scott's *Ivanhoe* and similar works of romantic medievalism, were intended to promote chivalry; after the war, they sometimes promoted sectional reconciliation. Jones delivered the "charge to the knights" at an 1870 tournament in Winchester, Virginia. See Esther J. Crooks and Ruth W. Crooks, *The Ring Tournament in the United States* (Richmond: Garrett and Massie, 1936), 3, 42–48, 87, 100–105.

48. A. A. Wiley, "Samuel F. Rice," 88 *Alabama Reports* (1890), ix–xii (quoted passage on xi).

49. *Report of the Organization and of the First, Second, and Third Annual Meetings*, 227–35.

50. See *Hamlet*, act 3, scene 1, line 72.

51. For brief discussions of pleading under Alabama's 1852 Code, see Pruitt, "Life and Times of Legal Education," 289–90. For subsequent rules of pleading, see Tony A. Freyer and Paul M. Pruitt Jr., "Reaction and Reform: Transforming the Judiciary under Alabama's Constitution, 1901–1975," *Alabama Law Review*, 53 (Fall 2001), 96–97.

52. *Report of the Organization and of the First, Second, and Third Annual Meetings*, 226–27 (quoted passage on 227), 236–41. Courtroom criticism of opposing lawyers was so common that Mark Twain could write (of a mock trial held in 1867) that "The opposing counsel were eloquent, argumentative, and vindictively abusive of each other, as was characteristic and proper." See Mark Twain, *The Innocents Abroad, Or The New Pilgrim's Progress* (1869; repr. New York: Signet Classics, 1966), 35.

53. Friedman, *History of American Law*, 467–87; and James W. Ely, *Railroads and American Law* (Lawrence: University Press of Kansas, 2002).

54. For a discussion of the early "plaintiffs' personal injury bar," see Edward A. Purcell Jr., *Litigation and Inequality: Federal Diversity Jurisdiction in Industrial America, 1870–1958* (New York: Oxford University Press, 1992), 150–54.

55. Thomas, *Lawyering for the Railroad*, 35–36; *Code of Ethics, Adopted by the Alabama State Bar Association, Dec. 14, 1887* (Montgomery: Brown Printing Company, 1887), ix (number 20).

56. *Code of Ethics, Adopted by the Alabama State Bar Association, Dec. 14, 1887*, ix (no. 20).

57. See Robert W. Gordon, "'The Ideal and the Actual in the Law': Fantasies and

Practices of New York City Lawyers, 1870–1910," in *The New High Priests: Lawyers in Post-Civil War America,* ed. Gerald W. Gawal (Westport: Greenwood Press, 1984), 51–74; and Thomas, *Lawyering for the Railroad,* 33–39.

58. [W. T. Sheehan], *Judge Jones and the Railroad Question: From the Montgomery Advertiser* (Montgomery: N.p., circa 1907), 3–4. The L&N was also upset with the Montgomery city government over its quarantine policy during the yellow fever epidemic of 1878—specifically over its refusal to allow refugee-bearing trains to unload in town. See Wayne Cline, *Alabama Railroads* (Tuscaloosa: University of Alabama Press, 1997), 115; and Maury Klein, *History of the Louisville and Nashville Railroad* (New York: Macmillan Company, 1972), 232–33. Jones supported the absolute power of governments to impose such bans on commerce. Jones, "Some Observations on the Law of Quarantine," 161–75.

59. [Sheehan], *Judge Jones and the Railroad Question,* 4.

60. Jones to Hilary A. Herbert, 27 January 1887, 6 February 1887, Letterbook, 1886–1889, (leaves 31–32, 46–48), Jones Collection.

61. Aucoin, "Thomas Goode Jones, Redeemer and Reformer," 65–66. For Alabama's ban on imprisonment for debt, see *Constitution of the State of Alabama,* 1875, Article I, section 21. The Wiley bill was sponsored by Ariosto A. Wiley, Jones' former law partner. See also *Journal of the House of Representatives of the State of Alabama* (1884–1885), 5, 862.

62. *Montgomery Daily Advertiser,* 24 March 1892, quoted in Aucoin, "Thomas Goode Jones, Redeemer and Reformer," 66–67.

63. On this point see Oliver Wendell Holmes Jr., *The Common Law* (1881; repr. New York: Dover Publications, 1991), 1. Holmes famously notes that "The Life of the Law has not been logic: it has been experience. The felt necessities of the time, the prevalent moral and political theories, intuitions of public policy . . . even the prejudices which judges share with their fellow-men, have had a good deal more to do than the syllogism in determining the rules by which men should be governed." See also Louis Menand, *The Metaphysical Club: A Story of Ideas in America* (New York: Farrar, Straus, and Giroux, 2001), 339–47.

64. Paul M. Gaston, *The New South Creed: A Study in Southern Myth-Making* (New York: Alfred A. Knopf, 1970), especially 119–50.

65. *Code of Ethics, Adopted by the Alabama State Bar Association, Dec. 14, 1887,* iii–xvi. Among many possible extracts from the 1887 code, consider two. First, from Rule 27: "An attorney is under no obligation to minister to the malevolence or prejudices of a client in the trial or conduct of a cause. The client can not be made the keeper of the attorney's conscience in professional matters." Next, Rule 57: "An attorney assigned as counsel for an indigent prisoner ought not ask to be excused for any light cause, and should always be a friend to the defenseless and oppressed." Generally see Andrews et al., *Gilded Age Legal Ethics.*

66. *Report of the Organization and of the First, Second, and Third Annual Meetings,* 235–36.

67. For overviews of Jones' gubernatorial years, see Pruitt, "Thomas Goode Jones"; and Huggins, "Bourbonism and Radicalism."

68. Rogers, *One-Gallused Rebellion,* 165–216 (quoted passage on 208). Kolb was a

hero of Alabama's small farmers, most of whom were members of the officially non-partisan "Farmers' Alliance." Convinced that he was unjustly denied the Democratic gubernatorial nomination in 1892, Kolb bolted the party and founded a short-lived, Alliance-based "Jeffersonian Democratic" party. He soon secured the endorsement of other opposition groups, including radical agrarians led by the Populists "Evangel" Joseph C. Manning and opportunistic Republicans.

69. Ibid., 221–26, 255. See also Chappel Cory to Jones, 14 August 14 1892; Tennent Lomax to Jones, 18 October 1892; and Milton H. Smith to Jones, 16 February 1893, Jones Collection. Officially, Jones won by a vote of 126,959 to 115,524.

70. Rogers, *One-Gallused Rebellion*, 236–40. The Sayre Act eliminated party symbols from ballots and specified an alphabetical listing of candidates. Under this law voters were required to enter a booth where only polling officials could assist them. The Sayre Act assured that Kolb, who ran as a Jeffersonian Democrat in 1894, would lose again. See ibid., 271–92.

71. For Jones' concern over white solidarity, see his 1890 inaugural address, *Journal of the Senate of the State of Alabama* (1890–1891), 179–80. At the same time Jones "dismissed talk of calling a constitutional convention to disfranchise African Americans"; see Aucoin, *Rift in the Clouds*, 54. By 1892, Jones was willing to endorse constitutional change, at least to the extent of an educational qualification; *Journal of the Senate of the State of Alabama* (1892–1893), 45, cited in McMillan, *Constitutional Development in Alabama*, 249.

72. C. Vann Woodward, *Origins of the New South, 1877–1913* (Baton Rouge: Louisiana State University Press, 1951), 321–49; and Edward L. Ayers, *The Promise of the New South: Life After Reconstruction, 1877–1906* (New York: Oxford University Press, 1992), 304–309. See also Wechsler, "Black and White Disenfranchisement," 25–29. For case law, see *Williams v. Mississippi,* 170 *United States Reports* (1898), 213. For earlier, related precedents, see *United States v. Cruikshank,* 92 *United States Reports* (1876), 542; the *Civil Rights Cases,* 109 *United States Reports* (1883), 3; and *Plessy v. Ferguson,* 163 *United States Reports* (1896), 537.

73. McMillan, *Constitutional Development in Alabama,* 229–62, 305. See also Wechsler, "Black and White Disenfranchisement," 39–41.

74. For Jones' persistent efforts to prevent lynching by means of both legislation and investigation, see Aucoin, "Thomas Goode Jones, Redeemer and Reformer," 48–54. Jones was one of several Alabama leaders opposed to the convict lease system, which had been rooted in the industrial life of the state since the 1860s. Jones and his allies nearly abolished the system in 1893, via an act that allowed the state to improve its own prison facilities and acquire farmland with a view to making prisons self-supporting. The plan was to transfer all prisoners from private confinement (typically in coal mines) by January 1895, but the Panic of 1894 caused such a decline in state revenue that William C. Oates, Jones' successor, persuaded the legislature to repeal the reform legislation. See ibid., 11–23. Generally, see Allen Johnson Going, *Bourbon Democracy in Alabama, 1874–1890, with a New Foreword by the Author* (1951; repr. Tuscaloosa: University of Alabama Press, 1992), 170–90; and Curtin, *Black Prisoners and Their World.*

75. *Journal of the Senate of the State of Alabama* (1890–1891), 175–79; Aucoin, "Thomas

Goode Jones, Redeemer and Reformer," 24–33; and see also Going, *Bourbon Democracy*, 158–61.

76. Jones' argument was somewhat diluted by an 1891 law that allowed superintendents of education in Black Belt counties discretion over spending; former laws had required equal apportionment per capita, regardless of race. Thereafter black schools were starved for funds. For this law, and for Jones' role in persuading black leaders that it would cause no harm, see Horace Mann Bond, *Negro Education in Alabama: A Study in Cotton and Steel* (1969; repr. Tuscaloosa: University of Alabama Press, 1994), 155–63.

77. By 1901 Jones was no longer thinking of himself as a leader in the mainline Democratic Party. During the gubernatorial term of his successor, William C. Oates, the Alabama Democratic Party had fallen under the influence of the "free silver" inflationist William Jennings Bryan of Nebraska. In Alabama, Bryan's supporter Joseph Forney Johnston (elected governor in 1896) had garnered a considerable number of former Populist votes. In the presidential election of that year, Jones had supported a bolting ticket of "Gold Democrats," not Bryan. See Rogers, *One-Gallused Rebellion*, 320, 325–26.

78. McMillan, *Constitutional Development in Alabama*, 305, 324.

79. For Jones' July 25 speech on suffrage, see *Official Proceedings of the Constitutional Convention*, 3:2886–96. See also McMillan, *Constitutional Development*, 292–94.

80. *Official Proceedings of the Constitutional Convention*, 2:2584–87. For a perceptive discussion of suffrage limitation in Alabama, see Robert Volney Riser II, "Prelude to the Movement: Disfranchisement in Alabama's 1901 Constitution and the Anti-Disfranchisement Cases" (PhD dissertation, University of Alabama, 2005), 219–348, especially 293–98 (for the "Episode" as the Knox-Jones shouting match on July 20 came to be known). The only scholarly explicator of this near brawl, Riser points out the astonishing fact that Jones drew a pocketknife to defend himself from forcible removal.

81. McMillan, *Constitutional Development in Alabama*, 283–309, especially 306; McMillan noted that the 1901 constitution's suffrage article was the "most intricate" yet adopted, with a "temporary plan" featuring "the newly invented soldier and fighting grandfather clauses," and a "permanent plan" that included "educational, property, and employment qualifications as well as the disfranchising crimes section and the poll tax." See also Wechsler, "Black and White Disenfranchisement," 35–39, 43–52.

82. Ibid., 350. The current discussion assumes that Black Belt election fraud was a vital factor in the ratification of the 1901 constitution, and that white opinion in the northern counties was divided. Glenn Feldman makes the case for racism as an ingrained and unifying tendency of white voters. Glenn Feldman, *The Disfranchisement Myth: Poor Whites and Suffrage Restriction in Alabama* (Athens: University of Georgia Press, 2004).

83. Jones to Booker T. Washington, 20 September 1901, in Harlan et al., *Booker T. Washington Papers*, vol. 6 (1977), 213. Washington wrote back in a tactful vein. His chief worry, he said, was whether the new constitution would be enforced fairly; see Booker T. Washington to Jones, 23 September 1901, ibid., 215–16. See also McMillan, *Constitutional Development in Alabama*, 302–304, 341.

84. See Freyer and Dixon, *Democracy and Judicial Independence*, 68; and Aucoin, *Rift in the Clouds*, 129–30, 147.

85. Jones sat as the trial judge in *Giles v. Harris*, a challenge to the 1901 constitution; see 189 *United States Reports* (1903), 475–504. He dismissed the petitioner's case on the grounds that his court lacked jurisdiction but certified Giles' appeal so the case could go before the U.S. Supreme Court. For the machinations in this case and for Booker T. Washington's schemes of litigation, see Riser, "Prelude to the Movement," 442–79. See also Wechsler, "Black and White Disenfranchisement," 56–57.

86. Daniel, *Shadow of Slavery*, 43–64; Freyer and Dixon, *Democracy and Judicial Independence*, 117–20; Aucoin, *Rift in the Clouds*, 58–61. See Jones' grand jury charge in the *Peonage Cases*, 123 *Federal Reporter* 671–92 (1903).

87. Daniel, *Shadow of Slavery*, 63–81; Freyer and Dixon, *Democracy and Judicial Independence*, 121–22; Aucoin, *Rift in the Clouds*, 62–64; and *Bailey v. Alabama*, 219 *United States Reports* 219–50 (1911). Jones had already declared Alabama's 1901 labor law to be unconstitutional, in that it sought to forbid laborers from breaking contracts without the permission of their employers, thus subjecting the former to a virtual state of serfdom; see *Peonage Cases*, 123 *Federal Reporter* 684–92.

88. For a full account of these events, see Aucoin, *Rift in the Clouds*, 64–72. As Jones sorted out his ideas, he was in contact with a number of judges and other legal officials, including Judge David Shelby of the Fifth Circuit Court of Appeals and Judge Jacob Trieber of the Eastern District of Arkansas. Trieber was thinking along similar lines. See his opinion in *United States v. Morris*, 125 *Federal Reporter* 322–31 (1903).

89. *Hodges v. United States*, 203 *United States Reports*, 1–38 (1906).

90. Aucoin, *Rift in the Clouds*, 72–79 (quoted passage on 78). For Jones' argument at length, see *Ex Parte Riggins*, 134 *Federal Reporter* 404–23 (1904), and *United States v. Powell*, 151 *Federal Reporter* 648–64 (1907). See also Thomas Goode Jones, "Has the Citizen of the United States, in the Custody of the State's Officers, Upon Accusation of Crime Against Its Laws, Any Immunity or Right Which May Be Protected by the United States Against Mob Violence?" *Proceedings of the Twenty-Eighth Annual Meeting of the Alabama State Bar Association* (Montgomery: Woodruff Co., 1905), 200–35.

91. See generally James F. Doster, *Railroads in Alabama Politics, 1875–1914* (University: University of Alabama Press, 1957), 102–225.

92. *Journal of the Senate of the State of Alabama* (1911), 64–67.

93. *Birmingham Age-Herald*, 12 March 1911.

94. Ibid.

# Chapter 6

1. Malcolm C. McMillan, *Constitutional Development in Alabama*, 283–339, 350.

2. See generally Rogers, *One-Gallused Rebellion*; and Samuel L. Webb, *Two-Party Politics in the One-Party South: Alabama's Hill Country, 1874–1920* (Tuscaloosa: University of Alabama Press, 1997).

3. For ratification, see McMillan, *Constitutional Development in Alabama*, 340–59. For analysis of convention personnel, Democratic tactics and strategy, and the process of ratification, see Hackney, *Populism to Progressivism in Alabama*, 175–229 (quoted passage on 179); and Riser, "Prelude to the Movement," 216–413. On regional disfranchisement, see C. Vann Woodward, *Origins of the New South* (Baton Rouge: Louisiana State University Press, 1951), 321–49. For Joseph Manning's post-ratification views, see his *Letting the South Alone: Class Government that Defrauds Whites and Blacks* (Birmingham: N.p., 1903), 6–7, 9. For Manning's retrospective summary, see Joseph Columbus Manning, *The Fadeout of Populism: Pot and Kettle in Combat* (New York: T. A. Hebbons, 1928), 49–50. One Black Belt statistic can tell the story of the 1901 constitution's ratification. Dallas County, with a voting-age male population of 2,525 whites and 9,871 blacks, voted for the new constitution by a count of 8,125 to 235.

4. Booker T. Washington, *Up from Slavery: An Autobiography* (New York: Doubleday, Page & Co., 1901).

5. See Chapter Five of this volume, in which Jones attempts to persuade Washington that disfranchisement will be a blessing in disguise for African Americans. It is interesting, though, that Jones' reformist work in the area of race relations dates from the period after 1901.

6. For child labor issues in the post-1901 era, see Paul M. Pruitt Jr., "Suffer the Children: Child Labor Reform in Alabama," *Alabama Heritage* 58 (Fall 2000), 16–27.

7. Feldman's *Disfranchisement Myth* argues the staying power of racism in turn-of-the-century politics. For the classic version, see Ulrich Bonnell Phillips, "The Central Theme of Southern History," in *The Course of the South to Secession*, ed. E. Merton Coulter (New York: Hill and Wang, 1939), 151–65.

8. For the crop lien and sharecropping system (most common in the hill country and Black Belt, respectively), see Woodward, *Origins of the New South*, 180–84; and Edward L. Ayers, *The Promise of the New South: Life After Reconstruction* (New York: Oxford University Press, 1992), 92–95, 252–53.

9. Joseph C. Manning, *The Rise and Reign of the Bourbon Oligarchy* (Birmingham: Roberts and Son, 1904), 18–21. On southern racial demagoguery, see W. J. Cash, *The Mind of the South* (1941; repr. New York: Vintage Books, 1969), 252–63; and C. Vann Woodward, *The Strange Career of Jim Crow*, 2nd rev. ed.(New York: Oxford University Press, 1969), 67–109.

10. See Going, *Bourbon Democracy in Alabama*, 41–60; and generally, Harold R. Hyman, *The Anti-Redeemers: Hill-Country Dissenters in the Lower South from Redemption to Populism* (Baton Rouge: Louisiana State University Press, 1990).

11. The previous four paragraphs are based on several books, including Lawrence Goodwyn, *Democratic Promise: The Populist Moment in America* (New York: Oxford University Press, 1976); Stephen Hahn, *The Roots of Southern Populism: Yeoman Farmers and the Transformation of the Georgia Upcountry, 1850–1890* (New York: Oxford University Press, 1983); and Rogers, *One-Gallused Rebellion*, 138 (quoted statistic). A recent (and persuasive) Alabama historian on these developments is Samuel L. Webb; see his *Two-Party Politics in the One-Party South*.

12. Paul M. Pruitt Jr. "Joseph C. Manning, Alabama Populist: A Rebel Against the Solid South" (PhD dissertation, College of William and Mary, 1980), 9–31.

13. Rogers, *One-Gallused Rebellion*, 188–222; Pruitt, "Joseph C. Manning, Alabama Populist," 66–108.

14. For election statistics and for discussion of the 1893 Sayre Act, a voting regulation law that was a precursor of the 1901 constitution, see Rogers, *One-Gallused Rebellion*, 221–27, 236–40, 272–86.

15. Ibid., 229–35, 241–44, 271–92; Paul M. Pruitt Jr., "A Changing of the Guard: Joseph C. Manning and Populist Strategy in the Fall of 1894," *Alabama Historical Quarterly*, 40 (Spring and Summer 1978), 20–36; and Pruitt, "Joseph C. Manning, Alabama Populist," 120–25, 156–205, 267–307.

16. Joseph C. Manning, *From Five to Twenty-Five, His Earlier Life as Recalled by Joseph Columbus Manning* (New York: T.A. Hebbons, 1929), 38–39. Manning recollected that he "encouraged to the front hundreds of country orators who sprang up amazingly, many of them with the guts and gizzard . . . to make it mighty disconcerting for the old-time local Democratic Party leaders."

17. For Manning's fund-raising among the Bimetallists, see Pruitt, "Joseph C. Manning, Alabama Populist," 125–31. For the Southern Ballot Rights League, see ibid., 235–47. See also ibid., 324–26. Many advocates of Alabama's 1901 constitution would use the argument that disfranchisement would purify politics; it was a well-spun version of the rationale behind Alabama's 1893 Sayre Act. See Chapter Five of this volume.

18. Pruitt, "Joseph C. Manning, Alabama Populist," 327–37.

19. Louis T. Harlan et al., eds., *The Booker T. Washington Papers*, vol. 4, (Urbana: University of Illinois Press, 1975), 285–86n1.

20. Pruitt, "Joseph C. Manning, Alabama Populist," 282–83, 326, 348–50.

21. Ibid., 351–53.

22. Ibid., 353–55.

23. *Alexander City Outlook*, 12 and 26 May 1899, quoted in Pruitt, "Joseph C. Manning, Alabama Populist," 356–57.

24. Hackney, *Populism to Progressivism in Alabama*, 170–73.

25. *Dadeville Free Press*, 3 October 1901.

26. *Alexander City Outlook*, 1 and 15 November 1901.

27. Joseph C. Manning to Senator W. E. Chandler, 28 September 1900, 24 and 27 November 1900, 13, 14, 15, and 24 December 1900, in the William E. Chandler Papers, Library of Congress (hereinafter Chandler Papers, LC) cited in Pruitt, "Joseph C. Manning, Alabama Populist," 355–56; see also the *Alexander City Outlook*, 5, 12, and 26 October 1900, 14 and 21 December 1900, 5 April 1901. Senator Morgan was well aware that his seat would have been in jeopardy had Manning's strategy (of congressional investigations) succeeded.

28. *Alexander City Outlook*, 17 October 1902.

29. *The Washington, D.C., Times*, 30 November 1901, quoted in the *Alexander City Outlook*, 17 October 1902.

30. Joseph C. Manning to Senator W. E. Chandler, 5 October 1901, Chandler Papers, LC. Jones' appointment, and the power displayed by Washington in securing it, intrigued perceptive political observers. Jones' appointment was decided on September 29, just prior to the furor over Washington's "dinner at the White House." See

Robert J. Norrell, *Up from History: The Life of Booker T. Washington* (Cambridge: Harvard University Press, 2009), 242–55.

31. Webb, *Two-Party Politics in the One-Party South*, 16.

32. Manning's story was that he and Montgomery lawyer Charles Scott had worked before the August meeting to form a statewide Republican Club on behalf of Roosevelt—membership open to all. Ironically, it appears that all who met in the hotel room with Manning were white. For slightly differing versions of the Montgomery fracas, see Pruitt, "Joseph C. Manning, Alabama Populist," 366–67; Webb, *Two-Party Politics in a One-Party State*, 20–23; Richard Sherman, *The Republican Party and Black America from McKinley to Hoover, 1896–1933* (Charlottesville: University Press of Virginia, 1973), 34–37; Louis T. Harlan, *Booker T. Washington: The Wizard of Tuskegee, 1901–1915* (New York: Oxford University Press, 1983), 8–9; and Norrell, *Up from Slavery*, 255.

33. It should be noted that in May 1908, Booker T. Washington circulated an editorial in which he accused Manning of supporting a "Lily White" faction of Alabama Republicans; by this time, Manning opposed the faction headed by Washington's friend James O. Thompson; see Booker T. Washington to Frederick Randolph Moore, 6 May 1908, in Harlan et al., ed., *Booker T. Washington Papers*, vol. 9 (1980): 528–29.

34. Joseph C. Manning, *Politics of Alabama* (Birmingham: J. C. Manning, 1893), 20–21.

35. J. C. Manning to Walter White, 20 December 1928, National Association for the Advancement of Colored People Papers, Library of Congress (hereinafter cited as NAACP Papers, LC). White befriended Manning during the latter's last illness, 1928–1930. The "yak-yak" was not apparent early in Manning's tenure; for articles variously praising Manning's organizing and business skills, his division of the post office into departments, and likewise the courtesy of his employees, see *Alexander City Outlook*, 11 January 1901, 8 February 1901, 5 April 1901, and 15 November 1901. By the following year, the town had a new post office, "fitted up with all the latest fixtures and conveniences"; see *Alexander City Outlook*, 24 October 1902. It is possible that Manning's regime of equal treatment began in this building.

36. *The Crisis: A Magazine of the Darker Races*, 2 (August 1911), 150; Petition by the "Undersigned Colored Citizens of Alexander City," sent to Booker T. Washington, 17 November 1904, in the Booker T. Washington Papers, Library of Congress (hereinafter cited as Washington Papers, LC).

37. J. C. Manning to Walker White, 20 December 1928, NAACP Papers, LC; see Guion Griffis Johnson, "The Ideology of White Supremacy," in *The South and the Sectional Image*, ed. Dewey Grantham (New York: N.p., 1967), 56–78.

38. *Alexander City Outlook*, 3 May 1901, 4, 20, and 27 June 1902; *Dadeville Free Press*, 24 October 1901; J. C. Manning to W. E. Chandler, 14 November 1901, William E. Chandler Papers, LC; Jennie Lee Kelley, *Alexander City Centennial, 1874–1974* (Alexander City: Alexander City Centennial Celebration Committee, 1974), part 3.

39. J. C. Manning to Walter White, 20 December 1928, NAACP Papers, LC; Manning, *Rise and Reign*, 21. For an example of legal persecutions, see *Alexander City Outlook*, 31 March 1905. For coverage of a twenty-year prison term given in 1905

to Josh Grimes of Alexander City, a "black brute" who had allegedly wrenched the arm of a little white girl, see Woodward, *Origins of the New South*, 350–55.

40. J. C. Manning to W. E. Chandler, 5 October 1901, Chandler Papers, LC; J. C. Manning to Booker T. Washington, 10 and 22 January 1905, Washington Papers, LC; J. C. Manning to Walter White, 15 and 17 December 1928, NAACP Papers, LC; Manning, *Rise and Reign*, 28. For another perspective on black Alabama Republicans in the early twentieth century, see David E. Alsobrook, "Mobile's Forgotten Progressive—A. N. Johnson, Editor and Entrepreneur," *Alabama Review*, 32 (July 1979), 188–202. For more information on Roosevelt's 1901 luncheon with Washington, see Sherman, *The Republican Party and Black America*, 27–29.

41. Washington's published papers show how he grew to distrust and dislike Manning. The latter's involvement in protests against the Roosevelt administration's handling of the Brownsville "affair" of 1907 particularly annoyed him, as did Manning's subsequent political stands. See Roscoe Conkling Simmons to Booker T. Washington, 2 October 1907, Harlan, *Booker T. Washington Papers*, vol. 9, (1980), 359–61. In a letter Washington called Manning a "discontented Alabama politician," saying that he was one of "a group of second or third rate white people who are trying to meddle into colored people's affairs and become their perpetual advisors." Booker T. Washington to Robert Russa Moton, 5 October 1907, Harlan et al., *Booker T. Washington Papers*, vol. 9, (1980), 364–65. Washington also wrote that Manning "scarcely knows a fellow before he is after his pocket book." Booker T. Washington to Samuel Laing Williams, 3 July 1909, Harlan et al., *Booker T. Washington Papers*, vol. 10, (1981), 142–43. Washington dismissed Manning as "too small and little for us to discuss." Booker T. Washington to Benjamin Franklin Riley, 27 May 1913, Harlan et al., *Booker T. Washington Papers*, vol. 12, (1983), 186–88. For Manning's reaction to the Brownsville affair—the Roosevelt administration's dismissal without trial of 160 African American soldiers in the fall of 1906—see Pruitt, "Joseph C. Manning, Alabama Populist," 382–86. For a sunnier picture of Washington as a constant (and constantly discreet) litigator for civil rights, see Riser, "Prelude to the Movement."

42. Pete Daniel, *The Shadow of Slavery: Peonage in the South, 1901–1969* (Urbana: University of Illinois Press, 1972), 43–64; see A. P. Fuquay to Booker T. Washington, 18 November 1904, Washington Papers, LC; see also J. C. Manning to W. E. Chandler, 28 November 1916, Chandler Papers, LC. For a useful summary of these events, see Norrell, *Up from History*, 299–301.

43. Manning had been building up his northern contacts even before the urgency of the peonage scandals. In April 1903, he delivered a speech before the Middlesex Club of Boston. This shrewd and fiery talk, which he subsequently printed as a pamphlet entitled *Letting the South Alone*, was limited in historical and statistical scope to the state of Alabama. By the time he wrote *Rise and Reign*, his thought embraced the whole region, and his sociological observations were more sophisticated. In addition, Manning published other pamphlets, including one in support of Republican presidential candidate Charles Evans Hughes, titled *Sectionalism: Rise and Reign of the Southern Political Oligarchy* (New York: N.p., 1916). For a selection of Manning's later newspaper articles, see the *Montgomery Colored Alabamian*, 14 March 1914, 18 September 1915, and *Washington, D.C., Bee*, May–August 1919.

44. Manning, *Rise and Reign,* 8 (quoted passage). During the latter phases of his career, Manning stayed in touch with fair-minded people, even Democratic officials. See J. C. Manning to Governor Emmet O'Neal, 11 April 1911, official Governor's Papers of Emmet O'Neal, Alabama Department of Archives and History.

45. Manning, *Rise and Reign,* 5–8, 9, 10–13, 17. Manning glosses over the Reconstruction era, a time when, he feels, the black and white masses were alienated from each other by the presence of the carpetbaggers. Even so, he has little respect for the Democratic "Redeemers." "Violence and fraud," he says, were "seemingly a pastime employed" by Democrats, whether the object was "to count out and intimidate 'Carpetbaggers' and 'niggers'" or to overrule the wishes of the white yeoman majority.

46. Ibid., 18.

47. Ibid., 12 (quoted passage), 14–16; Hackney, *Populism to Progressivism in Alabama,* 206–208; Woodward, *Origins of the New South,* 326–37.

48. Manning, *Rise and Reign,* 18–21. Manning was particularly disgusted with the racism of Mississippi governor James K. Vardaman and quoted one of his more notorious speeches: "I am just as much opposed to Booker Washington's . . . voting as I am to the voting by the cocoanut-headed, chocolate-colored, typical coon who blacks my boots." Ibid., 8. See also Sherman, *Republican Party and Black America,* 64.

49. Manning, *Rise and Reign,* 21–23. Concerning black material progress, see Henry Allen Bullock, *A History of Negro Education in the South from 1619 to the Present* (Cambridge: Harvard University Press, 1967), 191–93.

50. Manning, *Rise and Reign,* 26.

51. J. C. Manning to Booker T. Washington, 3 and 15 October 1904, Washington Papers, LC; Theodore Roosevelt to Owen Wister, 27 April 1906, in Elting E. Morison, ed., *The Letters of Theodore Roosevelt,* vol. 5, (Cambridge: Harvard University Press, 1952) 226; Sherman, *Republican Party and Black America,* 52–82.

52. *Alexander City Southern American,* 24 March 1909. This is the only known copy of Manning's newspaper. J. C. Manning to W. E. Chandler, 29 February 1908, 15 June 1908, Chandler Papers, LC; *New York Times,* 1 and 2 June 1909; and *New York Survey,* 12 June 1909; Charles Flint Kellogg, *NAACP: A History of the National Association for the Advancement of Colored People* (Baltimore: Johns Hopkins University Press, 1967), 28–45, 287n41.

53. Pruitt, "Joseph C. Manning, Alabama Populist," 400–401, 414, 415–17; Manning, *Fadeout,* 83 (quoted passage).

54. J. C. Manning to Walter White, 3, 5, 14, and 23 December 1928, NAACP Papers, LC; *New York Amsterdam News,* 21 May 1930; and *Chicago Defender,* 24 and 31 May 1930. Also see Pruitt, "Joseph C. Manning, Alabama Populist," 400–431.

# Chapter 7

1. For more on Thomas Goode Jones, see Chapter Five of this volume.

2. See Shakespeare, *Twelfth Night,* act 2, scene 5, line 157.

3. See Robert Merton, "The Unanticipated Consequences of Purposive Social Action," *American Sociological Review,* 1, no. 6 (1936), 894–904. See also Merton, *So-*

*ciological Ambivalence and Other Essays* (New York: Free Press, 1979). Clayton was more likely to have been aware of Aristotle, "Quite often good things have hurtful consequences." Aristotle, *Nicomachean Ethics* (Baltimore: Penguin, 1955), 1.3.

4. See Robert K. Murray, *Red Scare: A Study of National Hysteria* (New York: McGraw-Hill, 1964).

5. Clayton's parents were Henry Delamar Clayton and Victoria Virginia Hunter Clayton. The elder Clayton was a pre–Civil War fire-eater who ended the war with the rank of major general. He was subsequently a circuit judge (1866–1868, 1874–1886), a candidate for the Democratic gubernatorial nomination (1886), and president of The University of Alabama (1886–1889). His mother ran the plantation during wartime, subsequently authoring a book of memoirs entitled *White and Black Under the Old Regime*. See Henry James Walker Jr., "Henry Delamar Clayton: Secessionist, Soldier, Redeemer" (PhD dissertation, University of Alabama, 1995); and Owen, *History of Alabama and Dictionary of Alabama Biography*, 3:347.

6. For the Claytons' paternalistic racism, see Walker, "Henry Delamar Clayton," 144, 170–72, 205–206, 211–12. The Claytons, father and son, secured the legal guardianship of an entire black family as compensation for legal fees owed to Henry Jr. See also Victoria V. Clayton, *White and Black Under the Old Regime* (Milwaukee: The Young Churchman Co., 1899), 84, 124–32, 144–47, 152–53, 158–65, and 184–87.

7. Owen, *History of Alabama and Dictionary of Alabama Biography*, 3:348; and Albert B. Moore, *History of Alabama and Her People* (Chicago: American Historical Society, 1927), 3:65–67. In addition to the offices he held, Clayton was a presidential elector in 1888 and 1892, and served on the Democratic National Committee from 1888 to 1908.

8. Henry D. Clayton to Lee J. Clayton, 4 September 1918, in the Henry D. Clayton Papers, Hoole Special Collections Library, University of Alabama (hereafter Clayton Papers). For Clayton's pre-judicial background and views, see Richard Polenberg, "Progressivism and Anarchism: Judge Henry D. Clayton and the Abrams Trial," *Law and History Review*, 3 (Fall 1985), 398–401; and Richard Polenberg, *Fighting Faiths: The Abrams Case, the Supreme Court, and Free Speech* (New York: Viking, 1987), 95–99. It should be noted that Clayton had no children of his own and, for much of his career, no wife. In 1882 he had married Virginia Ball Allen from Montgomery, but she died the following year. Clayton was a widower until 1910, when he married Bettie Davis of Georgetown, Kentucky. See Moore, *History of Alabama and Her People* 3:67.

9. Walker, "Henry Delamar Clayton," 171–72, 174; and Clayton, *White and Black Under the Old Regime*, 162.

10. Walker, "Henry Delamar Clayton," 171, 183–90; and see Rogers et al., *Alabama: The History of a Deep South State*, 259–68.

11. Rogers, *One-Gallused Rebellion*, 165–335. The chief insurgent was another Barbour County politician, Reuben F. Kolb, leader of the political wing of the Farmers' Alliance and subsequently a Jeffersonian Democrat; see chapters Five and Six of this volume). Clayton Jr. had worked for Kolb in 1890. See Walker, "Henry Delamar Clayton," 223; and Rogers, *One-Gallused Rebellion*, 181.

12. For the background to the constitution of 1901, the most accessible survey is

in Rogers et al., *Alabama: The History of a Deep South State*, 344–54. For recent approaches to the subject, see Riser, "Prelude to the Movement"; and Feldman, *The Disfranchisement Myth*.

13. McMillan, *Constitutional Development in Alabama*, 342, 349; and Evans C. Johnson, *Oscar W. Underwood: A Political Biography* (Baton Rouge: Louisiana State University Press, 1980), 70–71.

14. Rogers et al., *Alabama: The History of a Deep South State*, 351–54; McMillan, *Constitutional Development in Alabama*, 354–56, 364.

15. For a persuasive argument that the Republican Party, invigorated in several north and central Alabama counties by coalitions with Populists, remained a viable force, see Webb, *Two-Party Politics in the One-Party South*, 152–54, 155–84, 185–212.

16. Rogers, *One-Gallused Rebellion*, 302–304, 314–16, 319–26; and Rogers et al., *Alabama: The History of a Deep South State*, 370–75. For Democratic inflationism and Bryan's presidential candidacy, see Elizabeth Sanders, *Farmers, Workers, and the American State, 1877–1917* (Chicago: University of Chicago Press, 1999), 101–47. For an account written with the benefit of hindsight, see Oscar W. Underwood, *Drifting Sands of Party Politics* (New York: Century Company, 1931), 241–321, especially 256–72.

17. These congressmen were (in alphabetical order) John Lawson Burnett, first elected to Congress in 1898, who served more than ten terms; Henry Delamar Clayton, first elected to Congress in 1896, who served more than eight terms; James Thomas Heflin, first elected to Congress in 1904, who served more than eight terms; William Richardson, first elected to Congress in 1900, who served more than seven terms; George Washington Taylor, first elected in 1896, who served nine terms; and Oscar Wilder Underwood, who was first elected to Congress in 1894, was successfully challenged after a year in office, then reelected in 1896, after which he would serve nine terms. Underwood and Heflin each represented Alabama in the U.S. Senate (1915–1927 and 1920–1931, respectively). Owen, *History of Alabama and Dictionary of Alabama Biography*, 1:344–46, 3:262–63, 347–48, 783; and 4:1438, 1649, and 1698–1701; Thomas M. Owen, *Alabama Official and Statistical Register 1913* (Montgomery: Brown Printing Company, 1913), 44–46; and *Biographical Directory of the United States Congress, 1774–1989* (Washington, D.C.: Government Printing Office, 1989), 709, 790, 1166, 1715, 1915, and 1967.

18. David Alan Harris, "Braxton Bragg Comer," in *Alabama Governors: A Political History of the State*, 150–56; Rogers et al., *Alabama: The History of a Deep South State*, 355–75; Sheldon Hackney, *Populism to Progressivism in Alabama*, 248–323; Owen, *History of Alabama and Dictionary of Alabama Biography*, 3:384–88; and Wayne Flynt, *Alabama in the Twentieth Century* (Tuscaloosa: University of Alabama Press, 2004), 37–57.

19. For Underwood see Johnson, *Oscar W. Underwood*, 81, 88, 91–92, 97–101, and 105. On Democratic factionalism, see Samuel L. Webb, "Hugo Black, Bibb Graves, and the Ku Klux Klan: A Revisionist View of the 1926 Alabama Democratic Primary," *Alabama Review*, 57 (October 2004), 249–55.

20. See Sanders, *Roots of Reform*, 3–4, 7–8, 173–77.

21. On Jefferson, see Underwood, *Drifting Sands of Party Politics*, 83, 84–90, 92–

93. For the continued impact of Jacksonian ideology on politics in Alabama, see J. Mills Thornton III, "Hugo Black and the Golden Age," *Alabama Law Review*, 36 (Spring 1985), 899–913; Samuel L. Webb, "A Jacksonian in Postbellum Alabama: The Ideology and Influence of Journalist Robert McKee, 1869–1896," *Journal of Southern History*, 62 (May 1996), 241–42, 269; and Webb, *Two-Party Politics*.

22. Sanders, *Roots of Reform*, 8–9, 197–200, 275–78; Arthur S. Link, *Woodrow Wilson and the Progressive Era, 1910–1917* (New York: Harper and Brothers, 1954), 6–24; and Nancy Cohen, *The Reconstruction of American Liberalism, 1865–1914* (Chapel Hill: University of North Carolina Press, 2002), 217–56.

23. Karl Rodabaugh, "Congressman Henry D. Clayton, Patriarch in Politics: A Southern Congressman During the Progressive Era," *Alabama Review*, 31 (April 1978), 110–20 (quoted passage on 111).

24. *Biographical Directory of the United States Congress, 1774–1989*, 709. Burnett was three times chairman of the Committee on Immigration and Naturalization. See John Higham, *Strangers in the Land: Patterns of American Nativism, 1860–1925* (New York: Atheneum, 1975), 191.

25. *Biographical Directory of the United States Congress, 1774–1989*, 1166; and R. M. Tanner, "James Thomas Heflin: United States Senator, 1920–1931" (PhD dissertation, University of Alabama, 1967), 10–20.

26. *Biographical Directory of the United States Congress, 1774–1989*, 1195–96; Johnson, *Oscar W. Underwood*, 228–29; and Richard N. Sheldon, "Richmond Pearson Hobson as a Progressive Reformer," *Alabama Review*, 25 (October 1972), 243–61.

27. *Biographical Directory of the United States Congress, 1774–1989*, 1967; Johnson, *Oscar W. Underwood*, 28, 30–32, 39–40, 83–84, 124–25, 135–36, 157, 195–96, 200–201, 225, 231, 252–53, 307–308; and Underwood, *Drifting Sands of Party Politics*, 112–17, 124–71, 171–84, 185–238.

28. The Clayton Antitrust Act is not a major topic of this essay, though the component measures as Clayton drafted them are a model of Wilsonian "New Freedom" reform. Generally, see Link, *Woodrow Wilson and the Progressive Era*, 68–70; and Sanders, *Roots of Reform*, 282–89, 344. See also Karl Louis Rodabaugh, "Congressman Henry D. Clayton and the Dothan Post Office Fight: Patronage and Politics in the Progressive Era," *Alabama Review*, 33 (April 1980), 148–49.

29. For Clayton in action as a federal attorney, see *Powell v. United States*, 60 *Federal Reporter* 687 (1894).

30. Jonathan Turley, "Senate Trials and Factional Disputes: Impeachment as a Madisonian Device," *Duke Law Journal*, 49 (October 1999), 63–64; and Kermit L. Hall and Eric W. Rise, *From Local Courts to National Tribunals: The Federal District Courts of Florida, 1812–1990* (Brooklyn: Carlson Publishing, 1991), 54–56. Swayne's case was complex, but Democratic partisanship played a role in his impeachment. The charges against him centered upon his absenteeism and alleged misuse of funds. Swayne had been the trial judge in the Clyatt case (1902), a peonage prosecution. See Daniel, *Shadow of Slavery*, 8.

31. Turley, "Senate Trials and Factional Disputes," 65. Archbald was removed in January 1913.

32. For the development of a climate favorable to reining in judges, see Stephen N.

Subrin, "How Equity Conquered Common Law: The Federal Rules of Procedure in Historical Perspective," *University of Pennsylvania Law Review* (April 1987) 950, 952, 955; Peter Graham Fish, *The Politics of Federal Judicial Administration* (Princeton, New Jersey: Princeton University Press, 1973), 17–18; and William Howard Taft, *Popular Government: Its Essence, Its Permanence and Its Perils* (New Haven, Connecticut: Yale University Press, 1913), 168–85.

33. Henry D. Clayton, "Popularizing Administration of Justice," *American Bar Association Journal*, 8 (1922), 44.

34. The first fruit of this movement was New York's 1848 Field Code, which abolished the distinction between law and equity, and launched the "civil action." See Friedman, *History of American Law*, 391–411.

35. For statistics on early twentieth-century state dockets in Alabama, see Tony A. Freyer and Paul M. Pruitt Jr., "Reaction and Reform: Transforming the Judiciary Under Alabama's Constitution, 1901–1975," *Alabama Law Review*, 53 (Fall 2001), 96–99.

36. See Alabama Chief Justice George W. Stone's address on "Judicial Reform," in *Proceedings of the Twelfth Annual Meeting of the Alabama State Bar Association, Held in the Court-House at Huntsville, Alabama, July 31, and August 1, 1889* (Montgomery: Brown Printing Company, 1890), 108–21; and Freyer and Pruitt, "Reaction and Reform," 96–99.

37. *17 Statutes at Large* (1872), 197. On the issue of federal rulemaking, see Tony Allan Freyer, *Harmony and Dissonance: The Swift and Erie Cases in American Federalism* (New York: New York University Press, 1981).

38. Erwin Surrency, *History of the Federal Courts* (New York: Oceana Publications, 1987), 138–41.

39. Subrin, "How Equity Conquered the Common Law," 944–56; Fish, *Politics of Federal Judicial Administration*, 18–24; Clayton, "Popularizing Administration of Justice," 44, 47–48; and Taft, *Popular Government*, 182–83. The formal name of the Committee of Fifteen was the Special Committee to Suggest Remedies and Formulate Proposed Laws to Prevent Delays and Unnecessary Costs in Litigation.

40. Subrin, "How Equity Conquered the Common Law," 955; and *House of Representative Report No. 462, 63rd Congress, 2d Session* (1914), cited in Charles E. Clark and James W. Moore, "A New Federal Civil Procedure," *Yale Law Journal*, 44 (January 1935), 389, 389n10. For Clayton's views, see his "Popularizing Administration of Justice," 47–51; see also Clayton to Joseph H. Choate Jr., 21 September 1921; and Clayton to Thomas J. Walsh, 26 May 1926, Clayton Papers.

41. See *Report of the Thirty-Fifth Annual Meeting of the American Bar Association* (Baltimore: The Lord Baltimore Press, 1912), 557–66 (or 37 A.B.A. Rep. 557–566).

42. The "Technical Error" act, for example, was not passed until 1919; 40 *Stat.* 1181. The passage of the Enabling Act was delayed until 1934; 48 *Stat.* 1064. By 1938, when the Federal Rules of Civil Procedure went into effect, Clayton had been dead nearly a decade; see Subrin "How Equity Conquered the Common Law," 910. On the other hand, the equity-to-law/law-to-equity proposal advocated by the Committee of Fifteen, of which Clayton's bill was a variant, was incorporated into new rules of equity promulgated by the Supreme Court in November 1912; see Robert M. Hughes,

*Handbook of Jurisdiction and Procedure in United States Courts*, 2nd edition (St. Paul: West Publishing Company, 1913), 421, 441, 606 (Rules 22, 23).

43. Clayton, "Popularizing the Administration of Justice," 44, 47, 50, 51.

44. Rodabaugh, "Congressman Henry D. Clayton and the Dothan Post Office Fight," 141, 143.

45. Polenberg, "Progressivism and Anarchism," 400–401. See also Jack E. Kendrick, "Alabama Congressmen in the Wilson Administration," *Alabama Review*, 24 (October 1971), 243–60.

46. Johnston signed a letter endorsing Clayton for the post of attorney general; see Senators and Representatives of the State of Alabama to Hon. Woodrow Wilson, President-elect of the United States (undated, circa 1912), Clayton Papers (filed with 1929–1930 correspondence). For Johnston, see Owen, *History of Alabama and Dictionary of Alabama Biography*, 3:918.

47. Johnson, *Oscar W. Underwood*, 226–28. Johnson cites, among other sources, the pro-Underwood *Birmingham News*, 12 October 1913.

48. Henry De Lamar Clayton to Woodrow Wilson, 11 October 1913, in *The Papers of Woodrow Wilson*, Arthur S. Link et al., eds., vol. 28 (Princeton: Princeton University Press, 1979), 391.

49. Johnson, *Oscar W. Underwood*, 230–31, 233–34, 235; Underwood, like Clayton himself, was a "local option" man, certainly not an out-and-out prohibitionist.

50. Johnson, *Oscar W. Underwood*, 228–30, 232, 236–37. For the political context of the Brownsville affair, see Richard B. Sherman, *The Republican Party and Black America from McKinley to Hoover, 1896–1933* (Charlottesville: University Press of Virginia, 1973), 56–63. For the reaction to Brownsville in Alabama, see Pruitt, "Joseph C. Manning, Alabama Populist," 382–85.

51. Johnson, *Oscar W. Underwood*, 242.

52. Rodabaugh, "Congressman Henry D. Clayton and the Dothan Post Office Fight," 148.

53. Ibid., 148–49. Arthur S. Link views the Clayton Act debate as "a storm of confusing dissent and criticism." There were controversies over the measure's interstate trade regulations and over its first-draft failure to exempt labor organizations from penalties. These battles occupied the spring and summer of 1914, during which time Wilson vacillated and the U.S. Senate made its own alterations. The issues were not settled until after Clayton had received his appointment. See Link, *Woodrow Wilson and the Progressive Era*, 68–74.

54. In a primary election held on April 6, 1914, Clayton defeated Steagall by a vote of 10,738 to 6,927; see Thomas M. Owen, *Alabama Official and Statistical Register 1915* (Montgomery: Brown Printing Company, 1916), 411.

55. *Montgomery Advertiser*, 7 and 9 April 1914. Headline is from April 7.

56. The other judge was William I. Grubb, on the bench from 1909 until his death in 1935. See Freyer and Dixon, *Democracy and Judicial Independence*, 272.

57. The caseload of private suits in the Northern District during Clayton's tenure was typically about three hundred per year, which actually represented a decline from the volume of cases that plagued Judge Jones (1901–1914). In all three Alabama districts, the yearly number of civil suits to which the United States was a party was

typically well under one hundred, though the number of such cases in the Northern District increased in the 1920s. The number of criminal prosecutions in the Middle District fluctuated, dropping below two hundred from 1921 to 1923 after ranging as high as 473 in 1918. Except for the 1920s Northern District criminal caseload, these statistics are below the national averages. See Freyer and Dixon, *Democracy and Judicial Independence,* 290–91, 300–301, 308–309.

58. For Clayton's Supreme Court ambitions (for the seat that went to Louis Brandeis), his interest in the Washington, D.C., Court of Appeals, and for his salary complaints, see Polenberg, *Fighting Faiths,* 99–100.

59. *Montgomery Advertiser,* 22 December 1929.

60. John A. Deweese to Clayton, 17 January 1920, Clayton Papers. Deweese claimed that this episode took place in El Paso, Texas, where Clayton was a visiting judge.

61. *Montgomery Advertiser,* 22 December 1929. For information on an incident in which Clayton acted to protect a witness from "unfair treatment," and for the remark that "I must be the judge of the proper conduct of the trial in any case. When I cannot so act as judge, then I will quit," see Clayton to N. D. Denson, 9 June 1922, Clayton Papers. See also Clayton to B.G. Farmer, 27 January 1919, Clayton Papers.

62. *Montgomery Advertiser,* 17 November 1929, 22 December 1929.

63. Hughes, *Handbook of Jurisdiction and Procedure in the United States Courts,* 695–96 (secs. 289–90); Surrency, *History of the Federal Courts,* 72–74. The 1911 Judicial Code was the product of lobbying as early as the 1890s by the American Bar Association and legal reformers. See Felix Frankfurter and John M. Landis, *The Business of the Supreme Court: A Study in the Federal Judicial System* (New York: Macmillan, 1928), 128–35. Clayton was silent in House debates on the Judicial Code; see 46 *Congressional Record* 3216–20, 3998–4012 (1911).

64. Hughes, *Handbook of Jurisdiction and Procedure in the United States Courts,* 626–27 (secs. 13–15). Several acts, including those of 1850 (9 *Stat.* 442–43), 1852 (10 *Stat.* 5) and 1869 (16 *Stat.* 44) had authorized reassignments in the event of the illness or disqualification of a judge, or in response to overcrowded dockets, and had given discretion over the matter to circuit judges, and in some cases, the Chief Justice of the Supreme Court. The 1911 Judicial Code allowed the Chief Justice, previously limited to selecting replacement judges from the affected circuit or a contiguous circuit, to choose a judge from any circuit. A 1922 act (42 *Stat.* 837), passed after lobbying by Chief Justice William Howard Taft, likewise allowed for inter-circuit transfers and established the Federal Judicial Conference as a mechanism for reporting such needs. See Fish, *Politics of Federal Judicial Administration,* 14–17, 24–30, 32–39. Clayton approved of temporary assignments but worried over the powers granted to the FJC. See Clayton, "Popularizing Administration of Justice," 45–47.

65. See cases at 222 *Federal Reporter* 732 (1915); 241 *Federal Reporter* 747 (1917); 3 *Federal Reporter 2d Series* 1019 (1925); 4 *Federal Reporter 2d Series* 519 (1925); and 250 *United States Reports* 616 (1919). See also Clayton to E. Perry Thomas, 15 March 1926, Clayton Papers.

66. Link, *Woodrow Wilson and the Progressive Era,* 20.

67. Link, *Woodrow Wilson and the Progressive Era,* 174–96, 223–30; Sanders, *Roots of Reform,* 387–408; and Thomas J. Knock, *To End All Wars: Woodrow Wilson and the*

*Quest for a New World Order* (New York: Oxford University Press, 1992), 129–31, 133, 135–37.

68. For Underwood, whose convictions were similar to Clayton's, see Johnson, *Oscar W. Underwood*, 252–53, 255–60, 264–65, 274; and Underwood, *Drifting Sands of Party Politics*, 119–23. Generally, see Dewey W. Grantham, *Southern Progressivism: The Reconciliation of Progress and Tradition* (Knoxville: University of Tennessee Press, 1983), 386–90. Twenty years previously, Congressman Clayton had opposed America's war with Spain. On April 2, 1898, he had written: "War is most deplorable and ought to be avoided unless absolutely necessary to prevent serious injury or national humiliation." He added that he "would not give one white faced, straight haired, blue eyed boy in Alabama for all the half breeds in Cuba." See David E. Alsobrook, "'Remember the Maine!' Congressman Henry D. Clayton Comments on the Impending Conflict with Spain, April 1898," *Alabama Review*, 30 (July 1977), 229.

69. The case discussions do not follow strict chronological order. The 1919 Alabama decision overlaps with the 1918 New York sedition trials covered below.

70. *Ex Parte Rush*, 246 *Federal Reporter* 173 (1917).

71. See Johnson, *Oscar W. Underwood*, 251.

72. *Ex Parte Rush*, 246 *Federal Reporter* 172–75; the 1916 National Defense Act (39 *Stat.* 186) allowed minors under age eighteen to enlist with parental permission.

73. *Ex Parte Graber*, 247 *Federal Reporter* 882–87 (1918); Croatia was a part of the Austro-Hungarian Empire. Graber was imprisoned under authority of a presidential proclamation of December 11, 1917.

74. Grantham, *Southern Progressivism*, 362.

75. Clayton's 1913 sneer at the "'cheap pauper labor of Europe'" quoted in Polenberg, "Progressivism and Anarchism," 402. For a pro-restriction vote by Burnett, Clayton, Heflin, and other Alabama congressmen, see 51 *Congressional Record* 2593–94 (1914).

76. *New York Times*, 7 January 1916, cited in Polenberg, "Progressivism and Anarchism," 402. Clayton was known for his involvement in the naturalization of soldiers at such posts as Fort Oglethorpe, Georgia, and Camp McClellan, Alabama; see Walter B. Jones to Clayton, 7 June 1918, Frank Stollenwerck to Clayton, 19 June 1918, and Clayton to "Dear Mary," 2 November 1918, Clayton Papers.

77. *Ex Parte Graber*, 247 *Federal Reporter* 884–85. Clayton observed that Graber's petition for a writ of habeas corpus was essentially a request for the court to determine a question of fact—inappropriate in a habeas corpus proceeding. For the precedent, see *In re Moyer*, 85 *Pacific Reporter* (1904), 190.

78. *United States v. Forbes*, 259 *Federal Reporter* 586. Clayton would assure assessment commissioners that the government had acted under "imperious necessity," stating further that it was "hardly necessary to say" that it "did no wrong in the occupation of these lands." See *United States v. First National Bank, et al.*, 250 *Federal Reporter* 300–301 (1918). Generally, see Wesley Phillips Newton, "'Tenting Tonight on the Old Camp Grounds': Alabama's Military Bases in World War I," in *The Great War in the Heart of Dixie: Alabama During World War I*, ed. Martin T. Olliff (Tuscaloosa: University of Alabama Press, 2008), 41–65.

79. *United States v. Forbes*, 259 *Federal Reporter* 586–87, 591–92. The sums of money

involved in the case were large for the era (the government proposed to pay in excess of $58,000), and the lawyers involved were well regarded. Forbes' lead attorney was Sidney J. Bowie of Birmingham, while five lawyers, headed by U.S. Attorney Thomas J. Samford of Opelika, represented the government. For Clayton on this intricate case (and his difficulties in following state-law precedents), see Clayton to Thomas J. Walsh, 26 May 1926, Clayton Papers.

80. *United States v. Forbes*, 259 *Federal Reporter* 588–90. For the 1917 act, see 40 *Stat.* 241. Forbes was convinced that federal authorities and the city of Montgomery had struck an underhanded deal to hand the land over to the city. Clayton held that the existence of any bargain was irrelevant. A technical objection aroused his wrath, and he asserted that "the federal court has the inherent power to so shape the adjective law" (i.e., procedural law) that "real questions of substantive law can be frankly and fairly presented and decided." See *United States v. Forbes*, 259 *Federal Reporter* 592–96 (quoted passage on 593). Clayton's rulings were affirmed; see *United States v. Forbes*, 268 *Federal Reporter* 273–78 (1920).

81. See David Stevenson, *Cataclysm: The First World War as Political Tragedy* (New York: Basic Books, 2004), 374–78.

82. 40 *Stat.* 553 (amending section 3 of the 1917 Espionage Act, 40 *Stat.* 219). The 1917 act prohibited false statements made with malicious intent; the Sedition Act added the language quoted in the text.

83. Paul L. Murphy, *World War I and the Origin of Civil Liberties in the United States* (New York: W. W. Norton and Company, 1979), 81–82, 266–68. Critics included Hiram Johnson, Learned Hand, Zechariah Chafee, Ernst Freund, and Harold Laski. See Zechariah Chafee, *Freedom of Speech* (London: George Allen and Unwin, 1920), 46–56; Mark DeWolfe Howe, *Holmes-Laski Letters: The Correspondence of Mr. Justice Holmes and Harold J. Laski, 1916–1935* (Cambridge, Massachusetts: Harvard University Press, 1953), 2:220–22; and Underwood, *Drifting Sands of Party Politics*, 352–63.

84. There were roughly two thousand prosecutions under the acts of 1917 and 1918. See Murphy, *World War I and the Origin of Civil Liberties in the United States*, 80; Zechariah Chafee, *Freedom of Speech*, 56–58, 387–93; and Burt Neuborne, "The Role of Courts In Time of War," *New York University Review of Law and Social Change*, 29 (2005), 558–59. For the trial of the editors of the *Masses*, one of whom was the famous radical John Reed, see Polenberg, *Fighting Faiths*, 70–72, 75, 93; and Alan Dawley, *Changing the World: American Progressives in War and Revolution* (Princeton: Princeton University Press, 2003), 156–60. For the Supreme Court's role in upholding prosecutions, see *Schenck v. United States, Baer v. United States, Frohwerk v. United States,* and *Debs v. United States,* 249 *United States Reports* (1919), 47, 204, 211; and *Abrams v. United States,* 250 *United States Reports* (1919), 616.

85. Polenberg, "Progressivism and Anarchism," 402–403; and Polenberg, *Fighting Faiths*, 101. See also Clayton to Mrs. Alice K. Davis, telegram, 4 June 1918, Clayton Papers. Bertram Clayton was a colonel in the Quartermaster Corps, a West Pointer and a former New York congressman; see *Biographical Directory of the United States Congress, 1774–1989,* 790.

86. Thomas B. Felder to Clayton, telegram, 3 June 1918; Thomas B. Felder to Clayton, 10 June 1918; and Clayton to Thomas B. Felder, 4 June 1918, Clayton Papers.

87. *Montgomery Advertiser,* 13 June 1918. See A. C. Davis, R. F. Ligon, et al., to Clayton, 13 June 1918, calling the vice problem "a specie[s] of German propaganda"; and Clayton to Attorney General of the United States, 15 June 1918 (copy), Clayton Papers. See also Newton, "'Tenting Tonight on the Old Camp Grounds,'" 60.

88. Frank Stollenwerck to Clayton, 19 June 1918, 11 July 1918, Clayton Papers. Stollenwerck was director of the Speakers Bureau, Alabama Council of Defense.

89. Clayton to Senator [John H.] Bankhead, 10 July 1918; Bankhead to Clayton, 20 July 1918, Clayton Papers.

90. For Clayton's arrival with his wife Bettie, see Clayton to George H. Ruge, 25 September 1918, Clayton Papers. They stayed at the Biltmore Hotel.

91. For examples, see *New York Times,* 19, 20, 25, 26 October 1918.

92. Murphy, *World War I and the Origin of Civil Liberties in the United States,* 220–24.

93. Clayton to Selmon [sic], 5 September 1918, Clayton Papers.

94. Chafee, *Freedom of Speech,* 131, 132; and Murray, *Red Scare,* 33–36.

95. Clayton to George S. Graham, 18 September 1918, Clayton Papers.

96. See Polenberg, *Fighting Faiths,* 36–42, 109–16. Officially, the American troops were sent to assist Czechoslovakian forces already in place.

97. Chafee, *Freedom of Speech,* 120–23, reprints the leaflets in full, one in its original English and the other, originally in Yiddish, in the English translation used at the trial. These and other documents, reproduced in *Supreme Court of the United States, October Term, 1918, Jacob Abrams, et al., Plaintiffs in Error, vs. The United States* (N.p., n.d.), 16–19 and in the microform set, *United States Supreme Court Records and Briefs* (Englewood, Colorado: n.d.) at 250 U.S. 616, 1919 Full Opinion No. 316 (hereinafter cited as *United States v. Jacob Abrams, et al., Plaintiffs in Error*).

98. Chafee, *Freedom of Speech,* 123–25; *United States v. Jacob Abrams, et al., Plaintiffs in Error,* 2–3, 22–41. For further details of the arrests and interrogations of Jacob Abrams, Hyman Lachowsky, Mollie Steimer, Samuel Lipman, Gabriel Prober, Hyman Rosansky, and Jacob Schwartz, see Polenberg, *Fighting Faiths,* 43–69. The mistreatment Schwartz received was a contributing factor to his death prior to the trial. For Clayton's reluctance to allow the defense to cross-examine policemen aggressively concerning the interrogations, see Polenberg, *Fighting Faiths,* 88–91, 105–107.

99. Clayton to Dr. Charles C. Thach, 16 September 1918; Clayton to Selmon [sic], 24 September 1918; and Clayton to George H. Ruge, 25 September 1918, Clayton Papers.

100. Chafee, *Freedom of Speech,* 125–26. The judges were Learned Hand, Augustus Hand, and Julius M. Mayer. Learned Hand had already presided in an action involving a radical publication, the *Masses,* and was, if anything, considered too lenient; see Chafee, *Freedom of Speech,* 46–54; and 244 *Federal Reporter* 535 (1917). As to Clayton's lack of experience, it is true that 1917–1918 saw twenty-five Espionage Act cases commenced in New York's Southern District, as opposed to two in Alabama's Middle District. On the other hand, fifteen such cases were commenced in Alabama's Northern District, and Clayton was probably acquainted with several of these. See *Annual Report of the Attorney General of the United States for the Year 1919* (Washington, D.C.: Government Printing Office, 1919), 121–22, 172.

101. For the complexities of this point, see Chafee, *Freedom of Speech*, 127, 130–138, 139 (quoted passage); Polenberg, "Progressivism and Anarchism," 404; and Polenberg, *Fighting Faiths*, 107–17. The defense also contended that the Espionage Act was unconstitutional; for their bill of exceptions, see *United States v. Jacob Abrams, et al., Plaintiffs in Error*, 20–22.

102. Chafee, *Freedom of Speech*, 133–34, 135, 137–39, 146–48. For Clayton's exchanges with Steimer, see Polenberg, "Progressivism and Anarchism," 404–407; and Polenberg, *Fighting Faiths*, 126–31. Polenberg also quotes the anarchist Emma Goldman, who called Clayton "a 'veritable Jeffreys.'" Polenberg, "Progressivism and Anarchy," 408. It is of some interest that Clayton had recently joined a league for "Constructive Immigration Legislation," formed by the Reverend Sidney L. Gulick, whose object was the establishment of quotas. See Sidney L. Gulick to Clayton, 25 July 1918, 8 November 1918, Clayton Papers; and John Higham, *Strangers in the Land*, 302–303.

103. Quote from *New York Times*, 26 October 1918. In his summing up to the jury, Clayton had attempted to mitigate his previous bias by saying that they were "to understand that any reference or comment or expression of opinion which the Court may have made or hereafter may make in respect to the evidence . . . or in respect to the contentions of the respective parties, is not evidence nor to be understood as expressing my own opinion or personal belief in either the guilt or innocence of the defendants." See *United States v. Jacob Abrams, et al., Plaintiffs in Error*, 226–39 (quoted passage on 230). See also Polenberg, *Fighting Faiths*, 135–38.

104. All quotes from *New York Times*, 26 October 1918. See also Polenberg, *Fighting Faiths*, 120–21, 132–34, 138–46. Clayton sentenced Jacob Abrams, Samuel Lipman, and Hyman Lachowsky to twenty years (the maximum), Mollie Steimer to fifteen years, and Hyman Rosansky (the government's informer) to three years. Gabriel Prober had been found innocent.

105. Polenberg, "Progressivism and Anarchism," 407. Polenberg cites praise from the *New York Times* and criticism from the *Nation* and Harvard president Abbott Lawrence Lowell; *Fighting Faiths*, 146–47, 281. In addition to the sources cited by Polenberg, see E. D. Smith to Clayton, 20 November 1918; R. E. Pettus to Clayton, 21 November 1918; and Martin W. Littleton to Clayton, 25 November 1918, Clayton Papers.

106. See, for example, Clayton to William J. Finerty, 15 November 1918, and Thomas H. Ince to Clayton, 14 April 1919, Clayton Papers. The later was from a Los Angeles filmmaker asking Clayton to endorse an anti-Bolshevik movie. For an indication that Clayton was worried about his image, see Martin W. Littleton to Clayton, 26 February 1919, Clayton Papers. Littleton had represented the defendants in *Blair, et al., v. United States*, a matter in which Clayton, holding court in the Southern District of New York, had jailed Littleton's clients for contempt after they refused to testify before a grand jury. *Blair, et al., v. United States*, 250 *United States Reports* (1919), 273–283. In response to an inquiry from Clayton, Littleton assured the judge that the appeal would not reflect badly upon him. In fact, it contended that the Corrupt Practices Act of 1910 (36 *Stat.* 822 [1910]) was unconstitutional. See *Ex Parte Blair, et al.*, 253 *Federal Reporter* 800 (1918).

107. Quoted passages are from Clayton to Bettie Clayton, 21 November 1918,

Clayton Papers. This letter is also quoted in Polenberg, "Progressivism and Anarchism," 403.

108. Clayton to Bettie Clayton, 21 November 1918; for Clayton's reading, see Hugo Grotius, *De Juri Belli ac Pacis* (1625), bk. 3, chap. 9.

109. For Clayton's involvement in setting bail for the defendants and other post-trial issues, see Polenberg, *Fighting Faiths*, 147–48, 152–53.

110. *Abrams, et al., v. United States*, 250 *United States Reports* (1919) 627–30 (quoted passages on 629–30). Holmes' dissent applies the "clear and present danger" doctrine in order to defend free speech; see Murphy, *World War I and the Origin of Civil Liberties in the United States*, 267. For the statement that "the Supreme Court's path to the modern First Amendment begins with the Holmes-Brandeis dissent in *Abrams*," see Neuborne, "Role of Courts in Time of War," 559n19. Clayton, though he claimed to have had no doubts that his decision would be upheld, had asked an assistant U.S. district attorney why "such people" as Abrams could not be merely deported; see Clayton to John M. Ryan, 17 November 1919, Clayton Papers.

111. Chafee, *Free Speech*, 51. For other examples of the post-war approach to social questions, see Frank V. Thompson, *Schooling of the Immigrant* (New York: Harper & Brothers, 1920), 289–92, 365–67.

112. Clayton's growing doubts about Progressivism did not extend to doubts about the Democratic Party, or even Wilson. For Clayton's prophecy that the Democrats would "continue as a militant force to advocate the principles enunciated by Jefferson and maintained by Jackson, Cleveland and Wilson," see Clayton to Harland B. Howe, 17 November 1924, Clayton Papers.

113. William Howard Taft, *The President and His Powers* (New York: Columbia University Press, 1916), 5, 12 (quoted passage).

114. Alabama was already "dry" by various forms of state action; see Rogers et al., *Alabama: The History of a Deep South State*, 416; and Moore, *History of Alabama*, 752–57. Clayton, by all accounts, was no prohibitionist; see James Benson Sellers, *The Prohibition Movement in Alabama, 1702 to 1942* (Chapel Hill: University of North Carolina Press, 1943), 143; Johnson, *Oscar W. Underwood*, 227; and Underwood, *Drifting Sands of Party Politics*, 364–67, 378–91.

115. Clayton to John Sharp Williams, 8 October 1918, Clayton Papers.

116. See Rogers et al., *Alabama: The History of a Deep South State*, 416. See also Thomas, *The New Woman in Alabama*, 199–203.

117. Rogers et al., *Alabama: The History of a Deep South State*, 416–18; and Paul M. Pruitt Jr., "Suffer the Children: Child Labor Reform in Alabama," *Alabama Heritage* 58 (Fall 2000), 24–26. For a negative view of federal child-welfare laws, see Underwood, *Drifting Sands of Party Politics*, 322–51.

118. To persons actually harmed, the atmosphere of demagogic racism was no mere political device. For a survey of extralegal violence during the period, see Glenn Feldman, "Lynching in Alabama, 1889–1921," *Alabama Review*, 48 (April 1995), 114–41.

119. V. O. Key Jr., *Southern Politics in State and Nation* (New York: Alfred A. Knopf, 1949), 3–12, 37–52.

120. Though no lover of academic jargon, Clayton would have agreed with Merton that "the empirical observation is incontestable: activities oriented toward certain

values release processes which so react as to change the very scale of values which precipitated them." Merton, "Unanticipated Consequences," 903.

121. Feldman stresses that immigrants made up 1.2 percent and Catholics only 3.4 percent of the state's 2.35 million people in 1920. Glenn Feldman, *Politics, Society, and the Klan in Alabama, 1915–1949* (Tuscaloosa: University of Alabama Press, 1999), 56, 60.On the other hand, Carl V. Harris notes that citizens of "foreign" stock (Irish, German, Italian) made up 15.1 percent of Birmingham's population of nearly 200,000 in 1920. Carl V. Harris, *Political Power in Birmingham, 1871–1921* (Knoxville: University of Tennessee Press, 1977), 33, 35. Wayne Flynt notes that in 1916 Catholics made up Birmingham's third-largest denomination, behind black Baptists and white Methodists and ahead of white Baptists. Wayne Flynt, *Alabama in the Twentieth Century,* 468–69.

122. Flynt, *Alabama in the Twentieth Century,* 467–68; and see Underwood, *Drifting Sands of Party Politics,* 373–75.

123. For immigrant and Catholic opposition to prohibition and Blue Laws, see Harris, *Political Power in Birmingham,* 55, 194, 197–98.

124. See C. Vann Woodward, *Tom Watson, Agrarian Rebel* (New York: Oxford University Press, 1963), 416–25; and Higham, *Strangers in the Land,* 178–80.

125. For Catts' speech, see *Birmingham Age-Herald,* 14 December 1916. See also Flynt, *Alabama in the Twentieth Century,* 468; and generally, Wayne Flynt, *Cracker Messiah: Governor Sydney J. Catts of Florida* (Baton Rouge: Louisiana State University Press, 1977).

126. Charles P. Sweeney, "Bigotry in the South," *The Nation,* 111 (November 24, 1920), 585; and Feldman, *Politics, Society, and the Klan,* 59. Both Catts and Kilby backed "Convent Inspection" acts. For the Alabama version, see *Acts of Alabama* (1919), 883.

127. Harris, *Political Power in Birmingham,* 85–86; and Sweeney, "Bigotry in the South," 585–86. For an example of the intersection of nativism, super-patriotism, and religious prejudice in post-war Birmingham, see the series of newspaper articles concerning a visit to Birmingham by Eamon De Valera, president of the Irish Republic. *Birmingham Age-Herald,* 4, 8, 10, 11, 12, 14, 16, 17, 18, 19, 20, 21, and 22 April 1920. Posts of the American Legion, a majority of the Birmingham City Commission, and a local council of Methodist ministers made it clear that they did not want De Valera in town. They denounced him chiefly for his Sinn Fein politics, but it is not difficult to read an anti-Catholic subtext in their pronouncements.

128. Feldman, *Politics, Society, and the Klan in Alabama,* 12–13; see also Ralph McGill, *The South and the Southerner* (Boston: Little, Brown, 1964), 129–44. For evidence that Clayton had seen and liked "Birth of a Nation," see Clayton to Dear Little Mother, 9 September 1918, Clayton Papers.

129. See Feldman, *Politics, Society, and the Klan in Alabama,* 17–18. Praise of the first Klan was common among Democrats of the period; see Virginius Dabney, *Liberalism in the South* (Chapel Hill: University of North Carolina Press, 1932), 163–64.

130. See Blaine A. Brownell, "The Urban South Comes of Age, 1900–1940," in *The City in Southern History: The Growth of Urban Civilization in the South,* ed. Blaine A. Brownell and David R. Goldfield (New York: Kennikat Press, 1977), 123–24, 145–50; and Kenneth T. Jackson, *The Ku Klux Klan in the City, 1915–1930* (1967; repr. Chicago:

Ivan R. Dee, 1992), 240–44. For a contemporary view of the perils of modernism, see "Address at the Ala. Polytechnic Institute, March [6,] 1922," Braxton Bragg Comer Papers, SHC M-168, Reel 7, Southern Historical Collection, University of North Carolina at Chapel Hill (hereinafter cited as Comer Papers). On pages 10–11 of this draft, Comer denounces "two monsters today threatening the youth of this land." One consisted of the violators of prohibition, namely moonshiners, bootleggers, and the "high[er] order of law defiers" who drink illegal liquor. The other monster was the movie industry, which was "daily—nightly in the very highest degree, in the most outreaching way corrupting and debauching our young people."

131. Feldman, *Politics, Society, and the Klan in Alabama,* 21–36, shows how the Klan combined violent repression with charity work, parades and other civic events, and substantial contributions to schools and churches. A number of influential Progressives (notably Kilby) were reluctant to criticize the Klan. Feldman, *Politics, Society, and the Klan,* 66. See also Thornton, "Hugo Black and the Golden Age," 901, 902–906.

132. For a Klan-generated figure of 115,000 Alabama members in 1924, see Feldman, *Politics, Society, and the Klan in Alabama,* 16, and 27–29.

133. For quoted passage, see Virginia Van der Veer Hamilton, *Hugo Black: The Alabama Years* (1972: repr. University, Alabama: University of Alabama Press, 1982), 65.

134. See Michael Mann, *Fascists* (New York: Cambridge University Press, 2004), 16–17, 28, 68–69, 98–99, 153–55.

135. See Clayton to T. J. O'Donnell, 5 July 1923, Clayton Papers.

136. Henry D. Clayton, "The Indefensible Usurpation of Governmental Functions by Secret Societies," in *Proceedings of the Fifteenth Annual Session of the Florida State Bar Association* ([Orlando, Florida]: The Association, 1922), 147–49, 150 (quoted passage). For the same argument on behalf of the original Klan, see Braxton Bragg Comer to John A. Lusk, 22 May 1924; and John A. Lusk to B. B. Comer, 24 July 1924, Comer Papers, Reel 12.

137. Clayton was hardly alone in his willingness to use procedural due process as a measure of civil rights. On just such grounds the military historian and editor Douglas Southall Freeman opposed lynching, the operations of the second Ku Klux Klan, and the unequal treatment of black defendants. See David E. Johnson, *Douglas Southall Freeman* (Gretna, Louisiana: Pelican Publishing Company, 2002), 190–205.

138. *Montgomery Advertiser,* 30 September 1919, 1 October 1919.

139. Quoted in *Montgomery Advertiser,* 3 October 1919.

140. See Rogers et al., *Alabama: The History of a Deep South State,* 453–54; and James R. Grossman, *Land of Hope: Black Southerners and the Great Migration* (Chicago: University of Chicago Press, 1989). For an indication that elite Alabamians viewed the Klan as a threat to the stability of their labor force, see Feldman, *Politics, Society, and the Klan in Alabama,* 70.

141. Braxton Bragg Comer to E. T. Comer, 12 January 1923, Comer Papers, Reel 9. In this letter, Comer notes that "Quite a few of my hands left—some to farming because of the high price of cotton and some to Chicago because of the high price of labor."

142. Of course the existing social relations, typically, were bitterly racist. For these

issues in all their complexities, see Steve Suitts, *Hugo Black of Alabama* (Montgomery: NewSouth Books, 2005), 241–91.

143. Feldman, *Politics, Society, and the Klan in Alabama*, 66.

144. Ibid., 64–66, 170–71; and Flynt, *Alabama in the Twentieth Century*, 54–55. For a summary of the Musgrove-Underwood race, see Johnson, *Oscar W. Underwood*, 275–93.

145. Feldman, *Politics, Society, and the Klan in Alabama*, 29–30.

146. Paul M. Pruitt Jr., "The Killing of Father Coyle: Private Tragedy, Public Shame," *Alabama Heritage* 30 (Fall 1993), 24–37 (quoted passage on 36). See also Roger Newman, *Hugo Black: A Biography* (New York: Pantheon Books, 1994), 71–88, 91; and Tony Freyer, *Hugo L. Black and the Dilemma of American Liberalism* (Glenview, Illinois: Scott, Foresman, 1990), 38–40. Suitts casts doubt on the Klan-infiltration theory and portrays Black as a lawyer doing his best (however offensively) for his client. Suitts, *Hugo Black of Alabama*, 337–65. It is true that Black did not formally join the Klan until 1923.

147. Underwood's 1920 opponent Lycurgus Musgrove had made an issue of Underwood's supposed subservience to the pope; see Johnson, *Oscar W. Underwood*, 286–87. Thereafter, anti-Catholicism became a staple of Alabama politics. In the 1920s, J. Thomas Heflin made a career of attacking the Knights of Columbus, a Catholic auxiliary, from the floor of the Senate. Because of these speeches, he received "a massive flow of letters from plain people who obviously thought of [him] as their champion"; see Tanner, "James Thomas Heflin," 100–25 (quoted passage on 112).

148. Pruitt, "Killing of Father Coyle," 34–35. Coyle was a remarkable man. A priest at St. Paul's in Birmingham since 1904, Coyle was a poet and an outspoken advocate of Irish freedom; in 1919, he had flown the Irish Republican flag from the rectory at St. Paul's. Since 1906 he had been an enthusiastic contributor to the local press on religious questions, taking on Protestant clergymen on a variety of issues. He was also a successful proselytizer for Catholicism; Ruth Stephenson converted to Catholicism under his teaching. See Vincent Joseph Scozzari, "Father James E. Coyle, Priest and Citizen" (masters thesis, Notre Dame Seminary, New Orleans, 1963), iii, 3–4, 8–35, 36–40, and 41–42.

149. B. B. Comer to H. C. Anson, 6 January 1922, Comer Papers, Reel 7. The former governor was responding to a December 21, 1921, letter from Anson; at issue was an incident in which, during a train ride from Birmingham to Montgomery, Comer had given offense to Anson's sister. Comer had mentioned the Stephenson case in connection with a discussion of Tom Watson's anti-Catholic activities. Anson's sister, whom Anson said had left her home in Florida to escape persecution by Governor Catts, overheard his remarks and objected to them.

150. Feldman, *Politics, Society, and the Klan in Alabama*, 67–68. The Klan did not claim credit for the attack, and some Alabamians did not connect it with the Klan. See Comer's statement in which he offers to contribute to a reward for information on "the parties who lynched Dr. Dowling." Comer asserted that the incident was the product of Chicago-style violations of prohibition. Draft statement of Braxton Bragg Comer, [24 May 1922], Comer Papers, Reel 8.

151. *Birmingham Age-Herald,* 18 June 1922; see also Feldman, *Politics, Society, and the Klan in Alabama,* 69–70.

152. Clayton to Frank S. White, 1 June 1922, Clayton Papers.

153. Clayton, "Popularizing Administration of Justice," 43n. On Clayton's Mississippi speech, see Hugh Henry Brown to Clayton, 2 June 1922, and Thomas W. Martin to Clayton, 2 June 1922, Clayton Papers.

154. Clayton, "Indefensible Usurpation," 156; and see Leroy Percy, "The Modern Ku Klux Klan," *Atlantic Monthly,* 130 (July 1922), 122–28.

155. Clayton to C. A. Culberson, 20 June 1922, and Clayton to Herman Ulmer, 20 June 1922, Clayton Papers; and *Orlando Morning Sentinel,* 14 June 1922.

156. For Clayton's comments on the Florida bar, see "Judge Armstead Brown Heads Florida State Bar Association," *Jacksonville (FL) Times-Union,* 17 June 1922. Clayton surely knew Armstead Brown, who had been a state judge in Montgomery for several years before moving to Florida; see *Florida Law Journal,* 8 (August 1934), 103.

157. David M. Chalmers, *Hooded Americanism: The History of the Ku Klux Klan* (1965; repr. Chicago: Quadrangle Books, 1968), 225–29; and Michael Newton, *The Invisible Empire: The Ku Klux Klan in Florida* (Gainesville: University Press of Florida, 2001), 37–73. Klan-like activities in Florida had included a 1920 Ocoee "race war" in which eight people were killed and several buildings burned.

158. Citations to Clayton's Orlando speech are from the official text, "Indefensible Usurpation of Government Functions by Secret Societies." For an edited, slightly abbreviated text of the speech and for the full text of the June 28 letter Clayton received from "A Klansman," see Paul M. Pruitt Jr., "Judge Henry D. Clayton and 'A Klansman': A Revealing Exchange of Views," *Florida Historical Quarterly,* 81 (Winter 2003), 334–47.

159. Clayton, "Indefensible Usurpation," 146, 147.

160. Ibid., 147–48.

161. Ibid., 148–50. Clayton admitted that "bad men" had imitated the original Klan, and he cited with approval the case of *Bacon, et al., v. State of Florida,* 22 *Florida Reports* (1889), 51, involving the suppression of a secret criminal society.

162. Clayton, "Indefensible Usurpation," 150–52.

163. Ibid., 153–54. For similar sentiments, see Underwood, *Drifting Sands of Party Politics,* 237–38, 375–77, 390–91, 403–11.

164. Clayton, "Indefensible Usurpation," 153–55. For further information on the Columbus episode, see Gregory C. Lisby, "Julian Harris and the *Columbus Enquirer-Sun:* The Consequences of Winning the Pulitzer Prize," *Journalism Monographs,* 105 (April 1988), 2–6; and *New York Times,* 28 and 31 May 1922.

165. Clayton maintains that in contrast to the work of the first Klan, "the recent activities have appeared to be free from color or political alignment." Clayton, "Indefensible Usurpation," 154. As to matters of religious prejudice, Clayton's attitude must have puzzled allies such as the Roman Catholic Leroy Percy. See Percy, "The Modern Ku Klux Klan," 122–25, 128. For Clayton's more considered opinion on the Klan's anti-Catholic and anti-Semitic bigotries, see Clayton to T. J. O'Donnell, 5 July 1923, Clayton Papers.

166. Clayton, "Indefensible Usurpation," 155–56.

167. See *Proceedings of the Fifteenth Annual Session of the Florida State Bar Association,* 11–17, 27–31, 34–42. The convention also celebrated Florida's territorial centennial.

168. *Jacksonville (FL) Times-Union,* 17 June 1922; *Orlando Morning Sentinel,* 17 June 1922; *Montgomery Advertiser,* 17 June 1922.

169. Clayton to Dr. L. L. Hill, 16 May 1927, Clayton Papers.

170. Clayton's excuse was his upcoming service on three-judge panels; see Clayton to Alex M. Garber, 19 June 1922, Clayton Papers. Two years later, Clayton gave an address to the Alabama State Bar Association. The occasion was an historic one, as the 1924 convention marked the transition between the old association, extant since 1878, and the state's new "unified bar." Clayton chose to discuss the history of the association. The rest of his speech covered his own interests, including the simplification of pleading, restatement and codification of the law, and the rightful place and importance of lawyers. He alluded to the "usurpation" of local rights by the federal government and to the outrageous views of anarchists; he made no mention of the Klan. See *Proceedings: First Meeting of the Alabama State Bar and of the Forty-Seventh Annual Meeting of the Alabama State Bar Association* (Montgomery: The Paragon Press, 1924), 45–46, 50–53, 105–29.

171. Thomas D. Samford to Clayton, 20 June 1922; M. S. Carmichael to Clayton, 20 June 1922; W. J. Carpenter to Clayton, 17 June 1922; and Jesse E. Mercer to Clayton, 20 June 1922 (quoted passage), Clayton Papers. Mercer was an officer of the Georgia League for Law Enforcement through Constituted Authorities. For thanks from a Texas lawyer who accused Judge William I. Grubb of Alabama's Northern District of having "Ku Kluxed" two Jewish litigants through unfair rulings, see Joseph W. Bailey to Clayton, 18 August 1922, Clayton Papers. For further comments on the speech, see Clayton to T. J. O'Donnell, 5 July 1923, Clayton Papers; and T. J. O'Donnell to Clayton, 12 July 1923, Clayton Papers.

172. Clayton to T. J. O'Donnell, 5 July 1923, Clayton Papers. Apparently, Clayton did not save most of these letters. The Clayton Papers contain no correspondence from persons claiming to be Alabama Klansmen.

173. "A Klansman" to Clayton, 28 June 1922, Clayton Papers. The letter is written on the stationery of the Hotel Empire.

174. Moore, *History of Alabama and Her People,* 3: 66–67. Moore cites the Orlando speech among Clayton's important addresses.

175. For Clayton's description of a "Southern Gentleman" as one "always reverencing God, believing in the atoning grace of the blessed Savior; morally, intellectually and physically honest and fearless; and at all times kindly and charitable towards men, women and children," see Clayton to John Sharp Williams, 30 January 1925, Clayton Papers.

176. By 1923, by a process of conflating past and present, Clayton had added Catholics and Jews to his list of modern Klan victims. He wrote to a friend stating that a number of Catholic and Jewish Confederates had been members of the first Klan. He then claimed, "The old Klan was not founded on any prejudice, religious or race; it was free from any hatred of Catholics, Jews, or even of the negroes." Yet the new Klan, Clayton continued, "proscribes Catholics on the ground of their reli-

gion; it proscribes Jews on both the grounds, religion and race. It claims to be 100% American. It is not entitled to be reckoned in any sense as an American institution or organization." See Clayton to T. J. O'Donnell, 5 July 1923, Clayton Papers.

177. *St. Paul Savings Bank v. American Clearing Company*, 291 *Federal Reporter* 212–31 (1923), see especially 228.

178. *Citizens' Savings Bank and Trust Company of Ohio, et al., v. St. Paul Trust and Savings Bank*, 10 *Federal Reporter 2d Series* 1017 (1926). For another example of praise for his out-of-Alabama work, see *City of New Orleans, et al., v. O'Keefe, et al.*, 280 *Federal Reporter* 92 (1922).

179. For brief biographies of Grubb (judge 1909–1935) and Ervin (judge 1917–1935) see Freyer and Dixon, *Democracy and Judicial Independence*, 270, 272. A survey via Lexis of the appellate records of Clayton, Grubb, and Ervin for 1922–1929 (the last years of Clayton's career) showed that Clayton was appealed 35 times and upheld 25 times (71 percent success rate); Grubb was appealed 111 times and upheld 84 times (77 percent success rate); and Ervin was appealed 37 times and upheld 23 times (62 percent success rate). Decisions partially affirmed were counted as having been affirmed. See also Clayton to E. Perry Thomas, 15 March 1926, Clayton Papers.

180. Hamilton, *Hugo Black*, 78.

181. The anti-Klan plank was narrowly defeated in the convention. See Johnson, *Oscar W. Underwood*, 397–400; and Feldman, *Politics, Society, and the Klan in Alabama*, 70–71, 91. Comer and other Alabama Progressive leaders were unwilling to derail Underwood's presidential campaign, but feared that Underwood might pack the delegation with anti-prohibitionists. Thus Underwood and Comer were each allowed to name half of the delegation. Underwood insisted on absolute loyalty to the anti-Klan plank. Comer, while he stopped short of embracing the second Klan, was unhappy with the prospect of denouncing it. For discussion of Underwood's doomed candidacy, see B. B. Comer to Oscar W. Underwood, 6 May 1924; Oscar W. Underwood to B. B. Comer, 13 May 1924; B. B. Comer to John A. Lusk, 22 May 1924; B. B. Comer to Thomas E. Kilby, 5 June 1924; Oscar W. Underwood to B. B. Comer, 7 June 1924; Donald Comer to B. B. Comer, 9 July 1924; Lister Hill to B. B. Comer, 15 July 1924; and John A. Lusk to B. B. Comer, 24 July 1924, Comer Papers, Reel 12.

182. Clayton, in New York holding court during the convention, asked a friend to tell one "Judge Carmichael" that "if he thought what I said about the Ku Klux was either ill-advised or extreme he would revise his opinion had he been here and heard all that has been said against the Klan, publicly and privately." See Clayton to "Dear George," 28 June 1924, Clayton Papers.

183. Johnson, *Oscar W. Underwood*, 406–407; and Feldman, *Politics, Society, and the Klan in Alabama*, 71.

184. Johnson, *Oscar W. Underwood*, 417–19; and Webb, "Hugo Black, Bibb Graves, and the Ku Klux Klan," 251.

185. For insight on the unsuccessful gubernatorial campaign run by the "Bourbon" Charles S. McDowell Jr., see Clayton to "Dear Charlie," 16 March 1926, Clayton Papers; and Feldman, *Politics, Society, and the Klan in Alabama*, 83.

186. In 1926 Black was a Birmingham trial lawyer whose previous office-holding had been limited to a term as solicitor of Jefferson County. See Hamilton, *Hugo Black*;

Newman, *Hugo Black*; Freyer, *Hugo L. Black.* In 1926, Graves was a lawyer and for-mer state legislator. He had been a high-ranking National Guardsman and leader of the American Legion. See Owen, *History of Alabama and Dictionary of Alabama Biog-raphy,* 3:693–94; Wayne Flynt, "Bibb Graves," in *Alabama Governors: A Political His-tory of the State,* 173–79; and William E. Gilbert, "Bibb Graves as a Progressive, 1927–1930," in *From Civil War to Civil Rights: Alabama, 1860–1960,* ed. Sarah Woolfolk Wiggins (Tuscaloosa: University of Alabama Press, 1987), 336–48.

187. See Hamilton, *Hugo Black,* 98–100, 119–20, 143–47; Newman, *Hugo Black,* 89–99, 114; Freyer, *Hugo L. Black,* 41–42; Feldman, *Politics, Society, and the Klan in Ala-bama,* 88; and Gilbert, "Bibb Graves as a Progressive," 336–38.

188. See Webb, "Hugo Black, Bibb Graves, and the Ku Klux Klan," 243–73, espe-cially 243–46. Webb's study of the 1926 elections casts doubt on the long-held belief that a Klan voting bloc dominated the campaigns. A complicating factor is that the primary election law in force from 1918 to 1930 allowed voters to cast "second-choice" ballots that counted as much as the first. Clayton believed that the law had allowed the Klan to elect "a governor with twenty-four per cent of the vote of Alabama." See Clayton to Dr. L. L. Hill, 23 May 1927, Clayton Papers.

189. Hamilton, *Hugo Black,* 127, 134–35, 143; Newman, *Hugo Black,* 114–15; and Feld-man, *Politics, Society, and the Klan in Alabama,* 81–82.

190. Hamilton, *Hugo Black,* 136–38; Webb, "Hugo Black, Bibb Graves, and the Ku Klux Klan," 243; Diane McWhorter, *Carry Me Home: Birmingham, Alabama: The Cli-mactic Battle of the Civil Rights Revolution* (New York: Simon and Schuster, 2001), 36; and Feldman, *Politics, Society, and the Klan in Alabama,* 81–87 (quoted passage on 87).

191. Thornton, "Hugo Black and the Golden Age," 904.

192. Thornton cites Black, Graves, future U.S. Senator Lister Hill, future U.S. Circuit Court of Appeals judge Richard Rives, and Alabama Supreme Court jus-tice Joel Brown as examples of public men who outgrew the Klan. Ibid., 902–904. See also Newman, *Hugo Black,* 154–230; Daniel J. Meador, *Mr. Justice Black and His Books* (Charlottesville: University Press of Virginia, 1974), 1–33, 34; and Gilbert, "Bibb Graves as a Progressive," 338–48. If Esdale underestimated Graves, so did Clayton, who hoped that Graves would prove to be merely a conventional politician. See Clay-ton to Graves, 30 October 1926, Clayton Papers.

193. Feldman, *Politics, Society, and the Klan in Alabama,* 92–105, especially 98–100.

194. Clayton to Grover Hall, 11 July 1927, Clayton Papers.

195. Feldman, *Politics, Society, and the Klan in Alabama,* 121–23 (quoted passage on 122), 125–26.

196. For a treatment that emphasizes the contexts of Hall's career, see Daniel Webster Hollis III, *An Alabama Newspaper Tradition: Grover C. Hall and the Hall Family* (University: University of Alabama Press, 1983), 24–40. See also Virginius Dabney, *Liberalism in the South* (Chapel Hill: University of North Carolina Press, 1932), 380–413, especially 399–400.

197. *Montgomery Advertiser,* 10 August 1927; and Clayton to Victor Hanson, 5 Au-gust 1927, Clayton Papers. Clayton's published letter also takes a swipe at "[t]ime serv-ing politicians, job seekers and 'job grubbers'" who had been afraid to criticize the Klan, and refers to defenders of the Klan as "shallow thinking individual[s]." As early

as the spring of 1926, Clayton had been mulling over another Florida speaking invitation, considering whether to speak on "Some of the Manifested Phases of Intolerance." See Clayton to Herman Ulmer, 30 April 1926, Clayton Papers.

198. See Edmund W. Pettus to Clayton, 21 July 1927; Travis Williams to Clayton, 27 July 1927; and Lawrence Cooper to Clayton, 12 August 1927, Clayton Papers. In the summer of 1927, conservative legislators battled with Graves' forces over several issues. Conservatives supported an anti-mask bill and a bill to abolish the state's double-primary law, and opposed proposed changes in libel law intended to temper press criticism of the Klan. The results were mixed—at the end of the day Klansmen could still wear masks and the primary law had survived, but the press was not "muzzled." The most important product of the term, however, was the passage of reform measures advocated by Graves, including abolition of the state's infamous convict lease system. See J. Mills Thornton III, "Alabama Politics, J. Thomas Heflin, and the Expulsion Movement of 1929," in *From Civil War to Civil Rights in Alabama*, 335–37; and Gilbert, "Bibb Graves as a Progressive," 338–46.

199. *Birmingham News* and *Birmingham Age-Herald* [combined edition], 14 August 1927. For insight into the editorial process, see M. S. Carmichael to Clayton, 14 August 1927, Clayton Papers.

200. See Clayton to L. L. Hill, 16 May 1927; and Clayton to Grover Hall, 11 July 1927, Clayton Papers.

201. These included the August 1927 Blount County trial of the floggers of an orphan, Jeff Calloway; here McCall secured unprecedented convictions that were overturned on appeal. McCall was frustrated in later trials in Crenshaw County, in which forty-five indictments resulted in no convictions. These failures were due in part to the fact that Governor Graves covertly used his resources to frustrate the prosecution. Feldman, *Politics, Society, and the Klan in Alabama*, 107–15, 145–59.

202. *Montgomery Advertiser*, 20 October 1927, quoted in Feldman, *Politics, Society, and the Klan in Alabama*, 159; see also *Montgomery Advertiser*, 21 October 1927.

203. For coverage of Bankhead's demands and for the anti-Klan activities of other "oligarchs," including Circuit Judge Walter B. Jones, son of Clayton's predecessor Thomas Goode Jones, see Feldman, *Politics, Society, and the Klan in Alabama*, 126–28. For Hall's war-is-declared treatment, see *Montgomery Advertiser*, 27 October 1927.

204. *Montgomery Advertiser*, 28 October 1927.

205. Feldman, *Politics, Society, and the Klan in Alabama*, 117. Feldman notes a decline in Klan membership from more than 115,000 in 1925 to more than 10,400 by the end of 1927.

206. John D. Dyer to W. B. Clayton, 30 April 1928; and Clayton to Joe Robinson, 30 June 1928, Clayton Papers. Robinson, in January 1928, had rebuked Heflin's anti-Catholicism; Heflin had responded that Robinson, should he ever come to Alabama, would be tarred and feathered. This incident was a bad portent for Democratic unity in the state. See Thornton, "J. Thomas Heflin and the Expulsion Movement," 361; and Feldman, *Politics, Society, and the Klan in Alabama*, 166, 171.

207. See Clayton to Peter O. Knight, 10 April 1928, Clayton Papers.

208. Thornton, "J. Thomas Heflin and the Expulsion Movement," 362.

209. Newman, *Hugo Black*, 138–39.

210. For Alabama's 1928 presidential election and related issues, see Feldman, *Politics, Society, and the Klan in Alabama*, 161–92, especially 172–79, 181–90.

211. Clayton to B. G. Farmer, 27 August 1928, Clayton Papers.

212. Thornton, "J. Thomas Heflin and the Expulsion Movement," 365; Feldman, *Politics, Society, and the Klan in Alabama*, 190–91. The official total was 127,796 to 120,725. Hoover did in fact carry six traditionally southern states, breaking the "Solid South."

213. Thornton, "J. Thomas Heflin and the Expulsion Movement," 364–73.

214. 43 *Stat.* 1590–91 (1925). Acceptance of such awards by government officials required congressional approval. This approval was not automatic in the jingoistic 1920s, but Clayton had the support of his friend Underwood; see 66 *Congressional Record* 4505–4506 (68th Congress, 2d. Session, 1925).

215. Clayton's death was front-page news; see *Montgomery Advertiser*, 22 December 1929. If the Klan had continued its practice of holding symbolic funerals, it could have held a ceremony for the political generation that had come of age with disfranchisement. Comer had died in August 1927, Underwood in January 1929. Clayton's actual death and Tom Heflin's political death nearly coincided.

216. See editorial in *Montgomery Advertiser*, 22 December 1929.

217. For the "compulsion to preserve cultural values" inherent in the region's early twentieth-century reformers, see Grantham, *Southern Progressivism*, 415.

218. See Freyer and Dixon, *Democracy and Judicial Discretion*, 215–55; and generally, Tony A. Freyer, ed. *Defending Constitutional Rights: Frank M. Johnson* (Athens: University of Georgia Press, 2001).

219. See generally Dan T. Carter, *The Politics of Rage: George Wallace, the Origins of the New Conservatism, and the Transformation of American Politics* (New York: Simon and Schuster, 1995).

# Afterword

1. Carl Degler, *The Other South: Southern Dissenters in the Nineteenth Century* (New York: Harper and Row, 1974); Virginius Dabney, *Liberalism in the South* (Chapel Hill: University of North Carolina Press, 1932); and Woodward, *The Strange Career of Jim Crow*.

2. Wilbur J. Cash, *The Mind of the South* (New York: Alfred A. Knopf, 1941). The edition read by all college students of southern history, however, is the reprint by Vintage Books.

3. Malcolm C. McMillan, *Constitutional Development in Alabama*; Rogers, *One-Gallused Rebellion*; Thornton, *Politics and Power*; and J. Wayne Flynt, *Poor But Proud: Alabama's Poor Whites* (Tuscaloosa: University of Alabama Press, 1989). The works of several other historians (e.g., Glenn Feldman, Allen J. Going, G. Ward Hubbs, William Warren Rogers Jr., Samuel L. Webb, and Sarah Wiggins) have also shaped this study.

4. Another figure briefly mentioned (see Chapter Six of this volume) is the Montgomery clergyman and child labor reformer Edgar Gardner Murphy. See Hugh C. Bailey, *Edgar Gardner Murphy: Gentle Progressive* (Coral Gables, Florida: Univer-

sity of Miami Press, 1968). Bailey has done much perceptive research on New South reformism; see his *Liberalism in the New South: Southern Social Reformers and the Progressive Movement* (Coral Gables, Florida: University of Miami Press, 1969).

5. Samuel L. Webb, "A Jacksonian Democrat in Postbellum Alabama: The Ideology and Influence of Journalist Robert McKee, 1869–1896," *Journal of Southern History*, 62 (May 1996), 266–73.

6. See Sheldon Hackney, *Populism to Progressivism in Alabama*, 288–323.

7. A tip of the hat, here, to W. J. Cash.

8. See Roger Newman, *Hugo Black*, 89–121, 247–63.

9. Robert Penn Warren, *All the King's Men* (New York: Harcourt Brace, 1946), 278.

10. *Hamlet*, act 3, scene 1. Of course!

# Index